Praise for

THE BOSNIA LIST

"A young New Yorker haunted by searing memories goes on a most unusual overseas vacation—not to sightsee or party but to confront the ordinary men and women who tore his family's lives apart. His journey takes us into a time of mesmerizing violence and betrayal when neighbors set upon each other as though it were the 1940s all over again—a world of twisted emotions and baffling brutality lying just below the surface of hip contemporary Europe. *The Bosnia List* is powerful, the flashbacks riveting."

—Tom Reiss, Pulitzer Prize–winning author of *The Black Count*

"With understated elegance and in highly personal pointillist dots, Kenan Trebinčević illuminates how the Bosnian tragedy blighted, and continues to blight, the lives of countless people both in his homeland and in its far-flung diaspora. This important and original work reminds us, in ways large and small, of the long half-life of an atrocity."

—David Margolick, author of *Elizabeth and Hazel* and *Strange Fruit*

"Kenan Trebinčević fights against the power of memory and his own rage in this remembrance of a time that seems like a medieval anachronism yet was barely a decade ago. This is a searing memoir of war and peace from a young man who sees through ancient rhetoric with stunning clarity, in both his home country and his adopted United States. Read this book for its impassioned honesty."

—Tom Zoellner, author of *A Safeway in Arizona*
and coauthor of *An Ordinary Man*

"I'm so blown away by this beautiful book. For the first time, a young Bosnian tells a riveting coming-of-age story about the brutal Balkan War when parents disappeared into concentration camps, teachers turned on students, and children betrayed children. Two decades later, now an American citizen, Kenan returns to his homeland to confront the guilty and honor the dead in this passionate, nuanced account of a man who refuses to forget."

—Julia Lieblich, human rights journalist and author of *Sisters*
and coauthor of *Wounded I Am More Awake*

"Kenan Trebinčević's courageous story of survival and remembrance is powerfully told, mesmerizing, essential for us all to hear. He makes a strong case for courage and human decency as the only way through the divisive madness of modern life."

—Ian Frazier, author of *Travels in Siberia* and *Great Plains*

"A harrowing and heart-rending journey. It's a graceful, taut memoir of family, friends, and faith: a moving recollection of souls being torn asunder and slowly beginning to heal."

—Laurence Bergreen, author of *Columbus* and *Marco Polo*

"A mesmerizing tale of survival and healing."

—*Booklist*

"*The Bosnia List* was difficult to finish because it touched me so deeply. Most powerful was how Kenan's mother's voice echoed in his head and became his morality, preventing him from getting revenge. She's one of the strongest, best-described female characters in Bosnian literature. And I was rooting for Kenan's father not to succumb to evil and stay a good man. That might be why his family survived. That shows us all: if we stay good, we have a chance."

—Dr. Esad Boskailo, psychiatrist, Bosnian war survivor, and
coauthor of *Wounded I Am More Awake*

PENGUIN BOOKS

THE BOSNIA LIST

KENAN TREBINČEVIĆ was born in Brčko in 1980 to a Bosnian Muslim family exiled in the Balkan War. He came to the United States in 1993, and became an American citizen in 2001. His work has appeared in the *New York Times Magazine*, the *International Herald Tribune*, the *Wall Street Journal*, *Salon*, and *The Best American Travel Writing 2012*, and on *American Public Media* radio and *NPR*. He lives in Astoria, Queens, and works as a physical therapist. His website is www.kenantrebincevic.com.

SUSAN SHAPIRO is an American-born Jewish journalist who has written for the *New York Times*, the *Wall Street Journal*, the *Los Angeles Times*, the *Nation*, *Salon*, the *Daily Beast*, the *Forward*, and *Tablet*. She is the author of eight books, including the memoirs *Lighting Up*, *Five Men Who Broke My Heart*, and *Only as Good as Your Word*. She lives with her husband in Greenwich Village, where she is a writing professor at the New School and New York University. Her website is www.susanshapiro.net.

THE
BOSNIA LIST

A MEMOIR OF WAR, EXILE, AND RETURN

———

KENAN TREBINČEVIĆ *and*

SUSAN SHAPIRO

PENGUIN BOOKS

PENGUIN BOOKS
Published by the Penguin Group
Penguin Group (USA) LLC
375 Hudson Street
New York, New York 10014

USA | Canada | UK | Ireland | Australia | New Zealand | India | South Africa | China
penguin.com
A Penguin Random House Company

First published in Penguin Books 2014

Insert photographs courtesy of Kenan Trebinčević
Photograph of Susan Shapiro courtesy of Dan Brownstein;
Photograph of Kenan Trebinčević courtesy of Eldin Trebinčević

LIBRARY OF CONGRESS CATALOGING-IN-PUBLICATION DATA
Trebincevic, Kenan, 1980–
The Bosnia list : a memoir of war, exile, and return / Kenan Trebincevic and Susan Shapiro.
pages cm
Includes bibliographical references and index.
ISBN 978-0-14-312457-3 (paperback)
1. Trebincevic, Kenan, 1980—Childhood and youth. 2. Yugoslav War, 1991–1995—Bosnia and Hercegovina—Personal narratives, Bosnian. 3. Yugoslav War, 1991–1995—Bosnia and Hercegovina—Personal narratives, Muslim. 4. Escapes—Bosnia and Hercegovina—History—20th century. 5. Trebincevic, Kenan, 1980—Family. 6. Trebincevic, Kenan, 1980—Travel—Bosnia and Hercegovina. 7. Muslims—Bosnia and Hercegovina—Brcko—Biography. 8. Brcko (Bosnia and Hercegovina)—Biography. 9. Bosnia and Hercegovina—Ethnic relations—History—20th century. 10. Bosnian Americans—Biography. I. Shapiro, Susan. II. Title.
DR1313.8.T74 2014
949.703092—dc23
[B]   2013035345

Printed in the United States of America
3 5 7 9 10 8 6 4

Set in Adobe Garamond Pro   •   Designed by Elke Sigal
Map Illustrations by Daniel Lagin

In Memory of Adisa Trebinčević

CONTENTS

The Bosnia List

1. Confront Petra about stealing from my mother
2. Stand at Pero's grave to make sure he's really dead
3. Visit the Muslim cemetery to honor my dad's fallen comrades
4. Leave lilies on Grandma Emina's headstone
5. Walk across the Sava Bridge that was destroyed and rebuilt by Americans
6. Take a picture of Dad and Eldin at the concentration camp where they were imprisoned
7. Put a karate robe back on at Partizan Sports Hall
8. Ask Zorica if she felt guilty living in my friend Huso's stolen apartment
9. Apologize to Huso for betraying him
10. See if Miloš will admit he regrets fighting against us
11. Find out why cousin Amela never kept in touch with me
12. Finish the story my mother wanted to write about how we survived

FORMER YUGOSLAVIA POST–1995 DAYTON AGREEMENT

HUNGARY

Zagreb

CROATIA

Sava River

Danube River

Vukovar

Bihać

Vrbas River

Banja Luka

Bosna River

Brčko

Bijeljina

Belgrade

Una River

Tuzla

SERBIA

BOSNIA

Zenica

Srebrenica

Sarajevo

Inter-Entity Boundary Line (IEBL)
(Dayton Agreement Line)

Drina River

Split

Mostar

Adriatic Sea

MONTENEGRO

Podgorica

Dubrovnik

Vienna

Austria

Hungary

Slovenia

Romania

Croatia

Serbia—
Vojvodina

BOSNIA

Central
Serbia

Montenegro

Kosovo

Bulgaria

Italy

Adriatic Sea

Albania

Macedonia

Greece

KEY

Bosniak-Croat
Federation

Republika
Srpska

Escape
Route

THE BOSNIA LIST

Marshal Tito in Astoria

Queens, New York
December 2009

"This is a recipe for disaster," Eldin said, as we ordered two Buds at the bar. My older brother eyed the closet-sized bouncer, standing at ease by the entrance. "The guy probably thinks he has the cushiest job in the world, overseeing a bunch of well-dressed, young, mild-mannered white patrons. He has no idea what he's in for."

I hoped Eldin was just being paranoid. "Why would anything bad happen here?" I asked as we sat down in the plush leather seats. I surveyed the scene in Marshall's, an ambitious new 4,500-square-foot lounge that had just opened in Astoria. We'd been invited by the owner, Gigi, a Bosnian Muslim like us. He had the romantic idea that a Balkan-themed dance club could unite all the antagonistic groups from the former Yugoslavia who were exiled in my Queens neighborhood. He mixed kitchen workers from Bosnia with waiters from Serbia, our old enemy. And Gigi chose a space right next door to the Scorpio Café, packed with Croatians who—in the southern part of my country—were no less culpable for what happened to my people in the 1992 war that my family barely survived.

Two cute waitresses with Serbian accents handed us menus printed in both English and Bosnian. They were dressed in white button-down shirts and black tights and had red scarves around their necks, the uniform of young Communist Pioneers in the era of Marshal Tito, the lounge's namesake. The salty aroma of red bean soup and smoked beef from the next table reminded me of when our mother, Adisa, stood on our balcony in Bosnia, beckoning me to lunch. In sixth grade, I'd rush home to eat between soccer and karate practice. The *štrudla sa jabukama* on the tray going by us couldn't possibly be tastier than the apple strudel my mom made, back before the killing started.

"Hey, Eldin, remember when you gave me your Kapetan Miki collection?" I pointed to the picture on the wall of my favorite comic-book character from childhood. He used to chase Indians on a horse, like John Wayne.

"There's a Croatian website where you can find it." Eldin was six years my senior, four inches taller, with ash-blond hair the color of Mom's.

"Really? Cool! Why didn't you tell me?" I asked.

I was surprised to hear our compatriot Dino Merlin's bittersweet ballad "Is Sarajevo Where It Once Was" on the sound system. I'd never had a chance to visit Sarajevo, the capital of Bosnia. On the wall behind Eldin, a framed photograph of eleven men in their twenties from the Yugoslavian National Soccer Team—my old heroes—caught my eye. The slim, muscular athletes with short, dark hair resembled me now. I realized it was taken in 1990, the last time Serbs, Croats, and Bosniaks played on the same professional team together.

As a twenty-nine-year-old single guy in jeans and sneakers who lived a few minutes away, I was comfortable here, delighted by every inch of this Tito-era lounge that glowed with ex-Yugo nostalgia.

Not so my brother. "Like this will make us forget the three hundred thousand dead."* Eldin clicked his beer against mine.

Gigi spotted us and came over. Ruždija Džidžović, aka Gigi, also owned DiWine bar, as well as our local hair salon. A slim six-foot-four bald guy in his fifties, he was wearing an ascot, stone-washed True Religion jeans, and suede shoes. He looked like an aging rock star. He was clearly pleased we'd taken him up on his invitation.

"Hey, get these two a drink on me," he ordered the bartender. "I want you to have some *rakija* on the house." Gigi offered us moonshine made from plums, which tasted like liquid fire racing down my throat. "You're the nicest Bosniak guys I've met here," he added, using the term for native Muslims from our region. "Your father raised you boys right."

I smiled, proud of my dad, Senahid Trebinčević, whose black hair and outgoing personality I'd inherited. As the prosperous and popular owner of the only fitness center in our city of Brčko, my father had been considered the unofficial mayor. Because of my surname, everyone had treated me special when I was growing up. My mother had a big job as the office manager at a clothing company; we lived in a breezy two-bedroom apartment with a wraparound balcony.

In 1993, as the Serbs were massacring Bosniaks across my country, the four of us—the last Muslim family in town—fled Brčko for Connecticut. There Dad slung fast food at Boston Chicken, painted houses, sanded yachts at a boat marina, bagged groceries at Stop & Shop, and toiled in a factory that made plastic tops for fruit cups, anything to avoid welfare. Mom took to babysitting while Eldin earned minimum wage as a busboy at a Mexican joint. I was thirteen,

---

* "Three hundred thousand dead" refers to civilian and military Croats, Bosniaks, and Serbs killed in the Balkans from 1991 to 1995. *All the Missing Souls: A Personal History of the War Crimes Tribunals*, by David Scheffer, director of the Center for International Human Rights at Northwestern University Law School (Princeton, N.J.: Princeton University Press, 2012), p. 28.

and my awkward, broken English had set me apart as the only Bosnian kid at Bedford Middle School in Westport. We were nobodies in our new home, and I hated feeling so invisible and insignificant.

But now, after two decades here, I'd become a proud citizen of the United States, and I'd chosen to live in New York's most culturally diverse borough. I was a pacifist more interested in the Yankees and *Seinfeld* reruns than bloodthirsty revenge. Yet more and more I found myself returning to this busy avenue known as Yugo Row, gravitating toward the other 10,000 expatriates in Queens, as if it wasn't too late to recover what was lost.

My brother and I ate *ćevapi*, our favorite beef sausages, at the Old Bridge, run by a Sarajevan also named Kenan. I bought my *pršuta*, long strips of lamb, from the Serbians behind the counter at Muncan Foods with no problem. Well, no problem once I learned that the butcher had emigrated to the U.S. thirty years ago and thus couldn't have been the soldier armed with an AK-47 who, in 1992, took my father and Eldin to the concentration camp.

Although they were released unharmed after two weeks, the experience had turned my gregarious brother more cynical and suspicious. Except, of course, when it came to women.

"Proximity alert. Eight o'clock," Eldin whispered to me. He'd noticed two pretty Bosniak sisters lingering close by.

I turned around to check them out. Like us, one was light-haired, the other dark. They were overly done up, wearing dark blush and pink lipstick. The brunette had on a tight black dress and stilettos; the blonde was in a sparkly top that shimmered like a disco ball. I could tell from their accents they came from Sarajevo. They were talking to each other in Bosnian about their jobs in the fashion business, but they kept making grammatical mistakes. They were already forgetting their past.

"So where are you from?" the blonde asked us in English.

"*Iz Brčkog,*" I answered, in Bosnian.

"But now do you guys live around here?" said the brunette.

"*Ovde na Broadway-u i 44 ulici*," I responded, giving them our address at Broadway and 44th Street.

"Oh, we live in the West Village," the blonde answered—in English again. She was probably just showing off how Americanized she was, but I felt rejected, as if she didn't trust me enough to share our mother tongue. Flirting in Bosnian would have been more intimate, offering a chance to create a bond from our common ground. After all, the Serbs did come close to wiping us off the planet.

Since we weren't offering to buy them drinks or dance or take them home, the girls soon gave up on us. Eldin called three male Bosnian buddies, who met us at Marshall's for a nightcap. I'd idolized my only sibling growing up. But he was six grades ahead of me in school, and he'd treated me like an annoying little kid, as though he felt he was too old to be my friend. During our years in Connecticut, we'd shoot hoops at the basketball courts. Taller and stronger, he would always win. It pissed me off. I was a bad sport and would hit him in the ribs with my elbow or step on his foot when he blocked my shots. Still, I'd missed him sorely when he left for college. So I relished finally getting to be his sidekick and joining his posse; it gave me the feeling of hanging out with the homeboys I never had as a teenager.

We shared stuffed cabbage while listening to Dirty Theatre, Croatia's Coldplay. My usual anxious energy was soothed by the guitar solos of Miki, a forty-year-old Serb/Croat string bean we knew from the reception desk at Gigi's hair salon. As both the featured musician and the DJ controlling the mood of the room, Miki was "the man." During his break he had a Beck's with us, making us feel like we owned the place. Miki was from Mostar, a town ravaged in the war, the Stalingrad of Bosnia. We had history together. Eldin and I usually kept our background quiet unless we were asked specifics. Our reticence had become second nature after we were almost slaughtered for our name and religion. But suddenly at Marshall's, we felt respected and important again because of who we were and where we were from.

I was psyched to return the next weekend. This time I dressed nicer, choosing slim-cut black jeans and a hunter green cashmere sweater. At the lounge I drank six Jameson whiskeys and got what my college pals called *drizzed*, dancing to trance and world techno with some hip olive-skinned girls Eldin and I met standing around the bar.

The tunes reminded me of the pop tapes Eldin and I used to like in Brčko, which fascinated my mother. She listened to them on a cassette player, singing along while she trimmed her houseplants because, she said, "Greenery demands music and constant attention." Since she had a green thumb, her friends would bring her their ailing flora that needed healing.

The first sacrifice of the war was her flowers. We kept our shades closed to avoid being sprayed with bullets. Without sunlight, her cactus and hibiscus withered. During the fighting, patriotic anthems took over the radio—when we had batteries to listen. To avoid any trouble, she turned the music off. She had to watch, mute, while her plants died one by one.

But it was more than familiar melodies that lured me back to Marshall's. I hadn't slept or eaten much since Nicole, the Manhattan girlfriend I'd adored, had left me six weeks before. We'd been together two years. She was a slim, dark-haired Latina beauty from an immigrant family, bilingual and hardworking like I was, the only woman I'd ever invited to spend the holidays with me, Eldin, and Dad. I wasn't ready to date anyone else. But it didn't hurt to see the flocks of beautiful ladies in high heels walk by, with their sexy Serbian accents, long silky hair, lovely faces painted with lip gloss and eyeliner. I was twelve when my family was forced into exile. So I'd never kissed a girl from home. I'd never danced to Bosnian music at a nightclub before. I'd never walked into a bar and ordered a beer in my own tongue. All the normal teenage highlights were postponed and experienced late, in a different language, through a foreigner's eye. At Marshall's I felt like I was traveling back in time to a life I never got to live but desperately wanted to reclaim.

Still, there were limits. After the bloody wars in the Balkans in the early 1990s, it would have been taboo to date, much less marry, a Serb. Eldin flirted with Snježana, a hot bartender who'd come to New York on a short-term tourist visa. She played along, but I told him she just wanted bigger tips to take home to Serbia with her. He insisted he was onto her ruse. But I worried about Eldin, who, like me, worked long hours as a physical therapist. I'd nicknamed him "Romeo" since he'd fall for a pretty face much faster and harder than I would. I was still inconsolable after my breakup—Nicole was the only girl I'd ever told I loved.

Despite Eldin's dire predictions that our old Eastern European cultural conflicts would spill over here, Marshall's remained altercation-free. We became regulars. The bouncer stopped asking to check our ID and greeted us with a double handshake. Gigi would wave. The bartender knew our drinks; the waitresses rushed our food.

One summer evening in June 2010, I sensed something was different the moment I walked in. The staff of enticing young Serbian women had evidently brought their guy friends to the lounge—in droves. Instead of the female Serb voices that were so melodious to my ear, we were surrounded by the buzz of deeper, more guttural accents that I found disturbing. The new crowd was the same age as the armed soldiers who'd threatened to kill us back in Brčko. I hadn't heard speech like this since the war. Their talk—filled with *bre?*, the equivalent of the Canadian "eh?"—was jarring, yanking me back to 1992. "You have an hour to leave or be killed," my beloved Serb karate coach, Pero, had told my father. Pero's men soon took Eldin and Dad to a concentration camp infamous for rape, torture, and mass murder. Even two decades later, the memory of seeing them taken away made my face tingle from fear. Hot blood coursed through my arms and legs, my heart pounding against my chest as if trying to escape.

Eldin must have felt the Serb menace at Marshall's that night too, because he muttered, "Poor Tito must be turning in his casket," pointing to the granite bust of Marshal Tito's head on the highest bar shelf. Bright lights flared beneath each side of Tito's face, as if it were in a permanent spotlight. Tito was the moderate Communist dictator who'd united all of my country's historically combative sects for thirty-five years. I was born in 1980, the year Tito died.

At school, I had diligently pledged in front of my classmates and my favorite teacher, Milutin, to respect my parents, honor my home-land, and spread the unity for which Tito fought. Then Slobodan Milošević came to power in 1989 and mobilized Serb nationalists in a deranged campaign to wipe Muslims out for the sake of "Greater Serbia," the way Hitler had envisioned an Aryan race. In the first month of warfare, I was crossing an intersection in Brčko, after buy-ing a loaf of rye bread, terrified of being struck by an errant bullet. I bumped into Milutin in full Serb uniform. I called, "Hey, teacher." He knocked the bag out of my hand. Holding me by my left side-burn, he shoved his rifle barrel against the back of my head. I would have been dead right there if his gun hadn't jammed. Running away, I turned back to catch him waving a three-finger salute—a symbol of Serbian separatism made by extending the thumb, index, and middle fingers of the right hand, like a peace sign with an added thumb. It was based on the way Serbs performed the sign of the cross, with three fingers, representing the Trinity. I'd never told any-body what my teacher did. I was too stunned to learn that the people we grew up with wanted us dead.

At the lounge that night, I noticed that a group of Serb men stopped singing and dancing when Miki played "Is Sarajevo Where It Once Was." A dividing line was drawn. Weeks later, we were upset to learn that the owners had fired Miki and given his DJ job to a Serb. Allegedly, Miki wasn't bringing in enough customers. Again I felt like we were unwanted outcasts being replaced. But I wasn't going to hide my identity this time. That Saturday night I showed up in a sleeveless shirt to flaunt my tats: my right shoulder showed the constellation Sagittarius. On my left bicep was the historical Bosnian flag, with its blue coat of arms, yellow lilies, and white sword. A pal from our old country looked impressed and said, "Hey man, that's some sick ink." But the Serb patrons eyed my blue shield suspiciously, as I'd expected.

Over the next year we continued to hang out at Marshall's, but the vibe slowly soured. Bosnians, Croatians, Montenegrins, and Serbians started sitting only with each other, in separate corners. I watched helplessly as my cherished hangout balkanized before my eyes. One evening I was dismayed when my stuffed cabbage came with bacon—strictly taboo, even for a secular Muslim like me. My mother had never cooked pork. "It's a filthy animal that rolls in its own dung," my father said. As I stared down at the greasy strip, my first thought was that someone in the kitchen was making a statement. But I learned the cook was an Orthodox Serb, so perhaps they now preferred serving meals with bacon. I removed the offending slice and put it on the bread plate filled with olive pits.

Later I learned that Gigi was just catering to the influx of Serbs who'd recently stepped off the plane. Eldin and I were annoyed that making extra bucks was more important to Gigi than not alienating his own tribe. The new DJ spun trumpet-heavy turbo-folk Serbian songs. Once again, I was becoming a minority on my own turf. I felt the way I did at twelve, when my karate teammates Velibor and Dalibor demanded that I return all the He-Man trading cards we'd collected together. When we'd venture outdoors between rounds of fighting, my onetime friends stopped picking me for their mini soccer games. They wouldn't even touch my black and white soccer ball, the lucky orb they'd once refused to play without. I'd have to watch the game from behind a shade in my living room, until they scattered at the sound of nearby explosions and gunshots.

When the new DJ at Marshall's spun pop singer Ceca's "Last Supper," we'd had enough and stormed out. She was Serbia's Madonna in her "bad girl" stage, but Madonna had never been in and out of jail for money laundering, possession of illegal weapons, and making death threats. Ceca's modern folk-pop dance music was laden with ethnographic hints that made my Bosniak skin crawl. I'd despised her since I'd read in the Belgrade news that she praised her husband, Arkan, a career international war criminal. He ran a paramilitary unit, Arkan's Tigers, that had raped and murdered Catholics and Muslims.

"Of course, he would play this crap," I muttered, looking over at the DJ booth. After Arkan was assassinated in 2000, before he could stand trial, Ceca had dedicated many of her songs to him.

"She was married to an animal," Eldin told his friend Admir.

"Their heroes never saw the front lines; they only murdered the elderly and unarmed," I added.

"You should see how many men his unit lost in our town," Eldin said.

"They only attacked the vulnerable in large numbers. When they faced danger alone, they ran away," I said. I caught the bartender's eye to give us another round.

Not long after that night, my neighbor texted me: "Do not go to Marshall's for a while."

The word was that the Montenegrins were planning to trash the bar. They were furious when a young customer waved that same three-finger salute while Ceca's song played. In my view it was like giving the "Heil Hitler" sign to a Jewish Auschwitz survivor. But those young Serbian punks were showing their pride to the wrong crowd. I was no longer a powerless little kid in Brčko.

My college buddies in America argued that everyone was free to express their beliefs without consequences. But they had not been the victims of an ethnic-cleansing campaign by vicious racists who were barely punished. They were not obsessively following the news of the International Criminal Tribunal for the former Yugoslavia, led by a United Nations court of law, like my brother and I were. They didn't know that almost twenty years later the Serbs responsible for mass murder had yet to be prosecuted. Or that while in prison, an ultranationalist monster named Vojislav Šešelj was able to publish his own version of *Mein Kampf*, inanely arguing that Serbia had legitimately waged war against us as self-defense to save Europe from an Islamic invasion. They didn't understand that the longer the trials went on, the more likely those responsible for the atrocities against my people would die in country-club prisons where they had access to TV, movies, music, and the Internet, and then be honored with a hero's funeral in Serbia, like the reception given Slobodan Milošević when he died in 2006. They didn't realize that in an ex-Yugoslav social setting, one idiotic salute could provoke a nonviolent man whose entire life had been ripped away from him because of his religion.

Even after being warned, I couldn't stay away from Marshall's. The illusion of recapturing some part of my childhood drew me back. In the winter of 2011, I persuaded my brother to give it one last chance. I wanted to bask in my Balkan haven a little longer.

But this time, walking into the Queens lounge one night in February, we immediately saw that we were the only Bosniaks in the place. Miki was long gone. The murals and Tito's statue reminded us that the make-believe brotherhood he'd created had died with him, thirty-one years ago. "Love Lives," one of Ceca's songs dedicated to Arkan, assaulted my ears. I turned to see a Serbian man in his twenties waving that three-finger salute to his buddies. Fueled by alcohol and testosterone, I felt years of buried rage resurfacing; heat rose from my chest to my pounding head.

I flashed back to the first of six times my family tried to escape Bosnia, when we were stopped at a checkpoint in Brčko and kicked off a bus. I was eleven, sweating under three layers of shirts and a jacket. We could each carry only one suitcase, so we wore extra clothes on our backs. A guerrilla fighter in a black uniform, a black hat, and a long beard cocked his gun and ordered us to march forward. Another armed man's face turned red as he stared into my father's eyes, then glanced down at his combat boots and said in a shamed mumble, "I'm sorry, I can't do anything, Keka." He knew my father, called him by an endearment while leading him to his possible death. I heard the sound of a chamber loading as we walked away in silence. "Don't turn around," my father warned. The soldiers laughed. I thought it was all over then.

I hated being too small to protect my family. I wished I could wake up the next day at eighteen and take revenge as a soldier. As an adult, I'd never once used a gun or knife or my fist. I was afraid of what I might do. But now I didn't care if I was outnumbered. I finished my last sip of beer. I picked up the empty bottle, ready to break it on the table and use the jagged edge as a weapon. My brain told me to simmer down, not to do anything that could destroy the nice world I'd managed to rebuild here.

Yet I felt like I was being disrespected in my home. I crumpled a napkin into a ball I threw from twenty feet away. It flew in a perfect arc, bounced off the top of the Serbian saluter's head, and landed in the middle of the table. I smirked. I used to stand on the banks of the River Sava, launching rocks that rippled across the water. "I'll never forget the time Kenan nailed the snake swimming in the river from thirty meters away," Dad had said proudly.

Now the guys at the Serb's table turned to look in my direction. I was no longer a scared five-foot, hundred-pound eleven-year-old. I was a muscular six-foot man in my third decade. I waved my index finger side to side, a silent warning that the saluter should keep his gesture to himself. My brother would fight alongside me. It would be two against six, yet I felt no fear. They could not imagine how much rage I had pent up. I'd had no idea myself until that moment.

Fortunately for us all, they stayed on their side, stifling their insults, but complaining to the bouncer. I walked over to one of the

Bosniak owners. "You'd sell your mother for a few extra dinars," I said.

Two months later, on April 10, 2011, while celebrating my brother's birthday elsewhere, we received a text that four Montenegrins had walked into Marshall's and caught the same three-finger salute that I had. That night, bottles and stools were smashed across the room, shattering and striking innocent patrons. The fight escalated on the sidewalk outside. Four young Serbs were injured. A twenty-six-year-old was stabbed in the back, and a twenty-one-year-old had his right forearm slashed. A twenty-four-year-old Serb received a chest gash, and a twenty-seven-year-old male was hit with a bottle. Each was treated and released from the hospital. Police were searching for the four Montenegrins, whom the *New York Post* referred to as thugs. I calculated that the youngest victim, at twenty-one, was a two-year-old toddler when the war began. His cluelessness about that time period, and his misguided arrogance, had given him a permanent scar. Marshall's closed on April 18, 2011.

I didn't need a haircut but scheduled an appointment at Gigi's salon anyway, dying to hear what had really happened. Gigi was in denial that the conflict had been triggered by nationalistic provocation. Kristina, the adorable Serbian brunette who washed my hair, had been working as a bartender that night. I gave her a kiss on the cheek as I walked in. She was still in distress that her friends had been stabbed. She recalled hiding under the bar as the bottles and chairs started flying. "They came to start trouble for no reason," Kristina insisted. I could have shared my opinion about the idiots who showed the three-finger salute, but I'd learned over the years that there was no point. There were always several sides to a story, but only one truth. I sat in my Croatian hairdresser Monika's chair and asked, "Did you hear?"

"Yes, what did you expect?" she replied.

The last time I walked by Marshall's I was sad to see it had turned into Portalia, an Italian restaurant serving homemade pasta.

It had been a worthy effort by Gigi. But Bosniaks like me, who lost our comrades, our home, and our country, could not be easily placated with prewar pop music, sexy Balkan miniskirts, and a foreign menu. Though the danger was years behind us, the memories were never far away. Having a drink with Eldin at DiWine a month later, we spied the statue of Marshal Tito hiding on a high shelf, behind a bottle of Bosnian moonshine.

"You know, Dad asked if I thought we should visit Brčko," my brother said.

"I thought we all swore we'd never go back there," I said, alarmed at the thought.

"Damn straight we won't. Though if we did, nobody could hurt us this time," Eldin said. He put his hand on my shoulder to let me know that, in case we ever did decide to return, he would be protecting me from our old enemies.

That wasn't my concern at all. Who, I wondered, would protect me from myself?

CHAPTER ONE

An Indelible Lesson in Self-Defense

Brčko, Bosnia
February 1991

"Kenan Trebinčević," I heard myself called over the microphone.

Beneath the tall windows of the Partizan Sports Hall, my second home, I marched to the middle of the lacquered wooden floor, my white kimono fastened at the waist with a blue sash. My bare feet were freezing, but I focused on my kicking. If I nailed this, at ten years old I'd be the youngest brown belt in my division. It was the biggest challenge of my life. One little slip could embarrass coach Pero, the brilliant black belt I'd looked up to for the last six years. I wanted to make him proud. I was nervous yet pumped, as though a swarm of butterflies were flying down my throat as I tackled the choreographed pattern of movements called katas, carrying out my slow, careful dance of kicks and punches.

When I was finished, coach Pero flashed two thumbs up, then winked at me. Yes! My father nodded, thrusting his fist in the air. We Balkanites took athletics very seriously.

I knew my performance was a reflection on my dad, who volunteered as president of our karate club. He owned a nearby fitness center in Brčko, training professional athletes. As a little kid, I sat beside him on the players' bench for our volleyball team matches. I'd hold the cans of cold spray he used to numb a player's pulled muscle. When the games were over, we'd hang in the locker room. I hated when the six-foot-ten-inch giants put me on their shoulders; my head would get dizzy and I was sure I'd fall off.

After my test, I waited impatiently as the judges for our team—Lokomotiva ("locomotive" in English)—filled out diplomas for those moving up the ranks and announced the winners. My friends Velibor and Dalibor were declared blue belts. When my name was called, all my teammates rushed to hug and high-five me. I ran over to my seventeen-year-old brother and then to Dad, sliding on my knees. Pero was grinning, squatting, his arms wide open. As I leapt into his embrace, he lifted me high over his head, triumphant. I wasn't scared this time.

"Super job, Keno baby," Pero said, draping my new brown belt around my neck. Then he tossed me over his shoulder, holding me by my feet, carrying me like a backpack. I laughed, happier than I'd ever been. Pero loved me most. I was special.

Then he put me down so we could observe our tradition, taking off my blue belt and officially handing it to Velibor. "*Evo ti plavi pojas*," I said. Here is the blue belt you earned.

"*Hvala*." He thanked me, slapping my palm.

I couldn't wait to tell Mom the awesome news. In the locker room I quick-changed back into myself, with my new belt around my neck, displayed over my street clothes. Returning to our apartment complex, I spotted my neighbor Igor on his souped-up neon blue BMX bicycle and ran ahead to greet him.

"I just won the brown belt," I boasted.

Igor had reddish hair and freckles and was taller than me, skinny like a tree branch. He was the bravest of our group, scaling the tops of cherry trees, popping wheelies on his bicycle, or riding downhill with his eyes closed and his hands behind his back just to show off. I hoped to impress him.

"Cool, Kendji," he said. "Check out my new bike."

"Where'd you get it?" I knew he'd stolen it. He was wearing his old, beat-up sneakers and a dirty gray sweatshirt my mom would have never let me out of the house in.

"Fell off a truck," he joked, laughing. "Want to ride with me and Huso?"

"Are you coming, Kenan?" Dad asked as he caught up to us on the sidewalk.

"Hey, Mr. Keka," Igor said.

Dad nodded hello, but he never liked it when I hung out with Igor, whom he called a "trouble-making punk." Igor's dad was a mean, sickly menace. He'd spent his last days in a wheelchair, his leg amputated below the knee because of diabetes. He would station himself outside here by the steps, chain-smoke, drink *rakija*, and swear at everyone walking by. He'd throw his shoe and spit at Igor if he didn't steal him cigarettes from the store, bellowing, "How dare you come home empty-handed, you worthless moron." After his father died last year, Igor's mom let her son "run rampant," according to my parents. But you could see Igor's other side in the way he treated dogs. He used to feed a stray black mutt he named Bobby bowls of milk and bones from his mom's chicken soup. When he found Bobby lying dead in the street—shot in the left eye—he arranged a funeral and cried for days. I felt so bad for Igor, who had it rough. Though at fifty-three, Dad was one of the older fathers, I knew he was the best one—showing me off to his sports buddies and giving me money to treat my friends to ice cream whenever I asked.

Just then my pal Huso came through the entrance, his Harley bicycle on his shoulder. "Hello, Kenan. Did you pass?"

I showed off the treasured brown fabric around my neck.

"Congratulations. Great job," said Huso. Out of the boys in the building, he was the neatest and tallest and had the biggest shoulders. He had a dark-blond crew cut and wore a blue shirt tucked into his jeans and clean white sneakers. He was fluent in English and spoke Bosnian formally since his father was a professor. "Would you like to come with us?"

"Yeah. Let's do it." I was ready to get a soccer game going. I wanted Huso on my side; he was two grades higher than me and had a lethal shot.

But Dad cut me off. "Your mom's made you food. You have to go upstairs."

"Sorry, can't." I shrugged to the guys.

"Let's go," Dad prodded. "Tell your father I say hi," he told Huso.

I rushed up the three floors two steps at a time, speeding so I was out of breath when I reached the top. The scent of roasted peppers filled the hall as I unlaced my Converse high-tops in a hurry. "Mom, Mom, check it out," I yelled, running in. "I won. I won."

She was sitting in front of the dining-room window overlooking the balcony, calmly pressing clothes with her new electric iron from Germany. She stepped on the pedal of her silver machine, humming to Dino Merlin's "Something Nice Needs to Happen" on the tape player. She'd had a wooden case built for the album collection my father had amassed during his jazz-band days. He liked the liquid-smooth trumpet of an American musician named Louis Armstrong best.

I held up my new belt. She hugged me, kissing the top of my head.

"Now go wash your dirty hands before we eat," she said.

"I already washed up in the locker room," I argued.

My mother, a pretty redheaded neatnik, was thirty-seven, sixteen years younger than my father, who—Uncle Ahmet said—robbed her cradle. She worked with Huso's mom at Velma, a clothing company. When she came home, her meticulous apartment was her sanctuary. The dining-room table was for eating only, so my G.I. Joes and miniature car collection were banned to the bedroom Eldin and I shared. Shoes were ordered off and left outside the front door. When my ski pants were soaked from sledding, they came off at the door too, so I wouldn't get her new rug wet.

"Wash again. I don't want your fingerprints on my furniture," she scolded. "I'll have to buy you colored socks. I'm tired of bleaching your white ones. Do you swim in the mud?"

When the phone rang, it was my best friend, Jasenko, asking if I wanted to test our new slingshots on pigeons outside.

"Jasenko and I are going to pick cherries," I told Mom.

"It's February, no cherries, you liar," she said. "Now wash up and eat your lunch. We're going to see Grandma Emina and Aunt Bisera today."

But who wanted old relatives when I could be testing slingshots with Jasenko or getting a pickup soccer game going with Huso? I'd earned the scabs and scrapes all over my arms and legs by playing outside, the best athlete and first-pick of all the neighborhood boys.

"Aunt Bisera and her kids will be there," Mom said. "She has a present for you."

"She gets gross lipstick all over me when she kisses," I lamented.

As we ate, I gave Mom the play-by-play of my karate award. She never liked sports, but she nodded, pretending to understand. Eldin reached for the carton of milk.

"Don't spill it. You'll stain my new rug," she warned my big brother, a notorious butterfingers.

She told everyone how special the dumb rug was. "So what's the point if you can't walk on it?" I asked.

"Just keep your sweaty feet off my carpet, you hellion," she answered, smiling.

After lunch she sat on her heels on the floor, framing my new karate diploma. Then the four of us walked across town to Grandma Emina's. I was hyper to show off my brand-new belt.

"Remember, keep your hands off the shelf so you don't break their aquarium," Mom warned. "No running like a maniac or playing tag in the house. And don't rattle the cage and scare her birds like you did last time."

Eldin won our race up the steep hill to my mom's childhood house. Inside Grandma hugged me—trapped! Aunt Bisera overkissed. Unable to escape her lips, my cheeks were red like a clown's.

"His coach Pero gave him that special belt," Mom announced.

I passed the brown fabric around for all to see.

"Very impressive, my honeybun," Grandma said.

"Look what I made you." Aunt Bisera served apple strudel warm from the oven, my favorite. "Want something to drink?"

"Can I have more milk?" Eldin asked.

"Just don't spill it," Grandma warned.

"When you come over, I have a yellow parakeet for you," Aunt Bisera promised.

"You can take all of them," said my cousin Mirza. He and his sister, Amela, hated their mom's coterie of turtles, birds, and fish, which she spoke to like her own children. Last time Mirza got screamed at for racing her turtles on the carpet.

"Adisa, this is for you." Bisera handed Mom a denim skirt and a silky beige nightgown. Then she gave me one hundred dinars (the equivalent of fifty bucks!) for climbing the karate ranks. I was totally psyched, thinking of all the things I would buy.

"Your Aunt Bisera's too nice," Mom said, hugging her sister. "If you compliment her shirt, she'll take it off and give it to you." Mom was younger, the feisty one. They looked alike, though Bisera had darker hair and blue eyes. Mom worried about her divorce. I never knew anybody who was divorcing before. I hoped I could continue playing with Uncle Nedjo and that he'd still be allowed to buy me miniature cars.

I wound up spending Bisera's cash gift on a customized soccer jersey. My teammates and I had numbers stenciled on our T-shirts to wear at our annual July karate camp on the Croatian coast. But that spring Dad told us the 1991 summer season was called off. "Yugoslav politics," was his excuse. "Bad timing."

The cancellation seemed so unfair. I wouldn't get to train for my black belt or snorkel or watch the funny American movie *Meatballs* outdoors again. "What's going on?"

"Remember the mass riot at Maksimir Stadium on TV last year?" Eldin said.

Scenes of rampaging fans popped into my mind. The fight between Dinamo Zagreb's soccer team from Croatia and Serbia's Red Star Belgrade was the most insane sports brawl we'd ever seen. Torn-off seats flew like Frisbees, and toilets ripped from the floor were thrown as missiles. The Serbs, led by an ex-con nicknamed "Arkan," sang "Zagreb Is Serbian." The police called in reinforcements and used teargas and water cannons to disperse the violence. Men were shot and stabbed, and hundreds were hospitalized; many Croatians were wounded by the police. A Croatian team captain came to a fan's defense by karate-kicking a police officer, knocking him down. The Croat was suspended from the soccer league for six months and had criminal charges filed against him. Afterward Dad said, "The Yugoslavian police have become the Serb police."

"Another soccer fight?" I questioned my brother now. How did I miss it?

"You know those tanks on television last week?" he said. "The Serbs were attacking Croatia and Slovenia."

"Why?" I asked Eldin, who never talked down to me just because I was younger.

"Because after Milošević rigged the election, the Croatians had enough and voted for sovereignty," he explained. "To get away from Milošević's sick obsession with creating an all-Serbian country."

"So they're both separate countries now?"

He nodded.

I recalled how, in second grade, I'd been called up in front of the class to point on the map and name the six different republics that made up my nation of Yugoslavia: Serbia, Bosnia-Herzegovina, Croatia, Slovenia, Macedonia, and Montenegro, along with the separate Serbian provinces Kosovo and Vojvodina. When Dad and I watched *Sands of Iwo Jima*, he'd told me Hawaii was one of America's fifty states, the way Bosnia was one of six Yugoslavian republics. Each state in the U.S. spoke English, he said, just as everyone in our republics used the same South Slavic language, though with different accents and dialects. I knew that Serbia was the biggest and that Dad and Eldin didn't like their leader, Milošević, calling him "that power-hungry ape."

"But why would he want to fight everyone?" I didn't get it.

"Historically, the Serbs see themselves as warriors," Eldin said. "They even celebrate wars they lost. They get trashed every June to commemorate the infamous Battle of Kosovo when the Turkish army wiped them out. It was in the fourteenth century, but they never got over it. They still think they're victims."

He pulled out his high school textbook to several paintings that showed the Turk's Ottoman Empire slaughtered the Serbs. In *The Kosovo Maiden*, a beautiful lady gave water to a handsome Serb soldier wounded by the Turks in the 1389 Battle of Kosovo. *Migration of the Serbs* depicted a Serbian patriarch leading a flock of thousands into exile after they were massacred by the Turkish army again in 1689. My brother explained that the Turkish occupation of our land started in 1463, when Turks brought Serbians to Bosnia as servants, along with Islam. Bosniaks had their own church, but the Pope accused them of heresy, Eldin said. Those who refused to convert to Catholicism instead embraced Islam, the main religion of the Turkish people.*

---

* The history of the Serbs and the description of the painting *Migration of the Serbs* were taken from *The Serbs: History, Myth, and the Destruction of Yugoslavia*, by Tim Judah (New Haven: Yale University Press, 1997), pp. 1, 110, 133.

"But the Serbs can't still be pissed off and blaming us for that," I told him. "They wouldn't hold a grudge against us for five hundred years."

"Why not?" he asked.

Could that be what Pero was mad at all of a sudden? The last time we saw him at Partizan, he acted strange and brushed me off. He hadn't shaved or combed his curly blond hair; he looked tired and scruffy. One afternoon, a brown-haired girl in a tight green dress came by, so our karate practice was rushed. He flirted with her while we finished our group exercises. When Dad came to watch the end of our session, he found us unsupervised, doing somersaults on the soft mats.

"The practice ended at two," I reported. "Pero left with a girl in a green dress."

"How can he teach you discipline if he leaves early with whores?" Dad growled.

At our next out-of-town martial arts event, Pero was supposed to walk us in front of the judges, but we couldn't find him.

"Goddamn flake," Dad muttered, pacing the locker room.

When our names were called, Pero was still missing. We were embarrassed. My father's face was red and sweating. Pero finally showed up, and he and Dad went to a corner. I could see Dad gesturing forcefully with his hands. Pero's own hands were on his hips, his eyes to the ground. Later Dad told me Pero was hung over and had been asleep beneath the arena's bleachers, where a janitor had found him.

"What's wrong with Pero?" I asked, worried.

The next morning at the team breakfast, another coach whispered in Dad's ear that he'd seen Pero sleeping between the mats, using *Oslobodjenje*, the freedom newspaper, as his blanket. Why was Pero partying so hard and missing practices? I needed him to show me more katas and help me spar, to win more tournaments, and give me hugs and high fives. But something weird was happening to him.

Dad said Pero was mad when his recent demand for a raise was denied. In retaliation, he quit coaching Lokomotiva. In a bold rebellion, he launched his own martial arts team at Partizan, pulling some of my teammates to his side and charging them separately. We were offended, but my dad couldn't fire Pero. Partizan Sports Hall, like the local library, was owned by the town. Dad made a good living running Fitness Keka, his own athletic training center, a few miles away. He only volunteered with our karate team to spend time with me and Eldin. My father hated confrontation. So instead of forcing a face-off, he coerced our old former coach out of retirement, rehired him, and avoided Pero.

What bothered me the most was that Pero didn't even try to take me with him. He left me with the beginners. Without his encouragement, I started doubting myself. If I was really good, Pero would have picked me for his new team. I thought I was his best. I missed him.

"*Djesi*, Pero," I said, the next time I saw him, as his team's practice finished. It was the equivalent of "What's up?"

He didn't answer. He didn't even look at me. I was devastated. Since first grade, Pero had been my idol. His whole family lived in Brčko, close by us. I knew he was twenty-six, that he worked as an electrician by day and did karate nights and weekends. He hung out with hip guys who wore leather jackets and aviator shades, like Tom Cruise in *Top Gun*. Pretty girls would stop by the gym just to flirt with him. All my teammates—and their parents—looked at him with respect. In bed that night, I couldn't sleep. I didn't know why Pero had abandoned me. I tried to think what I did wrong.

Our team weakened. For the next six months, the two karate squads shared the locker room at Partizan Sports Hall. But Pero never spoke to me again. Zoka, a Serb brown belt, became his new sidekick. He was two years older than I was. At six foot two, Zoka towered over me. I must have been too small for Pero, too weak.

"Pero's washed up," a teammate sneered as we changed out of our kimonos.

"Oh yeah? Is that why he's kicking ass in Croatia on weekends?" said Zoka.

Croatia? I wondered if Pero was coaching weekend karate there on his own.

"That's what they get for pushing to be independent," Zoka chided.

Eldin had mentioned the Croatians were trying to get away from the Serbians. But I didn't know they were still fighting about it.

Coming home on a cool October night, I listened to the low voices of Mom and Jasenko's mother on the balcony. No laughter, no music in the background. Bright red flashes lit up the northern Croatian plains. Suddenly the sky roared.

"Bombs in Vukovar," Mom told me, her eyes squinting with worry.

I told myself that the Croatian city was far away from us, at least an hour-and-a-half drive, and pretended not to be too scared.

As I ate my breakfast of Nutella crepes the next day, the morning news anchor announced that as a reaction to Croatia's declaration of independence from Yugoslavia, the Serb-dominated army was bombing the Croatians. Confused, I scanned Hollywood war movies in my mind: Americans troops battled the Third Reich, Russians, and Japanese. Nobody attacked their own countrymen. I wondered if the current Croatia-Serbia conflict was like *Gone with the Wind*. Mom said that America's Civil War was between two sides from the same country fighting racism against people of color. But the only blacks I'd ever seen were on the screen; all the people here were white.

In college, my father was an extra in the 1962 Yugoslav film *Kozara*. He played a German getting beaten up by a Yugoslav peasant. The actor was an old Serb mountain villager, Dad said, who'd hit him too hard with his cane. "Calm down, it's only a movie," Dad had yelled. He later told me the exterminators who shot stray dogs at five a.m. were Serb villagers who had been bused in. So I thought village people who came from the high hills resented city dwellers like us because we had nicer homes and cushier jobs. Our other differences had gone past me.

At lunch, Eldin pointed to an article in *Oslobodjenje*, a trustworthy liberal source, he said, published in Sarajevo. Their chart analyzed the election breakdown by region and faith. It showed that Serbia was mostly Orthodox Christian and Croatia Roman Catholic. Bosnia, where we lived, was the most religiously mixed: 32 percent Christian Serbs; 17 percent Croats, who practiced Roman Catholicism; and 45 percent Muslims like us. Growing up, the main difference I noticed was that we had Ramadan and no Santa Claus. Plus Catholics kids I knew got Christmas gifts in December, but Serbs had to wait till January. Geographically, Croatia seemed the most beautiful part of our country, filled with lakes, caves, and exotic natural beauty along the coast.

A TV newscaster mentioned "weekend warriors," Bosnian Serbs who were going to Croatia, where they were given a uniform and a gun to kill Croats from Friday to Sunday nights. After the bombing and deaths were reported, I understood why my Croatian summer camp was canceled. I figured out that Pero must have been fighting part-time in the war there. No wonder he was acting so weird, drunk, and tired at karate practice during the week. My coach was falling apart. My country was falling apart.

At dinner, my family watched the TV news in anguish. I tried to follow the new expressions: *Greater Serbia, nationalism, ethnic cleansing.*

"What's ethnic cleansing?" I asked my father.

"It means every fifty years a new politico turns us against each other," he said.

The Croatians were mad at the Serbians. But who was against us? And why? Dad explained that it was a land grab, that Serbia wanted to expand their territory and rule a bigger country filled with only Orthodox Christians like them. So Milošević ordered his troops to get rid of Muslims and Catholics in the other republics. My brother said this was the way Hitler had purged Germany of Jews in World War II, envisioning a pure race.

"But how can the Serbians get away with it?" I was outraged.

"They have the most cops, generals, and ammunition factories," Eldin said.

According to my brother, politicians and military bigwigs were already centered in Belgrade, the capital of Serbia. Since the end of World War II, they'd controlled the school curriculums and history books, the museums (filled with Serbian arts and Serbian heroes), and the media; the biggest TV station in Yugoslavia was based there.

After Tito died in 1980, Milošević began mobilizing, shoring up more power. When he'd touted his Greater Serbian Orthodox Christian vision to the Yugoslavian People's Army, Catholic and Muslim soldiers no longer wanted to serve. He let them quit, making sure Serbs controlled the army bases, supplies, and weapons. Even though I was only eleven, this sounded disastrous, like that demented soccer feud was spreading to real life.

As I was coming home from school one late October day, Velibor and Dalibor were cheering in delight, "Long live Serbia! Arkan is our hero."

Arkan was the crook who'd led the Red Star Belgrade soccer fan riot. Eldin said he was a murderer who'd escaped from jail and was wanted by Interpol, muttering that he was "a Serbian mafioso."

"Those stupid Croats are being slaughtered," Velibor roared, saluting a passing car that waved a Serbian flag.

"Don't worry, Arkan will come here too," Dalibor said, turning to me menacingly.

That week, Igor put Huso and me on the same side as our Croat neighbor, insisting, "Only Serbs on *our* team." Over the weekend, they were playing tag without me.

That fall, vans were passing through town every day, covered with enlarged pictures of Milošević's face, blasting turbo-folk music. Swarms of radical Serbs from the villages were bused in, rallying support for the upcoming primary elections for new party leaders. This politicking was more intense than any I'd ever seen. Billboards and posters sprouted up everywhere. On street corners men shouted speeches from megaphones and argued in parks, cafés, and public squares. Serbs waved three-finger salutes when their rally cars sped by. Croats and Bosniaks held up two fingers for victory. Eldin said everyone had to pick sides. I didn't totally get what our three main political factions stood for yet. But I noted that the Bosniak's color was green and the Croat's bloc was red-checkered. Milošević's Serb party, the most nationalistic and dangerous for us, showed a blue stripe. On it was an emblem with the Serbian cross and four *S*'s in their Cyrillic script.

"What do those letters mean?" I asked my brother.

"Only Unity Saves the Serbs," he told me.

My parents liked our Muslim majority group—called the SDA, Party of Democratic Action—who Dad wanted to vote for. But Mom said, "Rough times are coming. Look what happened in Croatia. Let's not be aligned to any side now." To be safe, they agreed not to vote. It didn't matter. Overnight we were all divided by background anyway: Orthodox Serb, Catholic Croat, or Bosnian Muslim. Igor and his boys—all with Serb backgrounds—stopped talking to me and stared as I walked by. They snickered and called me "Bosniak" behind my back. My teammates picked me last, though we still played soccer together every day after school. I felt ostracized, left out, ignored.

One chilly November recess while were eating salty *ćevapi* outside, Igor and I looked over the fence. Soldiers from the Yugoslavian People's Army military base, right next to our school, were cleaning their rifles. I was intrigued to see the weapons up close.

"The other day while I was stealing my bike, I saw them taking equipment out of the warehouse," Igor told me.

"What's in there?" I asked.

"They've got uniforms, gas masks, helmets, and duffel bags. I want some," Igor said, his bugged-out blue eyes hungry for looting. "I figured out a way in. We should check it out tonight. Meet me outside the building at nine. Bring plastic bags."

Robbery was a serious crime, but I felt flattered he still wanted me in his gang. Maybe my pals had stopped listening to the stupid slurs their parents were spreading. I was so glad they liked me again.

That night Igor, Velibor, Dalibor, and two other guys from school were waiting for me, holding shopping bags to cart away our booty. Igor led the five-minute walk to the edge of the school grounds. My heart was pumping fast as we sneaked up to a hole in the fence. One at a time we each squeezed through, slithering sideways to fit. Igor pointed at the young recruits with guns patrolling the base. We crouched on our hands and knees before a window in the warehouse and then lifted each other inside. It was too dark, so Igor turned on the lights. The whole place was overstuffed with military equipment in mounds taller than we were; you couldn't even see the floor. I wanted to wear a soldier's uniform like my father's. The crisp new merchandise smelled raw and woodsy.

"Grab what you can," Igor commanded.

I quickly took bandages, a canteen, a portable shovel for digging trenches, and a green flashlight. I made sure to collect four gas masks for my family, in case—as I'd overheard Eldin and my parents' friends predicting—the war in Croatia spilled over the river to us. Velibor and Dalibor grabbed shovels, combat sweaters, socks, holsters. Igor seized a green helmet, camouflage pants, a shovel, and some shirts. We all found backpacks and stuffed our stolen goods inside. We took turns as lookout. They were treating me as their equal. I was one of the guys, like old times. Nobody saw any guns or ammunition or we would have swiped that too.

"Hide!" Velibor sounded a warning. "A soldier is coming."

We hid under piles of blankets. I was so scared I thought I was going to pee my pants. The soldier looked through the window but didn't see us.

"Let's get out of here." I was shaking, freaking out that if we got caught, my mom would kill me. I didn't know who I feared more—the armed militia or my mother.

"Let's come back and get more tomorrow," Igor said.

Unlike me, he wasn't at all fazed; he'd been looting his whole life.

As we ran to the park, the weight of the stuffed pack was heavy on my back. We used our new shovels to dig ditches where we stashed everything. It was raining, so the ground was softer. When I came home at 10:30, I washed up and went straight to bed, pretending I'd just been out playing soccer and tag with the guys.

The next day at school, during our math lesson, the principal came in and took Igor and me out of class, into his office. Inside there were two military policemen waiting.

"Where were you last night, Kenan?" the tall one asked me.

"We were playing hide and seek." Igor took the lead, lying with ease.

The principal walked out and returned with Aleks, our short classmate who had braces on his buck teeth.

"I overheard them talking about breaking into the base last night," Aleks said boldly.

I knew my dad used to be ski buddies with Aleks's father, a doctor who was now president of the Serb Democratic Party in town. Dad said he'd become a "Milošević fanatic" who'd show off his Serbian accent any chance he got.

"When this is over, I'm gonna kick your ass," Igor hissed at the tattletale, then spat at him.

The principal pulled Igor by his ears and slammed him into the chair.

"You boys have ten minutes to bring everything back," the officer ordered.

I was trembling. If my parents found out, they would ground me for life. I would not be allowed to practice karate again. I had never been in this much trouble before. Running to get the stuff to return, Igor followed me.

"They don't know what we stole," he said in my ear. "Just give a few things back."

He had a point. And if I returned everything and Igor didn't, they might know he'd kept more of the loot. I didn't want him to see me as a wimp or Goody Two-shoes. Then he'd never include me in another feat of bravery again. So I retrieved the shovel, flashlight, and backpack, and left the bandages and gas masks behind. This way, if somebody threw a poison bomb like bank robbers on TV did, my family wouldn't breathe in the toxins and black smoke. We were then escorted to a military jeep by two uniformed men with armbands. The officer told us to get in back. Rows of my classmates' eyes gaped at us from the windows. I was shaking, scared to my bones.

"We are so screwed," I told Igor, sure they were taking us to jail.

We were separated and placed in two different rooms. The man in charge of the base came to interrogate me. He was really tall with a goofy mustache that draped around his chin. I recognized him as Milisav, a Serb friend of my father's. They had served together in the army reserves one month every year since I was born—or longer.

"Oh, it's little Keka," he said, sternly, not happy to see me. "I know his father."

I went to give him a handshake as I always did, but he refused. He kept his hands behind his back, standing very erect, scowling at me. "Sit down," he yelled.

I obeyed, sitting on a leather chair as two other men hovered above me.

"Did Senahid put you up to this?" Milisav used Dad's real first name.

"No. No," I stuttered. "We just thought it would be a cool game to see if we could sneak into the base."

"Wait until I tell your father."

I started crying.

"Are you a Bosnian, a Yugoslavian, or a Muslim?" his younger comrade barked at me.

What was I? Was it a trick question? I was baffled how to answer. I thought I was all three. "I'm from Yugoslavia," I sniffled. "I'm a Bosnian. And my religion is Muslim."

I was being honest, but judging from his scowl, I'd obviously flunked his test.

"You can't be all of them!" Milisav snapped. "What are you first?"

I heard the echo of a Serb politician I'd seen on TV who'd warned, "If Bosnians want independence from Yugoslavia, the Muslims will be extinguished."

"I'm a Bosnian," I responded. "Then a Muslim."

"I see." He shook his head disdainfully.

"Take him back to school," he ordered the younger guy.

"What did you do?" my homeroom teacher, Milutin, snarled at me in class. I'd always been a good student. He used to tell me, "I expect a lot from you because I respect your dad so much." I'd tried hard for him throughout grades one to six. He'd never scolded me before. "You're in big trouble now," he warned.

As Igor and I shuffled home together, I was embarrassed, my eyes to the ground.

"At least your dad isn't around to kick your ass, like mine will," I told him.

Turning into our building's courtyard, I looked up and saw my mother glaring down at me. "*Zadavi ću te,*" she shouted so everyone could hear. That meant "My hands will be around your throat."

I'd never seen her this mad before. I took a breath, bolting upstairs to get it over with.

"I was at work, and the radio news was on," she yelled. "I heard your name mentioned as the leader of a Yugoslavian People's Army theft!"

I was on the radio? Jeez. No wonder she was so upset. I had

humiliated her in public, smearing my family's good name. I was deeply ashamed. Now none of Dad's friends would shake my hand anymore. The owners of the candy store wouldn't trust me; they'd monitor my movements closely so I wouldn't rip them off, like Igor.

"But Igor was the leader, not me," I tried to tell her. "I took bandages and a gas mask for us, in case anything happened. And I returned the stuff anyway."

"Go to your room. You are grounded," she fumed, swatting at me. I ducked, racing to the bedroom I shared with Eldin, who wasn't home yet. I'd never been grounded. I dreaded losing my freedom to play outside and having my nights ruined with a curfew.

When my father returned from work, he marched in without knocking. I was sitting on the bed. He'd never hit me before, but I was sure this time I was in for it. He stood above me, hands on his hips. "Why did you do this?" he hollered.

"Everyone's saying the war's coming," I told him. "I took four gas masks, a shovel, a canteen, a flashlight, and bandages. I'm scared. I want us to be ready."

He didn't speak for a second. Then his eyes changed from rage to worry. "That's not your job," he finally said quietly, patting my head. "Don't go out of your room or make any noise or your mother will kill you."

I felt vindicated, but still nervous about Mom's wrath.

"Wow, that was wild. You were on the radio. How did ya sneak in?" Eldin asked when he came home, quite impressed with my newfound bad rep.

"Like Sylvester Stallone in *Rambo III* infiltrating the Russian base in the dark," I said. "It was like that, but there were no German shepherds."

I was not allowed to have dinner with my family. But hearing my mom's brother's voice down the hall, I called, "Can I please see Uncle Ahmet?" I hoped he'd protect me.

"No, you stay in your room, you thief!" Mom screamed.

"Get out here right now, Kenan!" Ahmet overrode her. My mom's macho older sibling was always bossy. Knowing she wouldn't dare argue with him, I slunk into the kitchen, where they were eating without me. Ahmet was in the middle of a plate of okra and rice.

"What did you do?" he demanded.

"I stole from the Yugoslavian People's Army," I confessed, head down, afraid he might slap me. "My classmate Aleks told on us."

"You know who Aleks's father is?" Dad said. "Head of the Serb Democratic Party."

"That's what you're punishing him for? You're not grounded anymore," Ahmet declared, magically granting me clemency. "Let him steal from those bastards who attack us with our own weapons." He lit a cigarette and gestured for Mom to make me food.

She pushed a plate of okra at me, scowling, and said, "Here, pig out, you animal."

I downed it all fast, wondering if stealing from bastards still counted as bad.

The next day at school, every period I was called to the principal. None of the other boys was. I missed all five classes. "Why am I the only one here?" I asked.

"Did your father get you to do this?" He kept pushing.

"No." I was mortified to think I'd gotten Dad in trouble. "It was just a prank with friends."

When they ordered my father to come get me, he barged into the principal's office, where I was waiting. "Why do you keep interrogating my son?" he yelled. "He is not a criminal."

The principal looked embarrassed. "It's just a standard procedure."

"They keep asking if you talked me into it," I told Dad. "At the base yesterday, your friend Milisav wanted to know if I was a Yugoslavian, Bosnian, or Muslim."

"What did you tell them?" my father asked.

"I said I'm from Yugoslavia. I am a Bosnian, and then a Muslim."

"Good for you," he said. "Is that why he's the only kid here? Because he's Muslim?" My father peered at the principal. He was a Serb, I now figured out. "If you call him into your office one more time, you'll lose your job," Dad threatened. Then we marched out.

At our apartment, Dad grabbed his army beret, belt, and first-class-captain uniform from the drawer. After his mandatory year-long army service at eighteen, he'd volunteered to stay in the reserves, leaving home for one month each year. Every spring when it was over, I'd wait downstairs for him to return, looking spiffy and powerful in his tidy green shirt and pants tucked carefully into his boots. I'd run into his arms; he'd put his cap on my head and carry me home.

"You're coming with me to the military base," he told me now.

At the gate he announced, "Tell Milisav that Keka is here."

"Keka, we need to talk," Milisav said as he approached. "This is not good for you."

"No, this is not good for you." My father pointed his finger at Milisav's face. "You asked my son if he's Muslim? How long have we been friends? How long have I volunteered to serve in this army?" My father ripped the red star from his beret and handed it to Milisav. Then he gave him the rest of his uniform. "I don't believe in this. I resign."

"I thought I could count on you," Milisav said.

"It's not my army anymore," my father told him before we left.

I was proud he stood up for me, but troubled by what it meant. We used to look up to the Yugoslavian soldiers marching around the base. We'd wave and bring them candy.

"Why didn't he ask Igor what religion he was?" I asked Dad.

"Listen, that kid didn't call Milisav," he said. "It was his father's dirty work."

At school that week, I was suddenly a dangerous celebrity. The guys wanted to know if we found any guns. The girls questioned how we managed to sneak by the armed soldiers. My teachers seemed fascinated that such a good, obedient kid had gone rotten, asking "When did you become a robber?" and "How upset are your parents?"

I relished my newfound bad-boy status. Yet I kept hearing Dad's and Uncle Ahmet's words. If the army didn't like Muslims or attacked unarmed, innocent civilians, I debated whether that justified my misbehavior.

"You're not going to need your braces anymore. I'll straighten those teeth for you," Igor hissed at Aleks the rat, right before we jumped him on the school's soccer court.

We got in trouble for that too, when Milutin told the principal, who phoned my father. But he never called me into his office again.

"We beat up Aleks for snitching," I admitted.

"Good," my dad said.

Weeks later, on the way back from karate one evening late in November, I saw Eldin and Mom rushing shopping bags of supplies from our apartment to the main boulevard across the street. I followed. Parked there was an endless line of dented buses caked with muddy tires, their windows ruptured. Hundreds of Croatians crowded outside, battered and wounded. A dark-haired woman cradling a baby cried, "They took my husband away. Where is he?"

An elderly man held gauze up to his bleeding forehead. A boy who'd taped his broken eyeglasses together helped an old woman in a torn coat bandage her hand. Was that her grandson? A blond lady who looked my mother's age wailed, "They murdered my son. He's dead." I'd never seen such misery up close before. Mom handed out cash and baby formula and medicine she'd bought, giving away our clothes and money. Feeling grateful I still had my family, I rushed home to get the blue panda sweater that Grandma Emina had knitted me for my birthday. I told Mom to give it to someone who needed it more than me. My best friend, Jasenko, brought his jacket to donate, and a blanket too. Jasenko and I stood on the side together.

"I bet foreigners attacked the Croats. Think it was the Hungarians?" he asked.

"Or Germany, like in *Battle of the Bulge*." I pictured the World War II movie about a secret brutal German attack that we had on VHS tape.

"No, it was the Serbs," Eldin said, filling us in: They'd forced the Croats to flee their city of Vukovar, only two hours north of here. Croatia bordered Serbia on the east, but wrapped around Bosnia on all three other sides. The Serbs had thrown rocks and shot at the passing buses, filled with fleeing refugees. It took three days to make a two-hour trip since they were forced to drive through Serbia. No wonder they looked dirty, tired, dazed. "I hope our Bosniak leaders are prepared when this happens to us," Eldin added.

At that chilly, wind-swept junction I knew: we were next. I was different from my Serb classmates and neighbors. Jasenko and I were bonded forever by our Bosniak blood.

"That poor mother has lost everything." My own mother shook back and forth, looking stunned. "Her baby is dead."

More of our Muslim friends brought jackets and blankets and food. The survivors said the Yugoslav People's Army, now controlled by Serbs, had set fire to their homes in Croatia, burning everything they owned. All that remained was ash.

"But aren't soldiers just supposed to kill other soldiers?" I asked Mom.

"You people will be next," a girl yelled out the bus window.

Later on Croatian TV, a refugee in Zagreb pointedly said, "I want to thank the Bosniaks and Croats in Brčko for coming to the aid of our people." Not the Serbs.

My parents were upset that no Serb citizens we knew helped. Instead, as we sat on the stairs, my pals laughed at the now-homeless

Croatians. Igor and the guys played war with Styrofoam guns, imitating soldiers killing Croats. I wanted to be the Terminator. But Velibor and Dalibor insisted they were Serbian generals and I was the enemy Bosnian soldier. I thought of the billboards contrasting the red-checkered Croats, green Bosniaks, and blue-striped Serbs: It seemed the whole neighborhood had been divided into three rival teams.

That winter Eldin told my parents that he was stopped at manned checkpoints on the way to karate practice in the next town.

"Will we be okay?" I asked. "Are we going to wind up like those Croatians?"

"Go to your room," Dad said.

I walked away, stung; he'd never blown me off like that before.

The trouble inched closer on Sunday, March 1, 1992, when we heard on TV that Bosnia had declared independence from Yugoslavia and become a separate nation. While secretly cheering the bold statement, we were troubled by the reaction. Politicians were screaming at each other. Neighbors were threatening us. On April 5, the Bosnian city of Bijeljina was attacked by Arkan's paramilitary units, who murdered unarmed Muslim civilians on the last day of the Islamic holy month of Ramadan, in a city just forty minutes from us. Arkan, the escaped convict who'd incited the soccer riot, whom Eldin called "a Serb mafioso," was now a military leader. Our town was dangerously in the middle, sitting on a highway connecting west to east. Jasenko's parents sent him to stay with his aunt and uncle in Zagreb, where there were no signs of unrest.

Standing outside after school that Monday, Dalibor came up to me. "Did you hear what happened to those Muslims on their holiday?" He smirked. "They all died."

"Fuck their mothers," Igor added.

They knew I was Muslim. What would they say about my

mother? I debated whether to swear back, retaliate, fight, or walk away. I wound up ambling alone to the corner store to buy myself a chocolate bar, kicking stones on the road. My friendships with Dalibor and Igor were over. It felt as if someone had pressed a button that turned the world lonelier, like everyone I thought I knew I didn't know anymore.

One late April afternoon, as I was out playing, I spied my dad meeting in the stairwell with all the other men from our building. One guy was drilling holes around the glass entry door to support protective metal bars. Hasan, my friend Huso's father, who lived downstairs, yelled that we had to watch out for Serbs running the army. Our next-door neighbor Obren shouted back, "We Serbs are peaceful people. It's the damn Croats we need to protect ourselves from." Hasan lunged at Obren. I watched Dad step in to pull Hasan away, talking him down in the corner. Why was Dad defending Obren against his own Muslim friend? Obren and his redheaded wife, Petra, were never very nice to us, barely saying "good day" when they passed us in the hall. Hasan had already sent Huso out of the country for safety.

"We'll be okay," my dad assured. But after school on Wednesday, April 29, he came home from the bank, swearing and shaken. All of our accounts were depleted, thousands of dinars erased. All we had left was in our wallets, our life savings gone.

"What happened to our money?" Mom paced, flipping out. "It just disappeared?"

"The Serb government is using it for supplies and weapons," Dad surmised.

"How are we going to survive?" she cried.

My father had been so popular and beloved throughout Brčko, he never really believed anyone would hurt us. He didn't think we would have to leave—until that day. Now it was too late. We had nowhere to escape to.

"Tomorrow you and Eldin go to Grandma's," Dad decided. "You'll be safer there."

The next day Eldin and I nervously walked half an hour to Grandma's, across the river, to the old part of town. After dinner, we watched TV with my cousin Amela. Then Eldin and I went to sleep, sharing the king-size bed in Grandma's extra room. We were shocked awake at 5 a.m. when two explosions shook her walls, flare-ups much louder than the firecrackers we lit on New Year's. These were no warning shots; they were meant to kill. We flipped on the lights and ran to check on Grandma. The ceiling had collapsed on the pull-out couch across from her bed.

"My God, I was lying on that couch but changed my mind and switched to the bed in the middle of the night," she said.

We walked outside to survey the damage. All her window frames were blown off, drooping over the sides, glass shards everywhere, as if a crane had demolished the side of her house. Neighbors came by to say the bridge connecting Bosnia to Croatia—just three hundred yards from Grandma's—had been detonated. The news blared on the radio.

"Come back right now!" Dad stammered over the phone, realizing he'd made a mistake—we were safer in the middle of the city than across town. "Don't walk by the Sava Bridge! Take the shortcut."

Eldin took my hand and rushed us home. His legs were so long I could barely keep up with his strides as we passed shattered glass on the sidewalk from every café, clothing store, and bakery. People were sweeping, silently nailing boards over their lost windows.

"Don't stop," my brother told me. "Walk faster."

"What happened?" I asked him. "Why didn't the stores burn from the bombs?"

"The pressure from the sound waves must have smashed all the glass," he said.

"Why did you want us to take the back road?" I asked Dad when we got home.

"I rushed to the bridge, but I saw it was severed in half," he told us. "On the pavement I saw human limbs and blood. Half a baby was dangling from the thick branch of an old chestnut tree." His voice cracked, his face white as bone.

He was speaking to me the way he spoke to Eldin and Mom. I somehow knew he would no longer talk to me like a kid.

"Do we have to go to school on Monday?" I asked Dad later.

"No, you don't have to go to school," he said.

At first it sounded like fun; I pictured a soccer game with Igor, Velibor, and Dalibor. Then I remembered they hated me because I was Muslim. They weren't my friends anymore.

"You're not going to school for a long time," Dad said in a low tone that spooked me.

"From now on the four of us are sticking together," Mom promised, hugging me close. "You're never going anywhere without us again."

On Friday, May 1, 1992, rapid, continual gunfire and mortars announced the war's arrival in Brčko as the Serb soldiers and tanks rolled in. Our friend Mujo and his wife—Jasenko's parents—came to stay with us. Mujo was a handball coach who had an office at the Partizan Sports Hall and worked with Dad.

"How's Jasenko?" I asked.

"He's safe in Zagreb, where there's no fighting," Mujo said.

Since the Serbs started the combat, I didn't get why they were battling in *our* town instead of theirs, in Serbia. "When is he coming back?"

"Not soon."

I overheard Mujo asking Dad why he didn't send Eldin and me to Zagreb too, though we didn't know a soul there. Then Grandma called to say cousins Amela and Mirza had packed their car to leave, barely missing the paramilitaries who were making their way up the hill.

"Should we go hide in the country with Amela?" I asked.

"No. We're staying together here," Dad said, his eyes jumpy, trying not to look unnerved.

That Tuesday, as Mujo headed for his office at Partizan, he was stopped right outside our apartment by Obren, our neighbor. Obren now wore a green Serb uniform and was armed with an AK-47 and two grenades.

"Where are you going?" he questioned.

"I can't sit indoors anymore," Mujo said. "I have to check on my office."

"I do too." My father put his shoes on, ready to go along.

"Don't be stupid. Don't go to Partizan. Don't go anywhere," Obren ordered.

When we passed her on the stairs, Obren's wife, Petra, told Mom, "Soon Brčko will be rid of all the Croats and your people too."

On Wednesday Mujo insisted he was going to the sports complex anyway and coerced my father to come. But then he ran back into the house, heading for the bathroom. "Mujo's sick with diarrhea," Dad said. "We'll go to Partizan tomorrow."

Yet on Thursday, Mujo heard Serbs were gunning for him because he'd voted wrong. Everyone who'd picked the Muslim party was on a death list. Mom had been right about remaining neutral. With the help of a rich Serb connection, Mujo and his wife fled the country. Dad said Obren was now a guard at Luka, the warehouse and river port. I didn't understand what Obren was guarding there—the barrels of sugar and wheat?

That morning, I went to brush my teeth, but no water poured from the faucet. Mom opened the refrigerator and the light was out. The lamp would not turn on. The stove did not spark. "Check the bedroom," she called. I flicked the switch—nothing. All the running water was turned off. The sunlight was flowing in from the windows, so we hadn't noticed all the electricity was gone.

"Don't open the fridge often or everything will spoil faster," Mom said.

Obren insisted all windows must be covered with shades from now on. If you are seen looking out the window, "you'll have an RPG coming your way," he warned. From war movies I knew that meant a rocket-propelled grenade.

We spent the next seven days on edge, holed up in our dim, dry apartment that seemed to grow smaller, darker, scarier. That Friday afternoon in my bedroom, one week into the war, I caught Mom covering her mouth as she peeked through the shade's narrow slits. I dropped to my hands and knees next to her, watching a truck filled with corpses pass underneath our third-floor apartment. Arms and legs hung off the back, looking like a crate full of broken dolls' limbs. Uniformed men in ski masks, armed like Rambo, marched down our streets. One pack stood by the park where we used to play soccer, only their eyes and mouths exposed. Obren said no men over eighteen should go outside. All civilians were stopped by soldiers demanding identification cards. Our Muslim names would get us killed.

We tried to eat what was in our fridge; everything else went bad. We finished the cookies and pita in the bin, then rationed cans from the cabinet, carefully splitting sardines, chicken pâté, beans, and vegetables. Soon we needed more food.

"Keka and Eldin should stay inside. It's not safe," Obren said. "Kenan should get supplies."

"It's too dangerous," Mom fretted.

"Obren said he'll be okay," Eldin argued.

"Run and buy us a loaf of bread." Dad gave me a few dinars. "Be careful, Kenan."

"If the soldiers ask, give a false name," my brother warned.

"They're making Muslim men pull down their pants to see if they're circumcised. Croats and Serbs never had circumcisions as babies, like we did," he explained. "Muslim boys are dying this way."

I tightened my laces. At eleven, I was short and quick. Nobody my age had ID. I wouldn't give my name. If asked, I'd lie and give a non-Muslim name: I'd say I was Igor. If they told me to pull my pants down, I would run away fast.

The streets were abandoned, except for army vans zooming around and the Serb soldiers who were now occupying our town. My stomach hurt from worry and hunger. The store beneath our building was closed. As I dashed across the boulevard to the closest open grocery, there were loud, ugly blasts of mortars and gunfire behind me. My legs were numb; I couldn't feel my feet touching the pavement. I hurdled over bushes and sidewalks, telling myself soldiers would never hurt a kid. But then I felt a warm breeze. Something grazed my left eyebrow. A whistling sound, then a vibration against my eardrum made me dizzy. Must have been a random bullet. Was I hit? I touched the left side of my forehead. It was sore, a little bit of skin torn off. But there was no blood on my hand.

I walked into the grocery and snatched the last remaining loaf of bread. I approached the cashier, who knew my parents well. She always asked me about school.

"Tell your mom you Turks won't be needing to eat much longer," she hissed while grabbing my money. She added, "You're not welcome here anymore."

Now I was Turkish? I thought I was a Bosniak. Neighbors and friends we lived close to our whole lives were abandoning us like rats scurrying from a shipwreck.

On the way home, I sprinted back across the boulevard. That was when I spotted my teacher, Milutin, my most respected mentor, a tough grader who'd refereed our soccer games during recess. He was in a uniform, holding a long gun.

"Hey, teacher," I called, relieved to see someone I trusted. I was about to blurt out that a bullet just almost hit me, hoping to hide behind his back.

"*Balije* don't need bread," he spat, knocking it out of my hand. He leaned his rifle barrel against my head. I froze. My favorite teacher was about to kill me in the street like a dog. His AK-47 jammed. I jumped, tugged away, swept up the bread for my family, and sprinted home so fast I couldn't breathe. I turned back to catch Milutin's three-finger salute at me, sure what it meant: he wanted me dead. Everything he'd ever taught me about brotherhood and unity was a lie.

Passing a soldier with an Arkan Tiger patch on his uniform, I feared Velibor was right. Arkan was coming to kill us too. Hoping they'd think I was Serb and leave me alone, I gave the salute myself to fake them out.

"A bullet nicked my head!" I told Mom when I got back, putting the bread on the counter proudly. I intentionally left out the part about Milutin for fear if she knew, she'd never let me out again.

"Oh no." She clasped her hands together, paced with tears in her eyes, then held a cloth to the nick on my brow, mumbling she was sorry for sending me to get us food. But I understood the new law. Dad and Eldin, of fighting age, hid inside or they'd be captured, killed, or tortured. I was mobile, the man of the family now.

"Hey, what's *balija*?" I asked.

"It's not important." She pushed my hair out of my eyes.

"It's a slur for Muslims. They want to wipe us out," Dad said quietly.

The next day, a year after my karate coach gave me my brown belt, Pero stepped out of a blue police van in front of our apartment complex. From the window we watched as twelve soldiers followed Pero, their commander.

"Oh, thank God, it's Pero," Mom said, eager. "I'll go talk to him." I wanted to go too, but Dad put his arm out, stopping me at the door.

My mother returned, looking startled. "He wouldn't look me in the eye." She was crying. "He yelled, 'Get back to your home.'"

We saw Pero hand his men a list. A moment later we heard the butt of a gun against our front door. Boom! Boom! Boom! "Trebinčevićs, you have one hour to leave," yelled a Serb soldier coming right inside.

"Where do we go?" Mom asked, her voice quivering.

"Leave or we kill you. One hour," he shouted in her face. Then he stormed out.

How dumb I was to think Milutin and Pero had ever loved me. Now they might shoot me and my entire family. My father was not the unofficial mayor in town anymore. He had zero power. All Dad's connections and kindness no longer counted for anything.

Mom covered her mouth with her hand, then went to the closet and pulled out pieces of luggage. "We'll go to Great-aunt Fatima's. Pack quickly," she said. In each suitcase, she threw in a photo album, saying, "Clothes are replaceable." I grabbed my favorite sports picture of me at Croatian karate camp on the Adriatic seaside, which Eldin had taken two years earlier. To my left was my friend Miko, a Serb. On my right was my pal Mate, a Croat. I was the smallest one of the trio, the Bosniak in the middle, wearing an orange belt. I wrapped the photograph, along with my 1991 karate diploma, in an undershirt, not knowing if I'd ever see either of my teammates again.

"Pero has eaten at our table." Mom was panicked, barely keeping it together as she ran from room to room, scrambling to figure out which few possessions from our life we could fit into our suitcases. In case we never came back.

I packed my kimono and brown belt in my duffel bag.

"You won't need these." Mom took them out, throwing my karate gear on my bed.

I'll come back for them, I told myself on the seven-minute walk to Fatima's, which we made breathlessly, dodging past Serb soldiers with guns who were all of a sudden everywhere.

"We'll be okay," Dad kept saying.

But then we learned that Luka, the river port where I liked to play, had been turned into a concentration camp. So Muslim and Catholic prisoners were what Obren was guarding now. And Partizan Sports Hall became a slaughterhouse for Bosniak and Croat boys and men. On the wooden floor where I'd kicked and somersaulted, my people were being gunned down by Pero and his comrades, their bodies left on the ground in pools of blood. In the gym's bathroom, where I showered, Serbs were slashing necks and blowing heads apart. The dead were stored on the outdoor basketball courts where I shot hoops, until frozen meat trucks came to take the rotting flesh away. If we'd gone to the gym as usual, we would have been murdered and loaded onto a truck. For the first time I doubted Dad's word.

Soon we figured out the only reason we hadn't been killed already: because my father had stood up for Obren at the meeting in our building, our Serb neighbor warned Dad and Mujo away from the sports complex. It turned out diarrhea wasn't the worst problem you could have. Mujo's upset stomach rescued the rest of him. Now he and his wife were out of harm, somewhere else. But as all the Muslims we knew were disappearing from Brčko, I was afraid there was nobody left to save us.

CHAPTER TWO

_____

Pressure Cooker

Queens, New York
May 2011

"So I hear you guys are taking your dad back to Bosnia this summer," my father's friend Esad said casually when I met him on the street in Astoria.

"What? Who's taking him?" I asked, surprised to hear—for the first time—that Dad had changed his mind and wanted to visit the country that tried to annihilate us almost two decades before. I was pissed off. I guessed yet another of Dad's cronies had flown back to the Balkans and returned to say we should go too. So this was Dad's way of floating the idea, secondhand. We'd vaguely fantasized about visiting at some point before we died—but it would be on _my_ clock, when I decided I could handle bumping into war criminals who'd tried to kill me walking down the street, now waving hello. I wasn't ready yet, and I did not want to be pushed. "No. We're not going!"

"That's okay," Esad said. "I'll take him then."

No way was I letting my father return to our homeland without me and Eldin to protect him.

That night in bed, I imagined what it would be like returning to my Brčko home. There I'd see Petra, our Serb next-door neighbor who'd taunted us the entire year we were trying to escape. While her husband, Obren, was working as a guard at Luka concentration camp, Petra had humiliated my mother by demanding she hand over whatever clothes and furniture she felt entitled to steal. This time, I'd find the hag, drag her down the stairs of our old building by her hair, then throw her into a meat truck, the way sadistic soldiers did to my people.

I was startled by the intensity of my fury. At thirty, I was an easygoing guy in a healing profession who hadn't had a revenge fantasy for nineteen years. But just because the political scenario in Bosnia had slowly improved and other Muslims we knew had trickled back to our town did not mean that *I* had to make the voyage now. A fleeting memory of my former apartment alone incited violent urges for revenge. I knew many survivors who felt this way. Sometimes, in the middle of breakfast, if the name of a turncoat from our town came up, even my gentle, mild-mannered father would mutter, "I would have no problem putting a bullet in his head."

The next day I bumped into Dad and Eldin outside Black Bull, a Balkan grocery store in Queens. Five blocks from my place, it was owned by a couple from our hometown.

"So when exactly did you decide Eldin and I were taking you to visit Brčko?" I asked Dad in Bosnian. He used to be fully bilingual. But after a stroke caused by a ruptured aneurysm ten years ago, he'd reverted back to our first language.

"What?" Eldin asked. I was blindsiding him, but I didn't care. I got the reaction I was looking for when he turned to Dad and barked, "What the hell is wrong with you?"

"It's safe to go back there now. And I'm not so young anymore. I miss Sead, Šabulja, Rizo . . ." Dad was listing his old gang.

"We're not going," I reiterated.

"Why not?" he asked. "I haven't seen my friends in twenty years."

"We can't," Eldin said.

"Then I'll go with Esad," Dad threw out, in a rare moment of defiance.

"You're not going without us!" I snapped. My brother nodded in solidarity.

Getting home from work at ten the next night, I saw Eldin's size 14 Adidas on the mat outside my front door. Walking in, I found him on my couch, watching *World Soccer Report* on my TV, drinking my beer. The downside of giving him my spare key.

"Got anything sweet?" He walked over to my kitchen cabinet.

"Hazelnut wafers." I handed over my five-dollar Jadros, a Croatian import.

He opened the box, took one out, put it in his mouth whole, then mumbled, "I need some milk." He went into my fridge and poured himself a glass.

"Bosnia," I said, still stewing.

"I know. Is he crazy? I'm not wasting my time off in that godforsaken place. Let's enjoy string bikinis in Brazil. *That's* a vacation." He plopped on my couch, resting his huge feet on my glass coffee table. "Taking Dad back there would be constant aggravation. It could be a catastrophe."

"You're right." I was perturbed to see the glass of papaya juice he'd left next to the beer bottle. How many drinks could he have at once? "Let's tell him no way."

"You tell him," Eldin said. He never liked confrontation, a trait he'd inherited from Dad. "Hey, check out Isabelle, the girl I met at the bachelor party." He scrolled through his pictures to a sexy Cuban brunette from Miami, this month's fixation. "Gorgeous, nice, and a chemistry major. Why does she have to live so far away?" he asked the love gods.

"Long distance is your type," I reminded him, checking her out. It was easier to discuss his current lady friend in Florida than our ancient ghosts in the Balkans.

"She sent me a picture of her knee to show me how swollen it is," Eldin said, showing me the pic with her index finger pointing to her leg injury. "She had an MRI, but a local doctor couldn't find anything. What do you think?"

"Nice knee," I said, squinting. "If her calf tightens, it's a tear. If it buckles or locks, might need to be scoped out. Make a house call. Instead of texting, go see her."

"I can't. But never close the door to any woman," he recited his motto. Or was it a rationalization for keeping a girl in every port but none living at his home?

Eldin's last serious relationship was with a beautiful Italian woman, but it ended in disaster. He'd been faithful for fifteen months, but she became too possessive, upset when he'd go to bars with me or his pals, falsely accusing him of picking up other girls.

"I'm having a tough time," he admitted one night over dinner. This was the most vulnerable he'd sounded since the war. I didn't know if it was our macho culture or proud temperaments, but nobody in my family spoke directly about our feelings. "I love her, but I can't deal with the jealousy," Eldin continued, looking tortured. "What do I do?"

He was asking *me*? I still wasn't over the breakup with my ex almost two years before. After we split, I'd tried going to clubs with my buddies. Their inane strategy was to say, "Fuck Nicole. You're better off without her. See those hot chicks around us? Take a few home with you. Then you'll forget her."

My father's reaction to my hurt was to walk around saying, "That's so terrible. I don't know what happened. She was so pretty and sweet and nice," over and over until I screamed, "Enough already!"

When I told Eldin, "I'm never giving my heart to anyone else again," I wanted him to understand my pain, guide me, say, "This happened to me before, so I know you'll feel horrible for a while. But it'll eventually fade and then you'll be happy again."

Instead he said, "You'll be fine, man. You're okay," which was more annoying than helpful.

After Eldin finally split up with his flame, I'd just listened, nodded, and bought him drinks. I didn't know how to console him emotionally either. This was what we needed girlfriends for. He somehow managed to remain friendly with her, quoting Dad's advice to "never leave a woman with anything bad to say about you." It occurred to me that over the years we'd fallen for women from all backgrounds—except ours. The only Balkan female we'd ever loved was our mother, Adisa.

Once we fled Bosnia, Mom swore she'd never go back. She kept that promise. She lived in Connecticut for thirteen years, never leaving the United States. After we lost her to cancer in 2007, we moved Dad from Westport into his own apartment in Astoria, near both of his sons. The three of us were on our own, living separately, but close by. Maybe the male Trebinčevićs had remained single because we'd never finished mourning her, or because nobody could compete with Adisa's imprint. After she died, Dad reminisced about Bosnia more often. I feared seeing his motherland might be his final passion.

On Saturday afternoon Dad and Eldin came over to my place. Unlike my college buddies, who shared beer and Doritos while watching sports on TV, we played "The War Game," a sort of demented *Jeopardy!* we invented. I put out hummus, carrots, and celery sticks and switched on my flat screen to watch the *World at War* series on the Military Channel. We'd seen most of these ancient videos before and found the history to be biased and one-sided, as if our people weren't worth mentioning. So Dad and Eldin would shout the missing Bosniak version at the television. To an outsider, our brand of male bonding might look nerdily pathetic. But it gave me a chance to pick their brains for the Balkan lowdown I wasn't taught at school—in Bosnia or Connecticut. I was still trying to catch up on what had happened to us and why, as if facts from the past could solve the mystery and soothe the rejection I still felt from being thrown out of my own country.

"In 1914, Europe had been at peace for forty years," began the crisp voice of the American woman narrating the World War I saga. Black and white clips of Russian and German armies aired as she chronicled the treaties signed by the German, Italian, and Austro-Hungarian superpowers pledging allegiance to fight together before the Great War.

"Started by the Serbs!" Eldin called out in Bosnian; we always spoke our mother tongue when we were together.

"How many other wars did they initiate?" I asked, sipping coconut water.

"Since then, four," Eldin answered. "Slovenia, Croatia, Bosnia, Kosovo."

It helped me to keep hearing that it wasn't just us, to put our exile in a larger geographic context. I wondered why my father—or any sane Balkanite who had a choice—would want to go back to that troubled region. I certainly didn't. I felt lucky—and safe—here.

Most of my American friends forgot, if they ever knew, that World War I began in the Balkans. It was triggered, the narrator recited, when a Bosnian Serb nationalist assassinated the Austrian Archduke Franz Ferdinand in Sarajevo in 1914. Up popped a picture of the mustachioed Ferdinand. He was the last surviving heir of Franz-Joseph, the emperor of Austria-Hungary.

"Franz-Joseph was a bitter old man whose wife was killed by a Serb," said Eldin, sitting beside me on the couch.

"He got back at them by ordering his army to invade Serbia," added my father from his leather chair, drinking coffee.

"A million Serbs died," Eldin explained. "Their military was so much smaller than the German, Turkish, and Austria armies, they seemed like the underdog. That's why the League of Nations gave Serbia the upper hand in the region after the war."

My brother often recited statistics, dates, and theories off the top of his head. His vast storehouse of knowledge awed me; he could have been a political science professor.

"The name of the country was changed to the Kingdom of Serbs, Croats, and Slovenes," the on-screen commentator reported.

"The language was switched to Serbo-Croato-Slovene," Dad filled in. "No mention of Bosnian."

"Why were we erased?" I asked.

"Serbs hated everything Turkish, so anything Islamic was hidden," Eldin said.

"Remember how the Serbs in Brčko called me Turk?" I slouched on the sofa, putting my feet up on the table, trying to place my memories into a historical time line. I struggled to find a clearer sense of where we fit in and why we were marginalized for so long. I felt better seeing the exclusion as part of a long-term pattern. It wasn't personal, nothing my family had done wrong.

"After World War I, it was hard for Muslims to become doctors or professors in Yugoslavia," Eldin told me. "Serbs made up laws to steal our land and banned the name Bosniak, which we'd used since the eleventh century. So tons of Muslims got the hell out. That's why two and a half million people in Turkey have Bosnian ancestry."

"Yeah, when I visited Turkey, the Turks were happy to hear where I was from," Dad said. "A shopkeeper there told me, 'My grandfather was Bosnian,' and he gave me a discount on a tablecloth. When I took your mother to Istanbul, we were at a museum and the tour guide was happy to find out where we lived."

I nodded at the story we'd heard several times.

"He snuck us into a room to show us this holy book from Bosnia that was brought over centuries before . . ." Dad dropped off, looking out the window.

"Okay, let's listen." Eldin jacked up the volume as the TV commentator moved on to Serbian army commander Alexander Karadjoredević, who became king in 1929 and changed the country's name to the Kingdom of Yugoslavia. He wanted to be known as Alexander the Unifier, to curb the tribal animosities, she said.

"Another lesson written in Belgrade!" Eldin cut in. "Alexander was just another oppressive dictator. He renamed our language Yugoslavian, as if that would help."

"We wanted to be recognized, not ignored," Dad said.

When it came to our background, I knew so little. I wanted to reach my father and brother's level of understanding so I could pass it on to my kids one day. It felt as if I'd flunked a required class. Yet no academic curriculum I'd ever encountered told the truth about our tribe. I didn't know if it was censored so much as never written.

More vintage clips, maps, music, and sounds of machine-gun fire followed as the documentary illustrated how, with typical Balkan volatility, that peace lasted only five years, until Karadjoredević was killed by a Croatian nationalist in 1934.

"In retaliation for a murder by a Serbian nationalist!" Eldin yelled.

"Damn, another Serb assassination," I echoed, chomping on celery.

I noticed that Dad wasn't eating anything. It was getting hard for him to chew vegetables with his brittle, chipped teeth. I needed to take him to the dentist. It troubled me to see him aging. Sitting there, hunched over, he looked more fragile than I cared to admit. I yearned for my childhood image of him as strong, swift, and immortal. As the World War II segment "Beast of the Balkans" started, I put a plate of strawberries, blueberries, and green seedless grapes in front of him.

Eldin, who often posted diet factoids on his Facebook page, preaching to his patients ("If you crave sugar, eat fruit"), scarfed up most of the berries himself while Dad ate one grape slowly, like a bird.

"Did you drink enough water today?" I asked him. He nodded.

On the video, marching music dramatized the rise of Eastern European nationalism in the 1930s, swastikas denoting Nazism. A different British male voice recounted how tensions between Balkan factions worsened in World War II. In 1941 German forces bombed Belgrade. A weakened Yugoslavia signed a pact with Hitler, leading to the German occupation. The narrator described how Tito, leader of the Communist Partizans, convinced most Balkanites to collaborate to defeat the Germans. Tito flashed on the screen in his general's uniform, wearing a green hat with a red star.

"Hey, I remember that photo! My first-grade classroom had that same picture," I jumped in. "On Republic Day, my teacher Milutin made us put our hands on our hearts and recite the oath on Yugoslavian unity: 'Today when I become a pioneer / I'm giving my pioneer word . . . that I will love my country . . . and spread brotherhood and unity,'" I recited. "That was before he put a gun to my head."

Dad stood up, crossing his arms. "What a fake brotherhood!" he told the TV Tito.

"When you were a kid, did you hate the Partizans?" I asked Dad. He was just five years old at the start of World War II.

"Why did my family have to fight for an army that didn't recognize us or our religion?" he asked, agitated. I watched as Dad shook his head and clicked his tongue. He wasn't even over World War II yet. A trip to Bosnia could raise his blood pressure and give him a heart attack or another stroke. It would be insane to go.

The Brit jauntily relayed how Tito's Partizans prevailed and World War II left devastation across the Balkans. He detailed how Serbs suffered a half million casualties while 86,000 Muslims were killed. The long tradition of regional blood feuds ceased in 1943, when Tito became prime minister. He was seen as a popular and benevolent dictator, promoting the peaceful coexistence of Yugoslavian factions. He was elected president in 1953, around the time my mother was born.

It depressed me that Tito's idealistic talk had been a lie. Our people were used. We'd never really been part of anything Yugoslavian. The hero I'd idolized as a kid turned out to be so deficient. "Maybe he was too busy shoring up his power to groom a successor to ease the transition after his death," I tried.

"We didn't realize it then," Eldin shrugged. "We should have known."

"Guess it's easy to be a Monday morning quarterback," I conceded, thinking how Mom used to say, "Everyone is a general after the battle."

"What's that quarterback expression mean?" Eldin asked.

"It means woulda, coulda, shoulda," I told him.

Eldin didn't go to high school in the United States, so I enjoyed filling him in on the English slang he'd missed. I recalled the first time I knew something he didn't, when Eldin came home from college, confused by Madden video games. "How many downs are there?" he'd asked me. I could never beat him at sports—he was way taller and stronger than I was—but it was a thrill being able to teach him American football and baseball, which we'd never played before. I didn't show off. I just told him the rules matter-of-factly, the way he used to help me.

"With Tito, the economy was good. Nobody was starving," Dad was saying. "He kept the Russians out and the Serbs under control."

"Yeah, until he died in '80. Those power-mad racial supremacists were only in hibernation," Eldin shouted, pointing a carrot at the screen.

If my brother got this fired up by video clips in Queens, what would he be like in Bosnia, confronting the Serbs who'd wanted us dead? I didn't want to find out. I ate a handful of grapes. "So growing up, you never noticed bias against Muslims?" I asked Dad.

"A little," he told me. "For decades they argued whether Bosniaks were an ethnic group, a religion, or a nationality."

"Which did you want?"

"Put it this way. A voting survey asked me whether I was a Serb, Croat, Slovene, Yugoslav, or other," he recalled. "I picked other."

"In '74 the Yugoslavian constitution was amended to list Muslims by nationality," Eldin said. "Better, but too broad."

"Thanks for finally recognizing us, but a religion is not a nationality," explained Dad.

"Picture if the U.S. government told a Jewish person, 'We're going to classify you as a Jew, instead of an American, in 1992," Eldin said. "Just like Hitler did in the '30s."

"Why did Tito take so long to acknowledge our existence?" I wanted to know.

"He was surrounded by those Serb politicians," Dad said. "He couldn't take a leak without their permission."

"All the Yugoslavian cookbooks were written in Belgrade," Eldin offered.

"We have to take Dad back at some point," my brother whispered as he was leaving that night. I was vaguely conscious that in some ways, the war had never ended for us and we'd never really left.

"Some point isn't now," I told him.

Since it was late and we were watching soccer the next day, my father decided to stay over, as he'd started doing a few nights a week. Later, as he slept in my spare room, I remembered how he'd bought me and Eldin all the fancy sports equipment we wanted as kids—shin guards, cleats, new sneakers, the fastest sleds. He paid for swimming lessons and drove an hour and a half to find us the best karate kimonos in the area. In the chaos of exile, when Vienna, Quebec, or Australia might have been options, my parents chose the United States for us, so we'd get a good education. "In America, your mom and I will start over. We'll be nobodies so you and your brother can go to college and become somebodies," Dad said.

Broke and exhausted in Connecticut, he remained generous. Working odd jobs from 6 a.m. to 11 at night in Stratford, he'd wake up from a nap to drive me to a soccer field to time my sprints in the scorching heat. Just last week when he'd seen me carrying heavy groceries, he took a bag out of my hand to help me carry them home—at age seventy-one!—and wound up missing his ride to a barbeque. It was selfish of me to deny him the trip home he wanted so badly.

Yet it could be too stressful and perilous to return to a town where the same people who persecuted us were still in power. The complex aftermath of all the Balkan bloodshed and stories we heard put me on edge. After we fled in January 1993, the fighting intensified. Eventually Bosnians and Croatians mobilized against the Serbs, whom we were finally about to overtake in 1995. Unfortunately NATO—led by the United States and Britain—intervened. It was the worst blow of our lives when Western leaders imposed the deeply flawed Dayton Accords in November 1995. The treaty unfairly ended the conflict before we could rightfully win the war we were forced into. For us that meant we were never going home.

Even President Clinton admitted this inequity. In controversial documents and recordings published in the book *The Clinton Tapes*, he disclosed that during negotiations, NATO allies felt "an independent Bosnia would be 'unnatural' as the only Muslim nation in Europe." The British, French, and Russians favored the arms embargo on Bosnian Muslims precisely because it locked in Bosnia's disadvantage. France's president Mitterrand told Clinton that Bosnia did not belong among European nations, and the British officials spoke of "a painful but realistic restoration of Christian Europe." When Eldin read me and Dad excerpts from the book last year, our rage was mixed with vindication at the former president's confession.

"It's like the World War I League of Nations treaty all over again," my dad said.

"It's a miracle Bosnia didn't lose all our land outright," Eldin added.

So that was why Dad always rooted against the French, British, and Russians—even at the World Cup. "Muslims and Jews were never welcome in Europe," he told me.

After the Dayton treaty, some areas, like Sarajevo—the largest city and cultural center of Bosnia—recovered quickly. But in Brčko turmoil and corruption continued to reign. Although my family wound up safe in Connecticut, we struggled financially, and for years it was too expensive and dangerous to visit our old region anyway. So we hadn't even considered going. In 1998, when my friend Jasenko's mom went to Brčko to file papers to evict the Serb family who'd stolen her home, American peacekeeping soldiers had to drive her to her apartment in a military jeep. She eventually won it back and sold their apartment at a devalued rate. (After the war we sold our two-bedroom place in Brčko—which had been worth $200,000—to Dad's friend Truly for $26,000.)

In 2000, international forces pressed the new local government to elect rotating multiethnic officials and start returning property to refugees like us. Yet later that year, the windows of Bosniak businesses were smashed, like a modern Kristallnacht, with Serb teenagers committing the hate crimes instead of Nazis. When my grandmother visited us in Westport in 2004, she said Brčko was still hazardous, that she'd been trying to rebuild her house and was wrangling to retrieve the pension the Serbs had tried to eradicate.

"Stay where you are," Grandma Emina warned. "You have no business coming back. You're better off in America."

I felt awful that in her early seventies she had to struggle to rebuild her life in Bosnia. Yet by my freshman year of college—amid a little success with grades, girls, and sports—I started seeing the upside of being an American. I realized Grandma was right.

"You'll live longer with better health care here," Mom told her, trying to talk her mother into moving in with us.

"I'm too old for change," Grandma insisted. "I want to die where I was born."

Despite the gradual return of Muslims to neighborhoods in Brčko, when my cousin Amela called, she relayed tales of riots and ethnic clashes in her children's school in 2006. It wasn't until Dad moved to Queens the following year that he got in with a group of Balkanites who planted the idea that it was now safe to travel to our old town.

Out of the six Bosniak guys my father palled around with in Astoria, Dad was the only one who hadn't been back to our homeland. Šemso, who owned a construction business, had spent the previous summer in Bosnia. He told Dad that all his old Brčko buddies were asking for him, which made Dad feel lonely and left behind. "Some of your Queens gang lived in parts of Bosnia that hadn't been occupied," I pointed out. "And your other friends escaped abroad earlier, so they never saw what we did."

I was less afraid of being assaulted there than of overreacting if a former neighbor asked, "What's that *balija* doing here?" Flashbacks played in my brain. I'd missed celebrating my twelfth birthday because we had no food or electricity in Brčko. Eldin joked, "No cake, bro, but plenty of candles." But I was no longer a small, starving kid. At thirty, I could carry out the vengeance I couldn't then. Mom used to say, "Don't let their evil corrupt you." I didn't while she was alive. But if I was in Bosnia without her, I didn't know if I could contain my resentment. What if I went back and lost it, barging into Petra's apartment, taking back everything she'd stolen from my mother? I would wind up in jail, destroying the future we'd worked so hard for in New York.

Eating *burek* in Astoria with my Bosniak neighbor Ado one spring morning, I said, "If I saw my classmates who turned on me, things could get ugly."

"Oh, all the guys who go back the first time have the same vengeful fantasies. Totally normal," Ado, a Bosniak engineer, reassured me.

"Really? Did anything happen when you went back?" I asked.

He nodded. "At a café, I see this Croat neighbor who'd held a gun to my head," Ado said in Bosnian. "He says hi to me, all friendly, like everyone just took a little hiatus. I sent him over coffee and announced, 'It's on me, because I have a good job. Your clothes are ripped, you don't have a dime to your name, you bum. There's forty-four percent unemployment in Bosnia now. Too bad you created your own poverty.'" Ado added, "I really wanted to throw a grenade under his table."

Among my people in New York, the Serbs' postwar financial ruin was our victory, vindication, and proof of their bad karma; their high jobless rate was our favorite mantra.*

A week later Dad stopped by my place, distraught that his seventy-three-year-old Bosniak pal Osman—whom he hadn't seen since 1992—had passed away. "I'm not going to be around much longer. I'm going to go down soon."

"Go down where?" I asked. I was tired from working late.

"I'll die."

"You're not dying. The States prolonged your life by twenty years. You'll outlive them all," I told him. But I didn't entirely believe my own cheerful prediction. He'd recovered from his stroke, but a ruptured Achilles tendon slowed his gait, and his left knee was worn down. He had a limp.

"The way Dad's ankle and knee are doing, he might not be walking so well five years down the road," I told Eldin that night. "It would be too hard for him to get around."

"Don't pressure me," he said. I felt pressured myself.

The next day, Aunt Bisera, my mom's sister, called from Bosnia,

---

* The 44 percent unemployment figure is from www.tradingeconomic.com, the federal office of statistics of Bosnia and Herzegovina, and the CIA *World Factbook*, which quote overall Bosnian unemployment rates between 43 percent and 46 percent in 2011 and 2012.

crying about how much she missed us. "Will I live long enough to see all of you?"

"I'm not ready," I told her.

"I feel bad we haven't seen Bisera," Eldin said, guilting me too. He'd always been the closest to our only aunt, who reminded him of Mom.

"So you guys will be in Bosnia this summer?" asked the owner of Black Bull, next time we went there. She was also from Brčko; she imported the food they sold from our old town. Dad was telling his whole damn crew about this trip I didn't want to make.

"We don't know. We're deciding when," Eldin said. What? We were? We'd switched roles, as usual. I was surprised he'd give up a South American beach for Bosnia.

"You guys would be doing a good deed if you took your dad," she added.

It was a conspiracy. Despite my good arguments, the world was pushing me to face down our past.

That night I invited Dad over for Chilean sea bass and couscous, cooking him a healthy dinner, as I did a few times a week. He showed me a picture of his postcollege jazz ensemble and said, "I miss my old buddies." Then he upped the stakes. "I really need to see my father's grave one more time."

He admitted he was afraid he'd die before seeing his home and making peace with the country that double-crossed him. Talk about a guilt trip. I realized he wouldn't be with me forever and worried how terrible I'd feel if we had to go to Grandpa's cemetery in Bosnia without him, knowing we'd denied my father his last request.

Having breakfast at an Astoria restaurant we liked, the Old Bridge, I told Eldin, "We need to go and get this over with." My brother had always been more malleable than me. I was known as the stubborn one, so once I changed my mind, there was no question. We were going. "If we wait, Dad might not be able to walk as well," I argued. "We should do it now because the timing is right," I reasoned.

"I'll only go out of spite," Eldin said. "To show the Serbs we have the balls to return. I'll spread the message: I survived, I'm healthy, strong, with a good career. Look at you, losers—you're out of work, drink beer and smoke all day. You can't even afford to take a lady out to dinner. You tried to get rid of us, stole everything we had, put me and Dad in your camp like animals. Now you're stuck in the hole you created."

I patted Eldin's back, wishing I'd let him talk me into sunny, carefree Brazil.

After he left, I imagined going back to our old apartment, where my teammates Velibor and Dalibor would run up to greet me, like we were still best friends. I would smile and hug them, playing along with the charade. I'd invite them to Aunt Bisera's for a barbeque in the suburbs. There I'd get those fickle, weak fuckers drunk on pear moonshine. I'd suggest a walk in the cornfields outside her fence, where it would be easy to cover up a crime. I'd surprise them, pull out a bat, and shatter their kneecaps and shoulders—so every time they had joint pain, they'd regret what they'd done to me.

Darkness brought out my wrath, but in daylight Eldin and I discussed rational reasons to go now, quieting each other's anxiety. "Brčko's become half-Muslim again, so there's a better balance of power with city officials and police," he texted.

"Yeah, the current climate makes it safer for us to return," I texted back. "And we could both get time off in July." Aunt Bisera insisted we stay with her so there would be no hotel fee. At $1,350 a ticket, we could afford the airfare, I told him. We'd split the cost of our retired father's seat as a birthday and Father's Day gift.

"Good, but I'll stay with Sead," Dad said, surprising us by announcing he'd lodge with his bandmate from the '50s. (Dad was the drummer, Sead on alto sax.)

"What? That's not fair," I cut him off. "We're only going for you. We're staying at Aunt Bisera's." I fought for my mother's only sister, whom we hadn't seen since we left, though she'd surely drive us all crazy with her overabundance of food, tears, and pets.

"Bisera's family," Eldin backed me up. "You can see Sead every day."

"You can stay with Bisera. I'll stay with Sead," my father insisted.

"You're making us go. And we're doing it for you," I yelled at Dad. "So at least stop being so self-involved and stay where Mom would want us to!" Usually I was quiet and agreeable with him, but all this talk of visiting Bosnia was freaking me out. The worst weeks of my life were when Dad and Eldin were taken to Luka concentration camp. Every day I'd feared they were dead.

"Why are you raising your voice? Can't we have a discussion like two grown gentlemen?" My father sounded hurt.

He was Mr. Chill until you disagreed with him. "You're killing a dead bird," I added, mixing up American sayings about birds and horses.

"We're staying with Bisera," Eldin insisted.

"Okay," he acquiesced.

Later that night I told Eldin, "Remember my classmate Igor, that douche who tripped me on the stairs at Brčko and called me *balija*? If I see him, I'm shattering a beer bottle on his face. Every time he looks in the mirror, he'll see the scar and think of me."

"This is why I'm not leaving your side," he told me. "I'll be your shadow, like the Secret Service."

"I can't guarantee anything," I told him. "But let's make sure Dad doesn't get mad at a Serb neighbor who shakes his hand, pretending nothing happened."

"Why do we have to go again?" Eldin asked.

"For Dad," I said.

When I told my work buddies I was going to Bosnia for a week, they thought it would be a cool trip, like sightseeing in Paris or Barcelona. Americans of my generation had no idea of the complex, volatile ethnic layers that made up Yugoslavia, a land still divided by medieval cultural hatreds. I couldn't explain that I wasn't just traveling to Eastern Europe for fun. I was reentering the hotbed of chronic religious unrest that haunted my past.

In the censured, Serbian-created version of Balkan history I was taught at school in Brčko, the Serbs portrayed themselves as defenders of the peace or innocent victims. During the 1992 war, power-hungry politicians had played on the Old World distortion that we were aggressors like the ancient Turks or modern militant Islamicists, using that illusion to justify ethnocide. Unfortunately, old prejudices spilled over to our new country. After 9/11, a Connecticut neighbor asked my mom, "What do you think about Osama Bin Laden?" My mother said, "He's an evil, horrible man. We're not terrorists," offended that anyone would connect us to violence or terrorism or suicide bombers. I'd never even seen someone wear a hijab until I moved to Queens.

Once I made the decision that I could handle returning to Bosnia, my next hurdle was figuring out which of the three Balkan airports we should fly into. Each had its own upside as well as headache, either logistic or historical. I suggested landing in Belgrade, Serbia. That was fastest; we could get to Brčko in an hour. My brother refused.

"I'm not scared of those genociders in Belgrade," Eldin said, his voice firing up. "But I'm not listening to Serb accents on the plane, going through their passport control, returning to the border where they degraded us by gunpoint. I'm not giving them one dollar of my business by buying airfare." Belgrade was out.

Dad wanted Sarajevo, Bosnia. To get to Brčko from there we'd have to drive four hours through winding mountains with no Serb border patrol. But I nixed that route since it wouldn't take us across the Sava Bridge. I had a special reason to venture that way. Dad and I used to fish along the Sava's banks, watching boat regattas and picnics there in peacetime. The bridge was blown up on April 30,

1992, killing hundreds of our civilian countrymen who were walking across. After rigging the underlying beams with dynamite, the Serbs opened the bridge at 5 a.m. and lured our refugees into the ambush. They were killed one kilometer, less than a mile, from freedom.

After a series of bridges were similarly detonated, there was no easy way to get from Croatia to Bosnia. Had the bridge been accessible during the war, it would have led us to liberty. It was rebuilt by U.S. soldiers in 1996. That was the only way I wanted to reenter my former country, symbolically saying, "You tried to destroy us, but we're back, marching down the steel pathway you blew up."

We finally compromised on the third choice, Zagreb, Croatia, so we'd land in a country where we'd never lived (thus nobody harbored bad associations). Then we'd drive three hours on the highway along the River Sava so I could cross my boyhood bridge. We'd stay on the Croatian side, so the border guard would likely be from there. Croatians had been fellow victims of Serbs, and our allies. That is, except for a treacherous stretch in 1993, when the southern Croats made a pact with Milošević to carve out Bosnia. They lost to Muslims, but after the 1994 Washington Agreement (another compromise urged by the Americans), our two republics joined forces again and had been friendly ever since.

There was also the peculiar matter of our passports. We'd kept the ones issued from Yugoslavia. The only problem: that country no longer existed. So they were of use only as souvenirs. We would have loved to get Bosnian passports in 1992, in our last year there, after Bosnians declared independence from Yugoslavia and became their own nation. They would have pictured our old flag—a blue coat of arms adorned with a white stripe and six fleurs-de-lis. But official documents were impossible to get during the Serb occupation of our town. Eldin and I obtained regular U.S. passports when we became American citizens in 2001. Dad—who couldn't pass the English test due to his brain injury—needed a doctor's note to be granted special dispensation for his U.S. citizenship. Mom, too sick to care, died in 2007 with just a U.S. Permanent Resident card that stated her country of origin; so Americans officially accepted her nationality as a Bosnian while she was exiled from the country that bore and betrayed her.

Eldin and I had been offered dual American and Bosnian citizenship, but we refused. We hated that the current passports from our original land had added Serbian Cyrillic script and no longer displayed our flag. The new one was blue and yellow, divided diagonally by a white stripe of stars. It resembled the European Union flag, representing nobody, managing to simultaneously offend all of the still-antagonistic ex-Yugoslavian factions. So we'd never become official Bosnians again. We'd be Yanks flying to Croatia on Lufthansa airlines, with a brief stop in Frankfurt. "Germans make more efficient machines anyway," Dad said.

"If we get into trouble with a Serb officer in Brčko, we'll call the 800 number for the American Embassy that's on our passports," I'd told Eldin, feeling protected by my U.S. identity.

"Good. Americans take care of their own," Eldin agreed.

Right after I made the reservations, we started to plan our itinerary—or at least discuss what our mission would be. My father's goal was to reconnect with his old buddies. So I pulled out Mom's old photo albums from the closet and went over them with Dad. He couldn't use a computer, so I scanned the old pictures for him, googled Bosnian names, and looked up people on Facebook to see who was still alive and living there. We found several e-mail addresses that I used to update contact info. Then Dad phoned his comrades. He first called his former sports club colleague Truly, who'd changed his name from Sejfudin when he'd moved to Germany. In 2006 Truly purchased our old Brčko apartment from us. He used it as a summer home and said we were welcome anytime. Truly promised to meet us there in July. When I asked, he confirmed that our Serb neighbor Petra remained next door. She was the only other person we knew who was still living in the building. The thought of seeing her made me wince, yet I anxiously anticipated her reaction. I pictured how nervous she'd be when I surprised her by showing up at her doorstep, all grown up, towering over her.

In the weeks before we left, I tried to focus on my job, but it wasn't easy.

"Hi, Zach, how's the heel?" I asked my noon client, a blond seventeen-year-old high school athlete with a surfer mentality barely affected by his Achilles tendinitis.

"Hey, dude, you gonna clear me for football camp?" he asked. "Lots of scouts."

"You call yourself a linebacker when you can't even squat?" I teased.

My cell phone whirred. "*Check out what that sick racist fuck Dodik just said,*" Eldin e-mailed, in our first language. "*Now he's claiming the 1995 Srebrenica massacre of Muslim men and boys never happened—and that Bosniaks dug up the bodies from other graves as a ruse!*" Eldin had been sending me links all day from www.24sata.info about the Bosnian Serb president Dodik. "*He's sprinkling idiocy over their minds.*"

"Let's start with juking drills," I told Zach, walking him over to the carpeted area. I pulled out an agility ladder. Zach began stepping in and out of it. My cell went off again.

"*Those psychopathic possums have been living their dream of greater Serbia for centuries, and every year they have less. It's going to be fifty percent unemployment soon.*"

"Hope that's a hot babe," Zack said, noticing my distraction.

"I wish, man, it's just my brother," I said. "Bend your knees. Lower."

Eating a chicken sandwich in the back room at work that day, I recalled the list we'd seen in Pero's hand of the Bosniak families his unit was evacuating in 1992. I thought of the Serb Death List I'd heard about that my friend Jasenko's parents were on because they'd voted for a Muslim party. Then I remembered that in the movie *Schindler's List*, the hero, Schindler, played by Liam Neeson, wrote down the names of the Jews who would work at his factory and survive. Now it was my turn to record my own foreign war-related agenda. While Dad collected phone numbers of his old pals and Eldin was scouring Bosnian newspapers, maps showing current ethnic breakdowns of towns and political blogs, I developed a different obsession. I took out a pen, tore off a sheet of notebook paper, and wrote: The Bosnia List.

Instead of the history museums, medieval castles, and waterfalls the Balkans were known for, I scrawled down names of Serb classmates and friends who'd turned on us. I'd track them down to ask them what changed overnight. My good memories of Brčko were ruined by thoughts of how defenseless I'd felt as our next-door neighbor humiliated my mother daily. So number 1 was: *Confront Petra*.

Number 2: *Stand at Pero's grave*. No, I crossed that out and wrote: *Piss on Pero's grave*. Then I changed it back again.

Since Dad insisted on seeing his dead friends and relatives, number 3 became: *Visit Muslim cemeteries*. I amended it to read *Visit the Muslim cemetery to honor my dad's fallen comrades*.

What was next? Maybe I'd locate Dalibor and Velibor, look them in the eye, and ask: how could you invite me to your home for your birthday party, then kick me and spit in my face a week later? Would you have let your dad shoot me in the back? I considered: *Track down my Old Serb karate teammates*. But then I decided I was more interested in getting our Serb neighbor Miloš to admit he regretted fighting against us.

I put my list in my shirt pocket but wound up pulling it out often, in between the dozen clients I treated that day, as well as on the subway home and when I ate dinner alone that night. I switched the order, crossed it out, then revised. Later, in the shower, I thought of the mass murderer from Luka and ran out, dripping wet, to jot down: *Find out where Ranko is imprisoned*.

Over the course of three months, finishing my list took me over. The closer we got to taking our trip, the more raw emotions I unearthed and felt a desperate need to resolve.

"We have seven days, let's figure out all of our priorities," I told Eldin over July Fourth weekend, as we ate *zeljanica* at Ukus, a Montenegrin-owned diner in our neighborhood.

"Dad wants to meet up with Truly and Sead and his jazz buddies and sports colleagues. Of course, we'll see Bisera and Amela and the cousins," Eldin said. "I want to visit the army cemetery and the statue for Bosnian war heroes in Brčko." While he focused on statues and stones, and my father longed to reunite with Muslim friends and relatives, I obsessed over the Serbs I wanted vengeance on—both living and dead.

"I can't wait to find Petra, the sadistic bitch," I admitted to Eldin, showing him my list.

"She's the first one you want to see? Really?" Eldin looked confused. "Why?"

He'd been a tall eighteen-year-old during the war, more in danger of getting killed than I was. So he'd spent most of 1992 hiding indoors with Dad. While they'd survived two weeks in the camp, most of their stress came from anticipation and claustrophobia. I was the little shrimp outside on the stairwell who every day was picked on by former friends, spit at, denied food in stores, hit, tripped on the steps, and shot at. My suffering was interactive. With so much face time on the street with Serbs, the confrontations I craved now were more personal. The list was becoming my scheduling book, security blanket, preparation tool, medicine to stem the pain, and symbol of my control. We had seven days in Bosnia. I might never go back; I didn't want to be left with eternal regrets.

Meanwhile I couldn't stop reliving all those times I'd walked through our building with Mom, watching the pain on her face as Petra toyed with her. "You won't be needing that carpet," Petra had said before taking the black and white rug my mother had treasured.

I was haunted by not being able to protect Mom when I was twelve. I couldn't even argue. I was muffled then since Petra could have turned us in to the police.

Petra loomed large in my Bosnian war memories. She was the first neighbor who'd turned on us. Right next door, she was the closest corrosive force through that dismal year. On our first five tries to get out of the country, we were forced back from the checkpoint. Each time Petra waited at the building's entrance, smirking when Mom told her the guards had refused to let us go. My tight-knit family of four was finally able to flee Bosnia together. When we returned now, Petra would expect to see my mom too. Would I tell her she had died? No. I would bang on Petra's door to demand she give back my mom's clothes, along with her carpet. I'd finally retrieve my mother's stolen belongings, bring her belated justice.

It would be bizarre for her trio of Trebinčević men to return without her. Yet despite my mother's heartbreak over what our country did to us, she'd be pleased with the reason we were going back. I could still hear her voice at the end saying, "When I'm gone, make sure you boys take care of Dad." She didn't have to ask. I would never put him in a nursing home or a hospice, no matter what. He was my blood. During the war and as we started over in a new country where we knew nobody, the four of us were our own team. We were all we had. I would take care of Dad forever, just as he'd taken care of me.

At 5:00 p.m. on Friday, July 15, 2011, we met up on my Queens street corner to hail a cab to the airport. I looked like a typical American guy in my loose-fitting black jeans, a yellow T-shirt, and suede Diesel sneakers. Eldin wore Adidas and cargo shorts with lots of pockets. My father was wearing his best navy suit and a tie.

"Way to be comfortable, Dad," Eldin said. "You'll melt in the heat when we land."

"Your grandfather always dressed like a gentleman," Dad said.

It was as if he was boarding the airplane in first class instead of being stuffed in the middle of the back row of cheap seats in coach. But I felt powerful, able to grant my father this crucial wish. It touched me, how excited he was to go home.

CHAPTER THREE

The Last Muslim Family in Brčko

Bosnia
May 1992

The tall paramilitary pointing his AK-47 rifle at us had a beard down to his chest and dark glasses. Despite the suffocating 95-degree heat, he wore an all-black uniform buttoned up to his Adam's apple. The bayonet in his holster hung halfway down his thigh. His *šajkača*, a flat hat decorated with a skull and two bones, showed he was a Chetnik guerrilla, a group notorious for cutting off the testicles and spooning out the eyeballs of civilians. The motherfucker gave me chills. My mother's chin was trembling.

It was the end of May and the first time we tried to escape Brčko. My stubborn father, believing the conflict would be over quickly and nothing bad would happen to us, made us wait too long. At eleven I already understood that the politics of my country depended on our strategically located city, lying close to the Croatian, Serbian, and Bosnian borders. Eldin said that whoever ruled Brčko ruled all of Bosnia. Unfortunately that was now the Orthodox Christian Serbs—like the psycho holding us at gunpoint.

When we'd boarded the bus to Vienna an hour earlier, we thought we'd make it out. But then, at the Pirometal factory checkpoint, the black-clad guerrilla had stomped aboard, demanded to see our ID. Then he yelled, "Get the fuck off." He'd obviously read our Muslim name, reason enough for us to be annihilated. "You're not going anywhere," he said. "I'm going to kill you."

We climbed off the bus and stood by the side of the road, as he'd commanded. A recent TV report I'd seen detailed how Chetniks had slit throats and sliced off Muslim ears and fingers. I was shaking. If he was going to murder us, I hoped he'd shoot us fast and not engrave crosses on our foreheads, the signature Chetniks left on their Muslim victims. As the guerrilla went to talk to another soldier, a four-door Stojadin stopped in front of us.

"That's my coworker, Slobodan Tešić!" Mom said, hopefully. I remembered him being a nice prankster from her company's soccer tournament; he'd called me "Little Keka" and showed me some soccer moves.

Slobodan rolled down his car window.

"We need help. We have the right paperwork. Would you vouch for us?" she asked breathlessly, sure if Slobodan said, "These papers are legit," they'd let us go.

He took the papers through the window and studied them. "These are no good." He threw them back at my mother, closed his window, and drove off.

My mother picked up the papers from the ground, shaking and sweating.

"I can't believe that piece of trash," Dad muttered under his breath.

I thought he was her good childhood friend. Then I remembered hearing two weeks earlier, from Todorović, another colleague of

Mom's, that Slobodan Tešić was the one who'd told soldiers Eldin and I had flown Islamic flags.

To our right, we saw four short men in green fatigues standing at the control booth, stopping cars and trucks driving past. As our tormentor walked over to say something to the group, a bald soldier in an oversized green uniform came up to us. "Hey, Keka," he said quietly.

"Milan?" My father recognized him from a soccer team he'd coached. Another chance!

"I'm so sorry, Keka. Srdjan's in charge." Milan looked down.

Nobody could protect us here. When the bearded psycho came back, he told Mom, "You, lady, you could come and cook us some bean soup." Did that mean he was going to rape her? I'd seen reports about what the Chetniks had done to Croatian women. My mother didn't move. He loaded his rifle and ordered us to march forward. We lined up next to each other, holding our bags by our sides. We started walking up the one-lane highway, away from Brčko. I heard the psycho cock his gun.

"Just keep going. Don't stop," Dad whispered. "Don't turn around."

Waiting to be shot in the back, I broke into a cold sweat. I was wearing three shirts and a thick jacket. We'd taken only one duffel bag each, so we'd dressed in layers. I struggled to keep up with Eldin. Mom, exhausted, was crying, falling behind. I took hold of a strap of her bag to help. Sweat stung my eyes. After a long flat block, the road climbed. When I eventually looked back, I could no longer see Srdjan the psycho. I wondered if he had been distracted by a car pulling up or by the arrival of other Muslims he could terrorize. Had Milan diverted his attention? I put my bag down, wiped sweat from my face on my shirt. I could breathe again. I relaxed my shoulders, thanking God we weren't going to be shot. Today. So they didn't kill us, didn't want us here, but wouldn't let us leave.

What now? We were stranded on the highway. The only way

back to the home we were thrown out of was blocked by the psycho at the checkpoint behind us. We couldn't escape to the suburbs in the south since the front lines dividing the Serb and Bosnian armies were drawn between us and our Brčko apartment. The sole way was east through Serbia—a sure path to death. To the left was the River Sava, dividing Bosnia from Croatia, but the bridge was destroyed. We worried that land mines would explode if we stepped off the pavement. Trucks of Serb soldiers passed, waving three-fingered salutes. Were they mocking us or did they think we were Serb refugees? When we realized we were heading toward Aunt Bisera's rural village, just five miles away, we decided to stay with her. It was a two-hour walk, carrying our bags in dry heat.

At her village's entrance, we now found a ramp with a Serb patrol who stopped us. "This is a detention center," a soldier said. "All men over eighteen have to sign in twice a day and get a number." Eldin and Dad complied.

"That's so no Muslim or Catholic males can escape to fight," my brother explained on the twenty-minute trek uphill to Bisera's. On the way, stray dogs, chickens, and cows who'd been let out of their stables roamed around, looking as lost as we did. This was farm country. The red-brick house Bisera had recently moved into had an unfinished roof and no garage door; it stood in front of a main road, totally exposed, overlooking the banks of the River Sava and Croatia. The back bordered on a cornfield where pear, apricot, and apple trees also grew. I'd been surprised months earlier when she'd relocated to this small, two-bedroom floor-through filled with mismatched rugs and elephant and turtle figurines to be with her new second husband, Halil. He was a riverboat captain who didn't make much money. "But he has the sweetest heart," she'd said.

We were let in by Halil, who was tall and quiet, with bushy eyebrows. He took our suitcases and gave us cold towels to wipe the sweat from our faces and glasses filled with water from the nearby well. Bisera embraced my mother and told us that Grandma Emina's side of town had been burned to the ground. Thankfully, my grand-mother had escaped with my cousins. "All the men who stayed behind were slaughtered at Luka," Bisera cried. "My friend Fadila was shot on her own doorstep. Dear God, what did we do to deserve this? Were we throwing rocks at You?" she asked the Lord.

Two parakeets in birdcages were squawking manically. The phones were turned off, and there was no electricity, but it was breezy, and the trees surrounding the open windows kept out the direct sunlight. A dozen Muslim refugees we recognized—mostly older female friends of Bisera's—were sitting on the floor, crying and shaking. They shared stories of husbands and sons who'd been shot, and how they'd been herded onto buses by the Serbs and brought here to be used for prisoner exchanges. "It's like a ghetto now," Bisera said, explaining that everyone who lived in the fifty homes in her subdivision took in Bosniak and Croat refugees.

"Keka, Adisa, how are you?" a woman called to my parents.

A retired volleyball player Dad had trained limped over to him, a black and green bruise on his head. "You wouldn't believe what happened. Our Serb friend Kišić beat me with a stick at the mosque."

"Kišić did that to you? That fucking animal," Dad muttered.

"I was trying to jump up and touch a live wire on the ceiling to electrocute myself," the volleyball player admitted. "But I will never forget you, Keka. If not for you, I wouldn't have been strong enough to withstand the beating. When you die of old age, I will put up your tombstone."

That night, the four of us crowded in Bisera's extra room, with Mom and I lying head to toe on the couch and Eldin and my father trying to sleep on the floor. The rest of the group slept on the floor of the long hallway between the front door and the main bedroom. We had no place else to go. We were stuck there. Despite the circumstances, Bisera was a noble host. She cooked eggs on her wooden stove and served bread, corn, tomatoes, and cucumbers from her garden. Halil gathered peaches, apples, and apricots from their trees, and milked the cows. Bisera served homemade sour cream. She extracted rose juice from flowers and cleaned clothes with soap and water from the well, then hung them up to dry outside. I played by myself in the backyard, trying to stay out of everyone's way.

On June 7, 1992, two weeks after we arrived, Dad and Eldin went to town for their morning sign-up but never returned. My mother, who was flipping out, completely frantic, ran to find them. I followed her. The streets were deserted. It looked like a ghost town from an old Western. As we passed houses in the Muslim village, all the doors and gates were open. Walking down a dirt road, we saw only one soldier. He looked like a young local boy. When we asked about Dad and Eldin, he told us all the Muslim men had been taken to Luka concentration camp.

"Don't go any farther or you'll be taken too," he said in a helpful tone, warning us.

Stumbling and sobbing all the way back to Bisera's, Mom crumpled into her sister's arms. Beside myself, I ran to the bathroom with the runs, my whole body erupting. It only stopped when Bisera fed me dry coffee grounds.

For the next six weeks, we heard nothing about Dad and Eldin. I felt sick, scared, and numb every day. At night, it was pitch-dark, ninety degrees, and there was no air-conditioning. Mom and I shared the small couch. I slept on my back, with my feet to her head for more room. She worried someone could walk by the ground-floor window and shoot us, so she only took a short nap at sunrise. It took me hours to fall asleep amid the sounds of crickets, croaking frogs, and gunfire. We were sleep-deprived, hungry, petrified that Dad and Eldin might be dead. Trying to be brave for my freaked-out and stressed-to-the-core Mom, I stayed quiet, spending hours digging sand in the backyard. It was hot and sweaty and I got bitten up by mosquitoes. Mom insisted I wear sweatpants and a long-sleeved shirt and put vinegar on my legs to repel the insects.

Two older Serb police officers came to the house to check up on us—one fat, one thin. "We know the men are at Luka and you're here. We're going to come and get you too," the fat one threatened, letting us know that Bisera's house was left alone only because it stood atop the hill and was exposed to the Croatians across the Sava River. Serb soldiers feared getting shot, so they didn't approach. Also buses wouldn't fit on the out-of-the-way, narrow gravel road.

A day later, as I was playing on the road in front of the house, I saw a four-door black Mercedes speed by, driven by a soldier in aviator glasses. When I heard shooting, I lay down flat on the ground and watched as a soldier in black jeans stepped out of his car, pulled out his RPG, and launched a rocket in the direction of Croatia. After an explosion in the trees, I ran inside and told Mom.

"You could have gotten killed. From now on, you just play behind the house," she said, pissed off.

The next morning I woke up disoriented, ready to meet Pero at karate practice in Brčko, as if the war were just a nightmare that had ended. But it had barely started. We were running out of food; there was just bread and corn left. The cow and chicken noises we used to hear during the day fell silent. Once the owners had left, no one fed the animals and they died, Bisera said mournfully. But the last call she'd received before the phones were cut off gave us hope: cousins Amela and Mirza had made it to free territory with Grandma Emina. Mirza enlisted in the Bosnian army. How I wished I were old enough to join too. But we heard nothing about Eldin and Dad.

Facing persecution for our faith was especially confusing to me, because we weren't religious. I'd entered a mosque only once, with my Uncle Ahmet, in a different town. I didn't fast for Ramadan or pray to Allah. Dad had studied the Koran in religious school when he was young, yet I couldn't make out the Arabic words at all. Mom's grandpa was an imam, but her parents just celebrated holidays. Nobody I knew wore burkas or followed conservative Islam. Women in our clan worked, dressed as they pleased, and bossed their men into sharing all cooking and household chores. In class we were drilled on Tito's separation of church and state. The Bosniaks, Croats, and Serbs I knew were mostly tall, slim white people I couldn't tell apart. All their accents seemed the same. Only names gave ethnicities away. But I started pondering whether Serbs had brown eyes, or darker hair and skin tone, or if their heads were bigger. After all, our lives depended on whether we could distinguish which guys wanted us dead.

I told Mom we should get to Croatia by swimming across the river to freedom in the darkness during thundershowers. "You're too young," she said. I argued that I'd taken swimming lessons two summers before. But she knew I'd never gone into the deep end without Dad. Even then I'd worn a life preserver or water wings, which we no longer had. I looked outside the window at the River Sava and felt spooked by the swirling currents. I felt guilty I was keeping her here. Along both riverbanks armed soldiers hid in bushes. Even if we reached Croatia, she said, it would be too dangerous to walk through the heavily mined woods to find a road.

We didn't know if my father and brother were alive. In bed I'd shut my eyes, hoping someone was taking care of them, praying that when I woke up they'd be back with us. But with my heart pounding off my rib cage, I couldn't sleep. Explosions traveled down the river, echoing for miles. My mother couldn't sit still and do nothing. The next time the fat-and-thin Serb police duo came to the house, on the afternoon of July 18, she begged for information about Dad and Eldin.

"If you really want to know, I can get you to town," said the thin Serb.

"What jewelry do you have?" asked his chubby partner.

My mother handed over her gold wedding band and a silver necklace so they'd drive us home to Brčko. We got in the back of their blue police Yugo, bypassing the checkpoints. I was afraid we'd run into the Chetnik guerrilla, but luckily we didn't see him from the backseat, and we were quickly waved through.

"I'm sure they're okay," I lied to console Mom, telling myself that Dad knew everyone and nobody would touch him, out of respect. But really I feared every second that they were being tortured or were lying in a meat truck, dead.

It was a twenty-five-minute drive to the apartment of Great-aunt Fatima, Grandma Emina's sister, our only other relative in Brčko. She was sixty-three, with short, curly black hair. She looked frail when she opened the door with Uncle Smajl.

She kissed and hugged us, then said, "Look who is here!" We turned to see Eldin and Dad sitting on the couch, in shorts and T-shirts. Eldin was wearing his big, yellow-framed glasses, reading an old soccer magazine.

"Oh my God, you're here! You're safe!" my mother shouted, overjoyed. "You're alive!" she cried as we all ran into each other's arms.

"We heard some of the buses with women and children from Bisera's village were blown up," Eldin said. "We thought you were dead." He picked me up high, hugged me, and messed up my hair.

When he put me down, I inspected him and my father carefully. They looked pale, scared, and thinner, but otherwise okay. They'd been detained at Luka for two weeks. Then they were among the few men miraculously released from the camp right before the Red Cross first came to report the atrocities to the world. For the last four weeks they'd been hiding at Great-aunt Fatima's place. With no phone lines, electricity, or radio communication available, there'd been no way to let us know.

"Pero was the one who took us to Luka," Dad said. "He made the men line up in rows. He walked by and ignored us. I hope someday he turns in his grave."

This was the worst Bosnian curse. He wished Pero would never find eternal peace. I couldn't imagine my father wishing Pero dead. I didn't know how to despise anyone yet, especially my beloved coach.

The radio station next door to Fatima's apartment had become a makeshift Serb headquarters, so we couldn't stay there. We sneaked back to our own home, a seven-minute walk. There were few civilians outside, mostly just passing army trucks and jeeps. We saw one couple walking outside, looking comfortable, as though they owned the streets, so we knew they must have been Serbs. Rushing with our bags, we feared we looked suspicious and trekked far off the road, underneath the awnings, to avoid soldiers. The streets smelled of gunpowder and metal, the sound of heavy and soft artillery in the background like an ongoing symphony. It was spooky, with no lights anywhere. Our feet crunched glass as we walked. I saw bullet casings on the ground.

We were unsure what we'd find at our apartment. On the stairwell, we didn't recognize new neighbors sitting on balconies in the hot sun. As we reached the top step, we found the door unlocked; a sign read "Property of the Brčko Police." Petra slinked out of her place next door with a smirk. She leaned against the wall, smoking, smelling of perfume, in my mom's beige nightgown, which she'd helped herself to in the six weeks we'd been gone. She said everyone kept their doors unlocked now so they wouldn't be kicked in by looting soldiers. A paramilitary commander had been living here, but he'd disappeared.

"When the conflict ends, Muslims will be defeated," Petra added. The new law dictated that we write our family name on the front door in Cyrillic. She insisted we use the Serb alphabet, as if they'd erased our writing, reading, and language too.

Nobody was inside our place now, but it was in disarray. The carpet on the floor was twisted. A bath towel with caked-on dirt was draped over the couch. The dining-room chairs were in the living room. The VCR and several of Dad's jazz records were gone. Mom's flowers were dried and shriveled—even the tree of life, her favorite.

"If there wasn't hope for the plant, is there hope for us?" I asked, wearing down, as we tried not to imagine what had happened here, within our walls.

"Petra's in the nightgown Bisera gave me, that whore," Mom swore as we checked for what else was missing or damaged. "I can't stop her. We're the only Bosniaks left."

In both bedrooms, the beds were unmade. It felt dirty to think someone had been sleeping under my covers. The toilets were filled and unflushed. Our always-clean house now reeked. When I saw maggots on the kitchen floor, I dry-heaved. The white, wormlike insects came up to my ankles. When I opened the freezer drawers, more maggots poured out. With no power, all the meat had gone bad, and nobody had removed it. The dining-room rug was wrecked by combat boot prints, muddy and sunken in.

I went to wash up, forgetting we had no water, soap, or toothpaste. Mom gave me baking soda to clean my teeth and to use as deodorant, and leftover laundry detergent for shampoo. On her knees, she started scrubbing the soil imprints away. We could be killed, and she was worried about her ruined rug? It got on my nerves.

"Walk softly, so the new neighbors on the floor below don't hear us," Mom ordered.

We didn't know which of our Muslim neighbors had escaped to Croatia or Germany, who was detained at Luka, how many were dead. Many families of the Yugoslavian People's Army lived in the building, the nicest complex in town; Eldin guessed that the soldiers hadn't bombed or burned it down because they wanted to keep it for themselves. The new tenants were Serb families who had their own places to live but stole second homes. Eldin's resister radio was still in the drawer underneath the TV. He turned it on quietly and searched for the latest news.

When I took the maggots out to the garbage in plastic bags, I saw that the Serbs occupying Bosniak homes had tossed wedding and baby albums into the dumpsters. Someone had used a black marker to block out the faces and heads shown in the pictures. They wanted to erase all signs we had ever lived.

I felt we should have swum across to Croatia. Or I could have insisted we go with our cousins Amela and Mirza to the free territory, where at least we had our own army. I wished we had gone to Grandma Emina's a week earlier and made it over the bridge to Croatia before it exploded. We had friends we could have stayed with on the Adriatic Coast. At twelve, my head was already filled with regrets.

"So what are we going to do?" I asked my parents.

"We're stuck here," Mom said. "Maybe it'll end soon."

In other words, we were screwed.

We had little food or water and only a few hundred dinars left, but we needed supplies. I was deemed the designated shopper. On the way out to buy bread and oil at the grocery, I bumped into Igor, Velibor, and Dalibor at the bottom of the stairs.

"Hey guys!" I greeted them, smiling, for a second forgetting we were on different sides now.

"Hey, *balija* is back," Igor frowned as they surrounded me.

"Dumb Turk," Dalibor said, rubbing my face with a poster of Alija Izetbegović, the leader of Bosnian Muslims.

"Kiss your president," Velibor yelled, then spit in my face.

"Why are you doing this to me?" I asked.

"We're not friends anymore," he said.

When his dad returned from the front lines, Velibor said, "I hope you killed a lot of Muslims," in front of me.

Over the next month, I watched from the outdoor stairwell while Velibor, Dalibor, and Igor asked the new kids in the neighborhood to play. When I walked by, they'd slap and punch me. A fifteen-year-old Serb kid two heads taller than I who lived on the fifth floor came up to me one day, called me *balija*, and spit in my face. Seething, I wished I was bigger so I could toss him off the balcony and watch him splatter like an egg yolk. I lost it, spun around, and gave him a karate kick in the ribs. He kneeled over and grunted. I'd never used martial arts outside of practice before, but I didn't regret it—even when he chased me up the stairs and kicked me in the back so hard I could barely walk.

"Why don't you ask Eldin to protect you now?" Igor laughed.

If my brother tried to intervene, Velibor's dad would knock on our door with his AK-47. Hiding inside, Eldin calmly crouched down on the floor, listening to the free-territory radio station for hours on end, hoping for updates on the fighting. He was like a serene, skinny Buddha who firmly believed we'd survive. He and my dad discussed the war, and politics, and geography. Mom cleaned as much as possible and made us all a daily small meal with a sardine, or an apple slice, or bread. I played miniature cars, on edge and fidgety, my stomach aching all the time. I felt like an anxious old man with an ulcer. Every day we heard gunfire and vacant homes being broken into with a booming combat boot or rifle.

During the long nights, crouching on the floor by candlelight, Eldin and I would try to guess which weapons were being fired. The noise AK-47s made reminded me of multiple nails being hammered into a door, as I'd heard on construction sites. Howitzers were like jets taking off from a runaway, then firecracker explosions. Mortar rounds seemed like glass smashing. Eldin said RPGs made the sound of a supersonic jet zooming by our window. VBR launchers were the equivalent of twenty-four rockets taking off within seconds of each other, whereas I heard M48 machine guns as a rapid sewing machine.

Oddly, days of endless mortar rounds, automatic gunshots, and bombs going off soothed me. That meant my old friends would stay inside so they couldn't beat me up. If the sounds indicated the fighting wasn't too close by, I'd walk seven minutes to the closest Turkish fountain on the hill, overlooking Luka. I'd fill two canisters with fresh spring water; there were many ten-foot *česmas* with fancy faucets the Turks had built that were still working after hundreds of years. This became our only water supply, for bathing and drinking.

It was still summer, so a quick wash did the job. I'd splash my face and under my arms and fill my stomach with the cold water. I was starving, so I wanted to feel full for a few hours.

Coming home with my mother one day, carrying apples we'd picked from a nearby tree to eat and use as mouthwash, we bumped into one of our new neighbors on the stairwell. He was a Serb kid who looked fifteen. "Mom," he yelled inside. "Mr. Keka is back. *Balije* returned." He spat at my mother's feet, blocking our entrance.

"Shame on you," my mom told him. I wanted to boot him in the head like a soccer ball.

We stepped over his feet, heading upstairs. The next day, after I'd filled two jugs of water, Igor stuck out his foot and tripped me on the steps. I fell on my hands, scraping my palms. I punched him while lying on the steps. He spat and slapped me. Dalibor sneaked behind me for a cheap kick.

Enraged, Dad came to the terrace, screaming at my old friends, "What crawled out of your asses into your heads lately?" They looked down, embarrassed.

Petra, as ever on the doorstep, told Dad to be quiet. "You could be killed for defending him," she said. In her pink silk dress and heels, she then walked down to two soldiers looking for apartments to loot, telling them which ones were vacant this week.

"While Obren's away, she gets dressed up to flirt with all the soldiers," Mom said, disdainfully.

One afternoon when I brought home a used disposable grenade launcher, my mother had a fit.

"Get it out of here! Don't let anyone see you with it!" she told me. "They'll think we're firing it at them. You'll get us murdered!"

Another day I saw the boy who'd spat at my mother holding empty canisters, walking next to his dad, who wore a red beret. The father was armed with two guns, a knife, and a stick. A cigarette dangled from his mouth. I knew from the red hat that he belonged to a paramilitary group that specialized in looting. Every day he'd return to his stolen apartment with someone else's stuff. He'd bring home bags full of electronics from abandoned homes.

After filling my water containers, I turned toward home, numb and tired. During intense fighting, Mom made Eldin and me sleep on the floor of the long hallway between our bedroom and the dining room, in hopes that the intervening wall would protect us from the bullets whizzing by the windows. If we heard a long whistling noise followed by an explosion, that meant a mortar round had landed a safe distance away. If there was a one-second pause after a high-pitched whistle, I'd brace myself against Eldin or the floor, close my eyes, and hold my breath. Everything would vibrate like a guitar string as the walls absorbed the sound wave. Soon I couldn't fall asleep without the noise. The rare nights of silence became a problem.

When the father in the red beret came home one afternoon with a bag of candy, a mob of kids surrounded him. I couldn't recall when I last had chocolate. I was sick of beans and bread. Since the man knew my dad, I thought he'd give me a piece. He asked me to walk over and said, "Tell your father to ask Alija to give you some." He meant I should ask our Bosnian Muslim president.

The next time I saw him we were both getting water. His son and daughter were with him. I filled my containers. On the trek back, my load was so heavy I stopped to rest. The three of them caught up behind me. The man took his handgun from the holster and shot my plastic jug. The bullet created two holes, and the water leaked out as they laughed. "Nothing lasts forever," I yelled at him, enraged, daring him to shoot me in front of his kids.

I told Mom the jug had cracked and I'd thrown it out. Now I saw why Dad wished Pero dead. I felt the same way about my old teammates and nasty neighbors. Two weeks later, a car pulled up in front of our building. Two Serb soldiers with red berets asked where the wife of the candy man lived.

"Why? That's my dad. What happened?" asked the boy who'd

spat at my mother. He jumped on his feet and screamed for his mother. The men were his father's comrades. When they took their caps off and walked up the stairs, I knew they were delivering condolences. The bastard who'd shot my water jug was killed fighting our soldiers. I told Mom the news with a smile. I couldn't recall the last time I'd smiled.

"Let God punish them," she said. "Remember, they're not all the same. Mr. Obren brought you plum jam. He didn't let your dad and Mujo go to Partizan."

If Obren was a good Serb, why did he let Petra steal from us? When she wasn't at her home, she was at ours. She'd enter without knocking, sizing up our furniture, light fixtures, Mom's electric iron and other household appliances, the artwork on our walls. Mom gave her whatever she asked for so she wouldn't turn us in. It was a sick dance I hated. One night Petra wore Mom's denim skirt as they sat drinking Turkish coffee. We took turns waiting for the water to boil, holding a metal dish over a candle flame. "You won't be needing that rug soon. I may as well have it before someone else," Petra said.

The next day Petra invited Mom over to their place for coffee, and I went too. Mom and Petra sat at the table, my mother's carpet beneath their feet. I looked around at the overstuffed boxes on Petra's floor and on the couch. There were blenders, clothing on hangers, boxes of soap, china, wineglasses everywhere. Petra hadn't just been taking our stuff. She'd obviously been looting all the Muslim homes in the building.

I pictured how I would feel if I could just enter my neighbors' apartments and take anything I wanted for free without getting in trouble. Would I go for it too? I hoped I wouldn't, that I'd understand it was wrong to take something I didn't earn and know that, when they came back, they would miss it. It had to be bad karma to cash in on someone else's bad fortune. But then I thought of the army equipment I'd swiped with Igor and the guys. Did that mean

I was the same as Petra? I consoled myself with Uncle Ahmet's inference—if I was going to be a thief, at least I'd chosen the right bad guys to rob from.

Obren let me play with his rifle. I kept pressing the trigger, wishing I could shoot his wife.

"Did you make sure it's unloaded?" Petra asked him. Unfortunately it was.

"Enough playing with the gun," Mom said.

One morning Eldin heard that the Bosnian army had overrun a Serb village. We waited for retaliation. Sure enough, a bus soon pulled up and two soldiers came to our apartment. Our family name written on the door gave our background away. They were taking Eldin and Dad to another concentration camp. Flipping out with fear, I paced back and forth, waiting for Mom, who had gone out for five minutes. I watched from my bedroom window as she ran indoors, frantically asking where they were.

"They got them again!" I told her. I tried not to cry. "What do we do?"

She insisted I stay put as she rushed downstairs, heading straight for the bus with Dad and Eldin inside. I did as she told me. But if they took her away too, I'd be the only one left. I decided I'd swim across the river to Croatia late at night. A half hour passed. I never felt more alone.

When they all returned, I was so happy. Dad looked ashen. Mom lay down on the couch, out of breath. She couldn't speak, and her hands and legs were trembling. Eldin told me the bus had never left. While they sat there with the other detainees, a police car had pulled up. Mom rushed out of the car, quickly showing a piece of paper to a soldier. Just then, Eldin and Dad were allowed to get off the bus.

After Mom rested, she told us what happened. It turned out that she'd recognized Jovo, a former coworker who was in charge of detaining men for the camp. He didn't want to rescue Eldin and Dad in front of everyone. So he'd hidden in a military jeep, instructing her to go to the police station and ask to speak to the chief in charge, who knew Dad. She told him they were being taken away and requested a document to ensure their release in exchange for giving up our property and leaving the country. The rest of the Muslim men in the bus wound up at the concentration camp. Just in time she'd saved Dad and Eldin. My mother was my new hero.

"I felt so horrible, all those poor men staring at me, wishing I was there to get them off," she cried.

The next day we carried our suitcases onto another bus. We rode for an hour and a half, making it all the way to the Bosnian-Serbian border. Since the bridges to Croatia had been blown up, this was our only possible route out of the country. But two soldiers pulled us off and made us walk back and forth across the bridge while they laughed. Their heavy machine guns pointed down to the River Sava, where the dead floated downstream for miles before passing underneath the bridge, an eerie procession of corpses dumped in the water at Luka. To cover the evidence, they'd shoot the bodies full of holes so they'd sink.

We escaped and made it home, where I kept hoping our town would be liberated. Every morning Eldin and I prayed more bombs launched from the Bosnian army would fall on Brčko. We both agreed we'd rather die this way, knowing freedom was on its way. That day never came. We just plugged along in a macabre version of what our lives used to be. Instead of soccer cards, I collected shrapnel and bullets I pulled from building walls. I had ninety-nine sharp pieces. When Eldin and I played poker, we used the ammo pellets as chips.

Once in the market, I was buying lentils when a mortar round landed across the street. It was fired from Croatia, intended for Serbs, but it didn't clear the building, hitting it instead. The sound shook empty shelves. Customers fell to the ground for cover. I didn't even move. Across the street, a glass window five floors up on an apartment building shattered after a direct hit by a missile. "All Croats should be exterminated," the merchant said.

I wanted Croatians from the north and our army from the south to join forces to save us. But I kept quiet or I'd need another place to buy food; there were no other open stores near us. Outside the market, I reached for the chunk of shrapnel that had just become embedded in the doorway frame. It was too hot to touch; I waited until it cooled off before pocketing my souvenir. I stood in the middle of the road and looked up at the fifth-story apartment, now missing half its terrace. A moment later the rest of the balcony crashed down. The scent of burned metal filled the air, smoke diffusing into the sky. On the pavement I found a larger piece of shrapnel, the size of my forearm. I wrapped it in the belly of my T-shirt so I wouldn't get a blister holding it. In the courtyard, Mom called out, "Where were you? You okay?"

"Aha, look, I got two," I said. "This big one is still cooling off. Touch it."

When Igor saw it, he was jealous. "Where'd ya get it?" he asked.

"It's mine," I said.

"You're not allowed out for the rest of the day," yelled Mom.

In September we first heard the Red Cross was giving out oil, flour, sugar, and canned food. We'd run out of propane as well. Dad was going crazy indoors. He was desperate for sunlight. So we walked a mile to the Red Cross food dispensary. Thirty people mulled around there. We were dismayed that no international workers were there. We were the only Muslims. Unfortunately, Serb soldiers had already seized control of the donated supplies. Dad and I stood in line, hoping for anything Mom could turn into a meal.

"Keka, your line is over there," yelled a Serb we knew, Dad's old friend Kišić's wife.

We were segregated, instructed to form a new line, just the two of us. After everyone got food, we were given two sardine cans and a package of flour from a different pile. "This pile is for you, Keka," the Serb scowled. On the way home Dad muttered to himself, a look of hate on his face. Mom checked the expiration of the canned fish, labeled "Denmark 1972." When she opened the flour bag, it was filled with dead black maggots.

"Probably left over from Vietnam," Dad guessed, shaking his head.

"I want all the Serbs to die," I muttered, furious.

"Don't wish that upon anyone," Mom told me. "I didn't raise you that way."

"But look what Pero did. He made me like this," I yelled.

"See everyone for who they are, not what they are. The best revenge you'll have is great success."

By this time I wasn't buying it. It seemed like nonsense. Wanting real revenge, I wished I had a rifle to kill the bad guys who'd mistreated my family.

A week later, Dad and I ventured to an outdoor makeshift market. He picked out a tomato and two potatoes, all we had money for. A Serb woman shouted, "Put those back. It's not for Muslims." Everyone stared at us.

"In time you'll be ashamed," Dad said, putting our lost purchase back. I told Dad to keep quiet and forget about it. As we walked away, a very tall, broad-shouldered armed soldier in his late twenties approached. I looked up at him; he must have been six foot four. I was apprehensive, not knowing what he wanted.

"Hi, Keka. What happened?" he asked.

"I never imagined that in my own town I'd be treated like this," Dad said quietly.

"What do you want?"

When Dad told him, the tall man returned with our tomato and two potatoes.

"Forget about her. Just go home. Is your family okay? Do you need anything else? This is Kenan, your youngest?" he asked, patting my head, brushing my hair back.

"This is Ranko. Say hello," my dad said.

I shook Ranko's big hand. He wore a camouflage uniform with an AK-47 machine gun strapped over his shoulder, a handgun in the holster. He touched my dad's shoulder and in a low, concerned voice said, "Take care of yourself."

At home, I told Mom that some tall guy named Ranko bought the food for us.

"Ranko Češić?" Mom asked. She told me that growing up near us in Brčko, Ranko was a troubled kid. A truant, he couldn't pass a gym class or finish high school without Dad's intervention. Ranko's mom had begged my dad, "Keka, you know all of those professors. They're your friends. Have them go easy on him?" After high school, Ranko delivered payroll to the company where Mom worked. When he made delivery mistakes, Mom covered for him. Her coworkers asked her why. She'd say he was a good kid, that she knew his mother.

During the war, Ranko was becoming known for torturing Muslims and Catholics in Brčko. He personally killed dozens—if not with a gun, he'd beat them to death with a bat. He kept my father's college roommate and his wife in captivity. Ranko raped her, then shared her among the guards. They even made her husband watch—to inflict the most pain. When Dad was at Luka, night guards would walk into the warehouse, calling out names. Some men returned beaten up; others never came back. When Dad's name was called, he thought it was over. But he was taken to the small office, where Ranko shook his hand.

"How are you, Keka?" Ranko had asked. "So you're here with your oldest son, Eldin. I want you to know that as long as I am here, nothing will happen to you."

I knew many good, innocent Bosniaks and Croats had been killed for no reason. Yet amid the surreal chaos, where nothing was fair or made sense, it seemed that all of my parents' good deeds added up to a shield just strong enough to keep us alive.

But our problems weren't over yet. My mother had been suffering from a toothache. Suddenly it worsened, and she ran out of painkillers. We'd heard the local hospital was open only to treat wounded Serb soldiers who had emergencies; the doctors would give injections for pain and any medication they had left. We weren't sure if any health services were still working or would help us, but we took a chance. The town was empty as we passed by all the roofless, demolished houses. The infirmary building was shot up with bullets like Swiss cheese. Four doctors, a few nurses, and the receptionist were there, with one other patient. We sat in the waiting room where I'd once sat before having braces made. Mom complained that the entire side of her face hurt. Her head was pounding. I heard fighting outside. I slouched against the outdoor wall. Explosions ricocheted off the infirmary's windows.

"She'll get the other filling. The real stuff's for our kind," I heard a dentist say.

"They didn't fill your cavity with the real stuff," I told her afterward. "They saved it for Serbs." She later learned they'd used a material like cement.

On the way home, a soldier in his late teens told us, "Don't hang around here. The three mosques will be blown up in two hours. Open your windows."

"He thought we were Serbs," I whispered to Mom.

When we made it back to our place, we unlocked our windows so the glass wouldn't be shattered by the shock waves. Mom opened the balcony. I left my bedroom door ajar to create a breeze. We sat in silence, staring at the clock. At exactly four in the afternoon, loud explosions roared through the sky. Despite our precautions, our windows shattered. As our three holiest houses of worship were demolished, I heard cheering. My heart cried when I overhead the Serbs downstairs say that a parking lot would be built on the land where our ruined mosques had stood.

"Why don't they fear God's wrath?" Mom asked. "Don't they know he's watching?"

"What God? He left us a long time ago," I told her.

"He's still here. Don't worry," she said, touching my shoulder.

After the horrors we'd witnessed, I couldn't see how the hell she still had faith.

That day, we bumped into Milan, the bald soldier from the Piro-metal checkpoint. "I'm sorry I couldn't help you," he said. "But tell Keka that Srdjan's dead. He was captured by a Bosniak soldier. He was found hanging by his balls over a pointed fence."

At home I ran upstairs to tell my father that the Chetnik psycho who'd threatened us had been killed.

"There you go. The motherfucker deserves it," Dad said; it was the first time he'd ever used that word in front of me.

Maybe there was a God, after all.

CHAPTER FOUR

The Reckoning

The Balkans
July 2011

Awake for twenty-seven hours, I was hungry, dehydrated, wired, tense, jet-lagged already, and paranoid all at once. I wanted to take in the hot Balkan air, the salty meat, the lush walnut trees, and the gorgeous, silky-maned women I'd missed. As we traversed Croatia's Pleso airport on Saturday afternoon, I was pleased to be surrounded by voices speaking Bosnian and Croatian—sounds with no bad associations. Aunt Bisera ran up to greet us at the baggage claim in a blur of blond hair, bright fabric, and pink makeup. I hugged her, dodging lipstick. "I haven't seen you in nineteen years," she sobbed, her face now wrinkled like Grandma's. She still had my mother's eyes.

It was hot, a cloudless, dry heat with a warm breeze, as we walked outside to the parking lot. I was anxious to get to Brčko to see my old home. My handwritten list was scorching my jeans pocket. On the way to the car, I was on edge, afraid of who we might see and what my reaction would be. The first time Dad's friend Esad went back to Brčko in 2003, he'd bumped into a Serb acquaintance in the town square who'd told him, "It was just the politics. It's in the past. Time to move on." Another former neighbor greeted a returning Bosniak refugee with a flippant "Hey, where've you been?" as if referring to a minor social slight last week instead of years of gruesome slaughter nobody ever admitted or atoned for. You'd think somebody would have the brains and balls to say, "I'm sorry for what we did to you." But what I craved more than an apology was to stare a Serb in the eye and see regret—and shame. No longer small and cowed by grown men with machine guns and grenades, I wanted the turncoats to fear what I might do for revenge.

We piled into Bisera's neighbor Alen's four-door Jetta for the three-hour ride to my aunt's current home. On the drive she told us what happened to her after we'd left the country. Rounded up for a prisoner exchange in 1992, she was bused to this other Bosniak village named Brka, just two miles and two letters away from my hometown of Brčko. She'd become separated from her second husband, Halil, who somehow ended up in Atlanta, Georgia, after the war. Then she met a Brka mechanic named Kemo, married him, and decided to stay. The few Serbs who used to live among them had been run off during the conflict. So Brka was entirely Muslim now—segregated, like most of the country.

I sat in front, rolling down my window all the way as we passed wide meadows of yellow dandelions and corn and wheat fields filled with cows and horses. I inhaled the aroma of honey and hay and horseflesh. The scent of the farm air—from the vegetables and all the nut and fruit trees—was acrid and fresh. Famished, I wondered how the milk and fat, red tomatoes would taste. We passed three-story Mediterranean houses with cinderblock roofs and windows that opened to balconies with beautiful carved rails, the kind I wanted growing up. If I could ever afford to build a home from scratch, it would look like that.

At the Sava Bridge, the Croatian border guard said, *"Dobar dan,"* bidding us good day, then asked for our passports.

"Wait. Slow down," I told Alen before we crossed the river. I wanted to take my time and relish returning to my favorite spot, where Dad took me swimming and boating as a kid. I loved to fish and splash around here with him. I remembered catching fireflies in a jar from the back of Uncle Sabit's brown boat, which had oval windows, our rods strapped to the top. And every year I'd eat too much fish stew at the annual contest. I recalled watching my father jump into the water to pull out a drunk who'd gone under. "How many people have you saved from drowning, Keka?" the fish champion had asked him. "That guy makes it five," said my dad, the hero.

"Remember when you saved all those guys from drowning?" I asked Dad.

He smiled, his brown eyes gleaming, pleased at the reminder of his past glory. I hadn't seen him look so content since before the war. Despite all my trepidation, I could see it was good that we'd brought him back.

"Look how green the river is," he said.

"Why is it so clean and quiet?" I asked Bisera, who sat in the back, between Dad and Eldin. "Where are all the boats?"

"There's no industry anymore," she explained. "And not many people can afford boating for pleasure."

"I can't wait to swim in the river again. You down for it?" I asked my brother.

He shook his head no. "Not after all those dead bodies were thrown in from Luka."

"They're long gone!" I was furious that he'd just gutted my best childhood memory. Who wanted to swim in a graveyard? Then I felt guilty; he was probably thinking one of the corpses could have been him. My brain was in a time warp, images of karate and soccer camp marred by menacing weapons shoved in my face and shouts of *"Balije* don't need bread."

After our car crossed the bridge, I was about to ask Alen if we could get out so I could have a picture taken of me triumphantly treading across. I needed to get rolling with my agenda—number 5 on my list was to walk across the bridge the Serbs had destroyed. But then the guard on the Bosnian side curtly said, "*Pasoš*," pointed to us, and asked Alen, "Are they here visiting?"

Alen said, "Yes."

"No shit, I'm visiting," Eldin muttered from the back. "What else am I doing here?"

It didn't take much to set my brother off: one word from a man in a uniform. They wore no name tags, so it was hard to tell who was a Bosniak, Serb, or Croat. Thankfully the guard didn't hear Eldin. Or perhaps he did, because he added, "They should go to the police station and sign in to make the local authorities aware of their stay."

"Yeah, I'm running right now to the police to tell them where I am," Eldin said.

I turned nervously to Dad, who kept silent.

"Yes, sir, no problem, they will," Alen quickly acquiesced.

The last time we were at a Bosnian checkpoint in 1992, the Serbs pointed rifles at us, laughing as they made us walk back and forth on a different bridge. Although the disposition of territory here was still an ongoing dispute, Muslims in Brčko had regained the political foothold we'd lost during the war. International pressure kept Belgrade from supplying weapons to the Serbs in Bosnia, and the Bosnian army was stronger and more heavily armed than it had ever been. We could not be legally turned away, persecuted, or hurt this time. I felt my muscles relax as the border cop ignored my brother's provocation.

As we drove on, he sat up straight, completely rattled. "Now they want to know where we'll be at all times. They have no right. It's not 1992, when they took a census so they could throw us in the camps." Eldin's cheeks grew red. "Did you see that guy without a name tag? It's obvious judging from his ugly Serb village face where he's from."

"Keep your cool. Chill out, man. You have to relax," I said in English. I felt simmering anger too. But I had to soothe his anxiety. That was my job on this trip—to protect him. I didn't want a confrontation to escalate and freak out Dad and Bisera. It was much easier to calm Eldin down than myself.

"You're right. I don't need stress," Eldin said, taking in a few long breaths to cool himself down. "In ten days I'll be back in New York, enjoying my work and my life while the Serbs have no jobs or money. They'll be stuck forever in the dead-end hell their hate created."

Reminding ourselves, over and over, how well we were doing in Queens was our ongoing balm; like ChapStick, we could apply as needed. It was as if we kept trying to convince ourselves that leaving had been our choice. Yet being better off financially didn't soothe our longing, our loss.

"We'll be home in ten minutes," Bisera said. "I have cold water and hot food waiting."

Pulling away from the bridge, I was frustrated that I'd missed a chance to walk across and check off that item from my list. We'd just landed, but I already felt behind. When I turned to my right, I was shocked to see a bunch of beige-brick storefronts stacked side by side.

"What the hell is that?" I stared at a Chinese dive on the corner. The closest I'd ever come to anything Asian in Brčko was on television.

"They opened Chinese restaurants and a penny mart here in 2000. The clothes fall apart; they're cheap," said Bisera.

"How bad can China be if they came to postwar Bosnia?" I joked, disheartened that our gorgeous Old World Eastern European town had come to resemble a Staten Island housing project. Instead of the regal architecture and luscious parks and greenery I remembered, there were newly built offices cluttered close together and cars parked everywhere. A mall overstuffed with tacky, glass-encased stores overpowered the stately nineteenth-century buildings from the Austro-Hungarian era.

On both sides of us we saw that the three mosques blown up in Brčko nineteen years ago had been completely resurrected. I smiled, my heart soothed. The houses of worship looked the same, but they were joined by a white, ten-story modern structure in the shape of a rocket.

"A Saudi Arabian donated money to build that one," Bisera told us.

"It's like stabbing Serbs in the eye with thorns when they walk by." Eldin smiled.

As we drove on the main road, we heard recorded prayers playing a hypnotic Arabic melody. The sound reassured me that we were no longer the only Muslims in Brčko. I couldn't be persecuted for my religion. Or at least the persecution wouldn't be state-sanctioned.

"Before the war they only did prayers during Ramadan month. Now they play prayers five times a day over a megaphone," Bisera said.

"For spite," Alen added. "Most of the town is secular. The women don't cover themselves, and people hardly ever go to the mosques to pray except on holidays."

"This side of town was burned to the ground during the war!" I said, pleased it was mostly rebuilt. "In 1992, I didn't see one soul here, it was a ghost town."

"Wow. I didn't know that," Eldin said. He'd been hiding inside our home with my dad; he'd never witnessed what happened outside.

Many homes had signs saying they were betting parlors and pharmacies. "Why are there so many?" I asked Bisera.

"Since unemployment's so high, people are desperate to make money quickly," she said. "The locals have given up on real jobs because their bosses don't pay them. Everyone takes antidepressants. It's the new Western way."

By the time we reached Bisera and Kemo's modest-looking rust-brick house at 2:00 p.m., I'd been up for thirty hours. Kemo, Bisera's third husband, was sitting outside, waiting for us. He was shorter than me, chubby, in his sixties. She'd warned us that he'd recently gone deaf and his hearing aid wasn't helping, but he was starting to read lips. He greeted us with hugs and kisses, and led us inside.

In the kitchen, we drank bottled water and ate cut watermelon, cold and soothing, as Bisera told us the story of how they'd met during the war, when she'd escaped to free territory in the suburbs south of Brčko.

"I found him very handsome," she said. "I was complaining that my nails were broken because I didn't have any polish. So he drove an hour and a half to a store to get me some." She smiled. I thought it was a pretty stupid reason to risk his life.

When Kemo's first wife had moved out, Bisera moved in. It was months after we'd fled the country, so we'd never visited this place before. It held no bad memories.

"I might be hallucinating, but I feel happy here," I told Eldin. There was no possibility of seeing Serbs from our past, zero chance of heated face-offs. I relaxed and took pictures while Bisera gave us a tour of her three bedrooms, two bathrooms, and big yard. The home was overstuffed with ceramic elephants and glass animal figures everywhere. The tables and lamps were outdated, like '80s IKEA furniture. Hardly anyone we knew who'd stayed had prospered.

"Hey, wasn't that from our old apartment?" I pointed to the painting of a pirate ship in a storm that was hanging in the living room.

"Yes! After you left, I went back and retrieved it. That was all I could find of yours. Do you want it?" Bisera asked.

"No, consider it a housewarming gift," I said. We'd also brought her two bags of Lancôme makeup from Macy's that she'd asked for, refusing to take her money for it.

Coming out of the shower in the guest bathroom, I heard Alen's mother, Sabira, scream, "Oh my God, Eldin, you're so grown up. Where's the little dark-haired, feisty one?" Sabira had been close friends with my mom. I dried off, dressed, and rushed out to greet her, giving her two kisses on the cheek, the way we did in Bosnia. (Serbs kissed three times, like their three-finger salute.) Sabira was still slim like my mother was, with curly brown hair. She gave me a strong hug and ten more kisses.

"You got so big and strong," she said. "So why aren't you married already?"

"She hasn't found me yet," I said.

Everybody laughed. I wished my mom could join us. She'd be comfortable here.

I snapped a shot of my favorite old meal, moussaka—oven-roasted eggplant with ground beef and vegetables—and then ate two huge portions. For dessert we had apricots Kemo had picked from their tree. I took pictures of Eldin and Kemo outside, disappointed that Bisera's son, Mirza, had moved to Italy, so I wouldn't get to see him. My cousin Amela was on vacation until Thursday. Instead I met Bisera's peacock, rooster, hunting dog, two doves, and four chickens, who ran around the yard in harmony as we talked and caught up the rest of the day.

"These are my kids from America," Bisera said, showing us off to her neighbors, who came by to meet us.

I felt appreciated and really taken care of by a female for the first time since I'd lost my mother. But I knew the sweetness would be ruined tomorrow, when I got to Brčko and started bumping into Serbs from my past. Would they say hello, look down, run away? Or worse?

By 9:00 p.m., we were fading. Eldin took the pull-out couch in the guest room. Dad and I shared a king-size bed in the second bedroom.

I slept well, though he snored like a bear. At dawn on Sunday I was woken by Bisera's damn black rooster, who wouldn't shut up. Through the open window I heard doves cooing and morning prayers from the mosque. I went to the kitchen in just my shorts and found Bisera.

"He screams this early every morning?" I pointed to the rooster, who'd followed me.

"Leave my Gigo alone." She petted him. Outside a branch broke. I saw Kemo, in his tank top, pajama bottoms, and oversized sandals, picking apricots and apples.

"That's for your strudel tonight," she said.

She had risen at 5:00 a.m. just to cook for us. God, I'd missed Bosnian hospitality. The last time I'd woken up in my country was to the sound of gunfire and explosions, with no electricity or running water. Birdsong and Muslim prayers were a blessing. I took a really long shower to make up for all those waterless months of the war. Wide awake, I went outside to work out, preparing myself for the rough day ahead. I did push-ups and sit-ups on a towel on the grass and strength exercises with the resistance bands I'd brought. Eldin joined me as Dad sipped coffee with Bisera.

"Good, don't skip too many days," said Dad, in his coach voice. "I exercised before you woke up."

You could see my father's deltoids and biceps in his sleeveless T-shirt. At five foot eight and 140 pounds, he'd never gained back the fifty pounds he'd lost during the war when we'd almost starved.

"What do you boys want for breakfast?" Bisera asked.

"How about fresh eggs?" I asked, panting, half out of breath.

After Bisera's duck laid an egg, Bisera kissed the duck's head. My mother would have laughed and said, "Bisera can't tell her animals from her kids."

I paced and fidgeted, waiting for my boyhood pal Jasenko to pick us up. His mom and mine had been classmates and workmates; his father, Mujo, was a coach colleague of Dad's. Jasenko was a mechanic now, about to get his pilot's license. He'd been sent to Croatia before the fighting started in 1992, so he had none of our miserable recollections of this country. Although he also wound up in the United States, he'd visited Bosnia six times already. He planned this trip so we could see our old town together.

"What's up, dudes? You know what I'm saying?" Jasenko said when he arrived, hugging us hello.

He'd shaved his head since I'd visited him at his home in Iowa two years before. "Hey, you need Miracle-Gro for that bald pate of yours," I teased, taking his picture.

"It's so shiny I use it as a mirror." We were both joking around in English, regular American guys now. I had Eldin take a picture of me and Jasenko.

As we stepped into his rented car, I warned him, "Remember, no NASCAR driving in Brčko," recalling how in Iowa he'd sped us around like crazy.

"Yeah, I survived the war here," Eldin said. "I'm not dying in a car accident."

I was glad Jasenko agreed to play tour guide; he could help us navigate our old terrain, both physically and mentally.

"Don't worry, the Serbs are powerless in town," he reassured us. "I'm not afraid to show my face in Serb neighborhoods. They're the ones who should be afraid to see us."

In the twenty-five-minute drive to our old place, we reminisced about cherry picking and slingshots. He reminded me how bad I'd felt when I'd once hit a bird with a stone. I'd never done it again.

Driving past the Bosnian-Croatian border, I said, "Hey, will you stop in front of the Sava Bridge?"

"Why?" Eldin asked.

"Because I want to see how high the bridge really is and throw a rock off."

"You're thirty years old and you want to go rock throwing?" Eldin crossed his arms.

"I didn't get to do it yesterday," I told him.

"Why do we have to do this at all?" Eldin was fidgety, in a rush.

"Dad and I used to do it when I was a kid," I said in a smaller voice. "It would be neat to do it again over the rebuilt bridge."

"But we don't have our passports with us," Eldin argued, still on edge from the day before.

"Just show them your ID," Jasenko said. "They'll let you."

"Come on, it's on my list," I pleaded with my brother, revealing my real motivation.

"Really?" Eldin asked.

"You saw me write it down."

"I thought we were jotting down ideas of what we might do," Eldin said. "Since when did your list become mandatory and etched in stone?"

"You didn't think I was serious?" I was offended. "It'll just take five minutes."

We turned to my father.

"Why not?" was Dad's verdict. "I used to fish off that bridge. We should walk across."

Eldin couldn't argue with that.

Jasenko pulled over, let us out, and said he'd wait for us in the car. I picked up two stones from the gravel by the parking lot, put them in my pocket, and led us toward the toll booth. Two men sat inside. Another guard stood outdoors.

"Excuse me, sir. Can we walk halfway across on the pedestrian walkway?" I asked in Bosnian, as respectfully as I could.

He looked at our New York identification and said, "Sure, go ahead."

The bridge was painted light blue and felt narrower than I remembered. I stood against the side rails that used to come up to my neck. Now they just reached my belly button. I took a picture. As we crossed, I thought of the refugees who'd died when the bridge was detonated as they were escaping to Croatia. At midpoint we faced west, looking down at the River Sava.

"The water is so pretty and clean," Dad said.

But the river didn't look the same. The banks were dried up from heat and the rainless summer. There were only a few small vessels anchored at the shores. There used to be dozens of motor- and paddleboats and kayaks out here on regatta days. I took the rocks from my pocket and handed one to my father. We used to compete over who could fling stones farther on the water.

"Throw it the longest distance you can," I instructed.

He laughed and did. He still had strong arms, but he was now seventy-one, and his stone didn't go as far as it used to, flying a few feet out and then straight down.

I flung my rock, hoping for a big splash followed by a series of plunks that skimmed the surface. Instead it took a sharp dive and sunk fast, barely causing a ripple. It used to be so exhilarating skimming rocks from here as a kid, playing the little mascot to my young, heroic dad and his robust friends. Now they were old, dead, or displaced after the war. My father's illness had aged him; he wasn't going to be fishing, swimming, or saving anyone from drowning in this river again.

Standing on the bridge, I couldn't forget the lost refugees. It could have been us, lulled into believing we were about to escape. The blood and bones of my people were floating beneath me. I felt mournful. Spooked. Sorry that I hadn't been old or strong enough to save anyone. The dried-up banks made it look like someone had sucked the liquid out with a giant syringe. I could see Luka to my left. My childhood love for the River Sava didn't translate into adulthood. All my early memories were tarnished.

I pulled my list out of my back pocket, along with a small silver pen, and put a check across number 5. It was out of order, but at least I was marking something off, even though playing out my bridge fantasy sucked. Eleven more to go. I felt a little lost and distraught, but finishing one item gave me the illusion of a tiny accomplishment.

"Okay? You're satisfied?" Eldin asked.

I wasn't really. We stood there in silence. Grandma Emina was right: I had no business still being here. I was done with the Sava River.

"Now what?" my brother wanted to know.

"We're meeting Truly at our old apartment," Dad told Jasenko back in the car.

"Yes, let's go see the old place." I hoped completing my next task would be more illuminating.

But the closer we got to home, the more my body tightened. My palms were sweating, and my face tingled with anxiety by the time he parked in front of our Brčko complex. I couldn't believe I was back. My stomach felt heavy as we stepped out of the car. In the entranceway, I didn't see the old sign "Milana Marinkovica Lamela C" anymore. It bothered me that they'd taken it down. I'd remembered this building as huge, grand, and elegant, the nicest in town. But it had become plain, worn, haggard. I pictured us playing soccer in the parking lot. I could see the outline of a soccer ball we painted on the side wall. There were shrapnel and bullet holes still stuck in the concrete; it had never been repainted or fixed. Everything was so much tinier and dingier than the images in my mind.

The gloom was swiftly broken by the sight of Truly and his wife, Magbula, who rushed down to greet us. Dad wrapped his arms around Truly's shoulders. He grabbed Dad's cheeks and said, "You still look like a young eagle."

"I work out four times a week." Dad flexed his muscles.

"It's about time you guys decided to come here," Truly said, hooking his arm inside my father's elbow and escorting him toward the stairs.

But I wasn't ready to go inside the rooms of my childhood yet. My throat was parched. I noticed a new, bodega-like store underneath the building. "I need to get some water."

Sensing my apprehension, Magbula accompanied me. "They're visiting," she told the girl at the counter, who looked about Eldin's age.

I bought a Bosnian bottled water for a mark, 75 cents, cheaper than in Queens. Everything was cheap here but Serb souls, I thought, as the girl kept staring at me.

"You look like Keka. Is that Keka's son?" she asked, excitedly.

"Yes, he's here too." Magbula nodded, looking pleased.

"You knew my sister Daniela from school," she chirped. "Do you remember her?"

"Of course I do," I answered. "When you see Daniela, ask if she remembers spitting in my face and calling me a *balija*."

The sister looked down. I probably shouldn't have embarrassed her in front of Truly's wife, her neighbor during the summers. The girl had done nothing wrong. Yet in my eyes, Daniela was guilty—and so was this whole town. Now that I was here, it was impossible to pretend everything was fine and back to normal. My former haunts were tainted, the scene of crimes against me—and humanity. Mainly Serbs lived in this area now. So many Muslims had been thrown out, threatened, or murdered, and most Bosniaks who survived, like my family, chose not to come back. It was easy to see why. The continued, collective denial was suffocating. I'd returned a strong thirty-year-old man shielded by my list of vengeance. Yet part of me was still a shocked twelve-year-old boy who wanted to scream, "But how could you do that to us?"

Strolling outside, I spied Truly's two pretty teenage daughters staring down at us from my old third-floor balcony and waved. The building had the same high steps and brown mailboxes; only the tenants' names were different, the Trebinčevićs long gone. I climbed the two flights of stairs leading up to our apartment. It used to seem like scaling a tall mountain, leaving me out of breath. Now it took thirty seconds. I showed Eldin how my foot was the size of a whole stair. I wasn't scared.

When I walked in, I headed straight for the bedroom that Eldin and I used to share. It was so much smaller than it used to be; I couldn't see how the two of us ever fit. I used to lie on the floor peeping through tiny holes in the shades, which were drawn all day and night so soldiers wouldn't see us and spray the windows with bullets.

"Do you remember anything?" Magbula asked.

"Like it all happened this morning."

"Well, make yourself at home," she said. "Like old times."

Back in 1992, when I looked out the window I saw streets filled with soldiers in uniform, trucks driving dead bodies from the concentration camp half a mile away, tanks driving down the road that would catch fire.

"Get away from the window, Kenan," my mother would yell.

Now I heard laughter coming from the living room. I went in and sat on the sofa, leaned against the cushions, and took a long breath. None of our furniture was here; it had all been replaced. Truly told his daughters, "If the two of you were only a few years older, you could marry one of the boys." They blushed.

"After they turn eighteen," I said, trying to make them—or me—feel less uncomfortable.

All the Balkanites we knew here who were our age married and had kids in their twenties. If we'd stayed, Eldin and I would already be husbands and fathers. I thought of the decade delay. Marrying later meant our marriages would be stronger, I'd convinced myself. We'd love our wives even more when we did settle down. But they would surely be American women. I thought of the movie *Back to the Future*, where one kiss could change a family's destiny. The war had transformed the course of our bloodline for eternity.

"Your father is a great man. You and your brother should know what he did for this city," Truly told me. "That's why you're all alive today."

I was surprised that he seemed to know more about Dad's past than I did. I recalled, with pride, how adored Dad had once been in Brčko. But other equally kind and good Muslim men had been killed here. I didn't know how much my father's past reputation had protected us. I'd long ago attributed our escape to a mix of calm, perseverance, and pure luck. But now Truly's statement fascinated me. Could the legacy of compassion my father left really be the reason we'd survived?

I stepped out on the balcony overlooking the front entrance. The railing, once up to my neck, now reached my waist. People I didn't recognize on nearby balconies whispered to each other, staring at me. I imagined the mostly Serb tenants here knew who I was: a Muslim man come back to witness the damage their war had wrought. I felt tall and mighty, as though I had prevailed—without using a weapon in retaliation or losing the humanity my parents taught. No longer afraid, I looked down, surveying the dried lawn where I'd played soccer with abandon. A row of cheap cars was parked on the dried, burned-out grass. There were no kids biking or kicking a soccer ball or jumping rope on my old block. Paper, bottles, and garbage were strewn everywhere. Amid the rubble I made out a figure coming up the stairs.

As she moved closer, I could see it was Petra, holding two bags of groceries. I froze. My heart went crazy in my chest. Daniela's sister, the counter girl, had done nothing horrible to me. But Petra had. Our next-door neighbor was the first Serb betrayer I was about to confront as an adult. My eyes followed her unsteady shuffle as she climbed the steps slowly. She was shorter now, her hips wider, in a skirt down to her ankles; she wore a long navy blouse in this heat, like an old religious matron. She must have been sixty-five. Time had not been kind to her. I remembered her as slim, wearing red lipstick and miniskirts to show off her legs to the soldiers. Now she was just a pathetic old lady. I pictured kicking the bags out of her hands, then watching her on her knees, picking up her splattered tomatoes.

She caught sight of me and stepped back, startled. Good, she recognized me. She knew she was about to stand face-to-face with her old neighbor. She was afraid, as I wanted her to be. I could overpower her easily. I could kill her with one hand, and she knew it. She put down her bags, sat on the stairs, and lit a cigarette. I bet she was hoping I'd go away, but I held my ground.

I pictured the night she barged into our dining room and demanded my mother give up her light-blue denim skirt, a cherished present from Bisera. Then Petra had wanted my mom's special rug. A week later, I came along when she'd invited Mom for coffee. How dare she humiliate my own mother right in front of me, our feet resting on that stolen carpet.

When Truly and his wife purchased our apartment in 2006, my mother told Magbula all about Petra over the phone. "Do me a favor and don't befriend the neighbor. Don't ever trust her or let her charm you," Mom warned. Magbula promised to never even acknowledge Petra's presence and later reported to us: "All summer long I walk by her as if I'm walking by a grave."

Petra was the one who'd told the paramilitaries where Muslims were living so we could get carted away in meat trucks. But her husband, Obren, had protected my father and Jasenko's dad, warning them against going to Partizan Sports Hall when they could have been killed. Late at night he would knock on our door to make sure I wasn't hungry. He brought me canned beans and plum jam, not knowing that by day, Petra was requisitioning my mom's belongings. I guessed that he'd forced his wife not to turn us in and she had resented it. Right after Truly bought our place, he told us that Obren had died of esophageal cancer in 2006. Petra had lasted almost as long as a Galápagos tortoise. The monsters always live.

I walked from the balcony to the front door, wanting to drag Petra down the stairwell by the roots of her dyed hair. Did she still have the rug after nineteen years? My heart was banging against my chest as I pictured barging into her apartment and taking the rug back so she could no longer wipe her feet on my mother's stolen treasure—to avenge Adisa Trebinčević and everything they'd done to us. But all of a sudden I heard my mom's soft voice saying, "Don't ever be rotten like them, Kendji. We have to be better," as if my mother was standing there, beside me.

Petra ground out her smoke, got to her feet, and resumed walking up the stairs. Conscious of my menacing stare, she watched me from the side of her eye, in silence. As she approached our floor, her footsteps were halting, her breathing more labored. She fumbled nervously for her key. I strode right up beside her and stood too close, my foot pressed against our open door. There was sweat on her forehead, her face flushed. She looked petrified. Or was it ashamed? Her eyes would not meet mine.

"No one has forgotten," I said.

She put her head down.

The door opened with a long sigh, then closed. There was silence.

I reached into my pocket for my list and crossed off item number 1.

CHAPTER FIVE

Daca and Her Uzi

Brčko, Bosnia
August 1992

Peeking through Mom's white curtains on a boiling-hot Tuesday afternoon at the end of the summer, I was frightened by a tall bleached-blond lady in fatigues and white Adidas inspecting our courtyard. Her index finger hovered over the trigger of an Uzi machine gun. At eleven I was learning the distinctions between the dozen different weapons Serb military men carried. But I'd never seen a woman soldier before. Everything about her screamed *trouble*. I lay flat against the floor and closed my eyes tight.

For four months we'd hidden inside with no electricity, running water, or phone, and little food. The endless shooting kept us from the balcony; we crawled on the floor to move from room to room. Since as far as we knew we were the only Muslim family left in town, we barely opened the windows and spoke in whispers so our Serb enemies, in the apartments surrounding us on all sides, wouldn't hear.

I missed boating on the River Sava with Dad during the warm months and swimming lessons and karate camp. Everything good had been taken away, replaced with worries that hurt my head. Because a young boy was less likely to get harassed by the military men patrolling the streets of Brčko, it became my job to keep our canisters filled with water and to buy bread with the dwindling wad of bills Mom took out of her sock or bra. The liquor in the cabinet was gone. Our bowl of coins was getting smaller each week.

Whenever I left home, I was afraid I'd be shot or return home to find my family gone. I had no friends anymore, no sports, no chance to run around. I couldn't listen to music or watch my favorite action movies on the VCR. Eldin stayed quiet in his candlelit room, relaying tiny bits of news he'd heard on the free-territory radio. All he told us was the fighting had intensified throughout Bosnia. No word of a cease-fire, prisoner exchanges in Brčko, or international intervention. Evenings were the worst, sweltering, spooky, and pitch-dark. Every male voice could be a soldier coming to take away Dad and Eldin. After each thud of footstep on the stairs, Mom would say, "Shh, be quiet." I would think silently: *This could be it.* Any visitor might spell the end.

The blond Amazon strutting in front of the building looked directly into our window and pointed her finger, showing our place to the huge armed soldier next to her. It was five in the afternoon. These two were obviously looking for us. Someone had given up my family. My hands went clammy. I slithered to the kitchen, where my mom was sitting on the floor, splitting a sardine can so my brother and I would each get two little fish. I told her what I'd seen. She sneaked to the window to spy on the bleached blonde, who was walking up the steps with the giant, who reminded me of an action hero. He must have been six foot seven, broad and blond. From their perch on the stairs, Dalibor and Velibor stared in awe at the sight of these oversized warriors.

"Not this," Mom said. "Keka, Eldin, they're coming to get you again."

I hid behind her, grabbing her arm. We heard a loud knock. We didn't know what to do. If we ignored them, they could shoot through the door. Mom's hand was shaking, and she bit her lip before letting them in.

"Good day. How are you?" she asked in a formal way.

Without a word of greeting, they barged in, the man so tall he had to duck to pass through our door's frame. In the foyer, they snooped around.

"I am Daca, and this is my husband, Boban," the blonde said. With her sleek weapon, slicked-back hair, and red lipstick, she was like a female cyborg from a foreign adventure flick.

"I'm Ada. This is Keka." Mom used my parents' nicknames. "These are my sons, Eldin and Kenan."

This angry Serb couple—clearly younger than my parents—stalked through our living room, matching Uzis draped over their shoulders. They plopped down on the sofa like they owned the place. He was so tall that when he sat his knees poked up above the cushions. His green camouflage pant legs were tucked inside his black midcalf boots. Two olive-green hand grenades hung on the right side of his brown belt. When my mother saw them, she flinched.

My parents sat down on the other sofa. Dad was being very quiet. Eldin crossed his knees on the floor. Why were these visitors here? What did they want? We'd been taught to respect elders, but the war had destroyed all the rules. I pretended to play with my miniature cars, racing my American Mack truck, Ford police cruiser, and red Bosnian Yugo. Since I was closest to Daca, I sneaked peeks at her black semiautomatic. I'd never seen one so up close before. The pointed muzzle looked lethal. The bullet cartridges were longer than the handle. A few dozen rounds of ammo could fit in there.

"We are here from Belgrade, and I fought in the Croatian war last year. We are good friends of Arkan," Boban boasted. His speech was stilted, as if he was reciting from a script. On his shoulder was the patch of Arkan's Tigers, the militia notorious for swooping in after battles to kill civilians, rape women, and loot houses. "Most recently I was in western Bosnia, where I got my boots bloody walking over dead Muslim bodies." He smirked, pulling a pack of Drina cigarettes from his pocket, sparking one with a Zippo lighter. My mother ran to get him an ashtray. He could wipe us all out in a second with one long pull of his trigger. A minute later, when he leaned forward to flick his ashes, his elbow bumped against the grenades on his belt, and I saw Mom close her eyes. She was probably praying they wouldn't dislodge, roll onto our carpet, and blow us all up.

"We're now residing in Brčko," Daca said. "Across the street from the church. Do you know Sanela Delić?" She pulled her own pack of Drinas from her pocket.

My mother gasped. "I do know her. We went to school together."

Had they slaughtered Sanela when they'd moved into our friend's furnished three-story house? It was just a ten-minute walk from here. Were they going to shoot us?

"We heard Sanela went abroad," Daca said, taking her husband's Zippo to light her smoke and take a drag. She got lipstick on the filter. "Local officials gave us the addresses of wealthy, undamaged properties where nobody lives anymore."

That made me feel better; I hoped Daca was just stealing from Bosniaks who were killed or sent away or had fled, and not shooting them dead herself.

She looked over at Eldin. "How old is he?"

"Eighteen," Eldin replied boldly.

"He looks like he can fight for us," she said.

I glanced at Eldin, then smashed my Mack truck against the Yugo, worried they were here to force my brother to fight for them, digging trenches, and picking up the dead—until they shot him dead too. My forehead felt hot. My ears tingled. The combination of heat, smoke, hunger, and fear was making me dizzy.

Daca turned to Dad. "Why aren't you guys fighting?"

Rather than answer "I wished we could join the Bosnian army and kill scumbags like you, but every time we tried to escape, we flunked," he said nothing.

"We attempted to leave five times," my mother jumped in. "But we were turned back at checkpoints and the border. Eldin and Keka were recently released from Luka. We were never in a political party. So we didn't think we had any reason to flee. We have nothing against Serbs. We would never hurt a soul." She sounded desperate, pleading for our lives. "I'm a mother, I just want my boys." Boban was scowling, but Daca inched closer to her, nodding, as if Mom was getting through her skull.

"Can I get you some coffee?"

"That would be lovely," Daca said, pursing her red lips.

I joined Mom in the kitchen, pouring myself a glass of warm water from the canister while she used the last of our beans and propane gas to make Daca coffee. I went back to the floor as she served the adults on her good china, as if she was just entertaining old friends who'd come by to catch up.

Boban glared at my father. "What do you do?"

"I trained athletes at my own fitness center." I noticed Dad used the past tense. Was his job over from now on?

"Do you own a gun?" Boban barked.

"No." Dad was lying. I knew he'd bought a revolver after the Croatian war started five months earlier, because I'd heard Mom yell at him to get rid of it. He'd refused, saying he needed to protect us. She insisted he stash the weapon at his office. Some protection, like it could have stood up to these twin Uzis.

While Mom and Daca spoke, Boban never stopped glowering. Then Daca stood. "We'll be back," she said, as Arnold Schwarzenegger threatened in *The Terminator*. With that, they barged out.

"Human garbage," Dad muttered.

"Thank God they didn't take you away." Mom looked sheet-white.

"How do you work the grenade?" I asked my father. "You squeeze the lever?"

He nodded. "Then you pull the safety pin out. Some explode on contact with the ground," he said, "others three seconds after you release the lever."

My father had done his mandatory service in the Yugoslavian People's Army when he was eighteen; he knew about these things.

The next day, at the same time, Daca kept her promise to return. As she opened the door, my mother was standing very straight, her back tensed. Daca still had her Uzi, but she was alone this time. She handed Mom a bag of coffee. My mother relaxed. If Daca was going to shoot us or take Dad and Eldin away, she would have come with her menacing husband instead of a gift.

"Ada, make us a cup," Daca said in a fond way, like she and Mom were close girlfriends.

As they drank and chatted, I swayed back and forth and back on the rocking chair in the living room, pretending I was a little kid, but listening hard. What was she doing back here?

"Can I see the rest of your apartment?" I heard Daca ask. "Your building has a good location." My mother gave her a tour. "You have a classy style. You could help with my new place." Did she want Mom for her decorator? Or slave?

"I like decorating," Mom said as they sat back down with us.

"Your chandelier would fit nicely in my Belgrade home." Daca smiled.

Mom looked at Dad. His eyes were helpless, dim as rocks. My parents had picked out the gold antique fixture, with its twelve frosted bulbs, four years before, at Šipad, a furniture store. It was a splurge to celebrate Dad's opening his gym and Mom's promotion at her company. The chandelier had been installed before we moved into the new apartment complex. My mother fed the construction workers beef stew and Cokes, so ours was the first home they'd finished. She loved that light. When I'd bounce a ball in the dining room, she'd yell, "Don't you dare break my chandelier, it cost me three months of work." Now she asked Daca calmly, "Would you like it?"

"Yes. Keka can take it down. He can bring it over to us this weekend." Daca caught her gun strap from sliding down her shoulder. "Let's finish our coffee first."

That was all she wanted—our lamp? I didn't know why she'd asked when she could have just pointed the gun and taken it. Were we supposed to pretend it was a gift? Pero had taught us about betrayal. Petra had broken us into the ways of Serbian thievery. Our old next-door neighbor was more interested in free loot she could lift easily, like Mom's clothes, small artwork, and the round carpet. Daca—with her bigger eyes—set her sights on major appliances and fixtures that required hammers and screwdrivers to unhinge. It was as if we were watching our happy lives get dismantled and erased one item at a time.

The plants were all dead, the blinds were down. With so much stuff missing, our home looked spotty and discombobulated, as though it was undergoing construction. By now we understood Daca's subliminal message: hand over the rest of your valuables or we turn in Eldin and Dad. It was getting easier to let go of things as we told ourselves we'd also be leaving here soon.

On Friday Daca returned with Boban and a cart for Dad to transport our light. She surprised me with a bag of black licorice. I chewed a few pieces, then threw one to Eldin. I knew they were bad guys robbing us, but I hadn't had a sweet in months. It tasted good and chewy in my mouth. I popped in another. I liked red licorice better. I hoped she'd bring me that next time.

"Kenan looks like my little boy," Daca said. "He's staying with his grandmother."

I gave her my sweetest smile. If she called me by my name and saw me like her son, she wouldn't hurt me. And I'd get more candy. And I bet she'd even protect us if Pero and his soldiers came back.

I went with Dad to the dining room to dismantle the overhead fixture. He held a screwdriver and stepped onto a chair.

"I'll hold your feet so you won't fall when you unscrew the nails." I held him steady at the ankles.

"Wish I could unscrew her head from her shoulders," he whispered.

Back in the living room, Boban was standing, his gun still over his shoulder. Daca was sprawled out on the couch, her Uzi on the pillow next to her like some kind of a pet. I came and sat down beside her. I could smell the oil she lubricated the gun with and the leather from her holster.

"I have one too," I said. "I'll show you." I ran to my room and brought down the gun case where I'd parked my water pistol.

She laughed. "Where did you get the holster?"

"I found it outside."

"Kenan can come with his father to drop it off," Daca told Mom.

"Please, keep them safe," Mom pleaded to Daca, who nodded, looking at our dismantled light.

I walked alongside Dad as he wheeled the wagon transporting the fixture to our Bosniak friend's stolen home. Boban led; Daca walked behind, gripping her gun.

"I feel like their prisoner," Dad said quietly.

"I feel like a donkey," I told him, and he winked.

When Daca opened her garage door, I was stunned to see haphazard stacks of television sets, VCRs, stereos, typewriters, tables, lamps, chairs, tables, large framed paintings, bikes. She was warehousing merchandise! Wow, so much loot. So many Muslim homes robbed. If Petra's apartment was like the corner store, Daca had a whole mall stuffed in here.

As Boban went inside, Daca thanked us for helping her steal from us. Then she walked me and Dad home, staying close by us, keeping her promise to Mom to protect us.

"Fuck her mother, the ugly bitch," Dad said after she left.

"Yeah, fuck her mother," I repeated, wishing Dad would beat her up.

"Let her crawl back into her mother's cunt with those maggots," he muttered.

I'd never heard Dad say bad words like that, especially about a woman. He was usually a gentleman, an expert tango dancer with polite manners who'd open doors and carry bags for Mom. He used to warn me and Eldin, "Don't ever let a woman have anything bad to say about you." In photographs with his jazz band before he married, at thirty-six, he was always in a snazzy suit, his arms around a pretty girl. He'd bring carnations to Mom, Aunt Bisera, and even Grandma Zekija, though Mom said Zekija should fly away on her broom. I didn't figure out what that meant till I saw a Bosnian witch cartoon.

Later in the week, Daca came by alone, with more coffee for Mom and four pieces of Bazooka gum that she slipped into my pocket. I gave two to Eldin. She told Mom of her parents in Belgrade, how much she missed her son. After an hour, she pointed to Mom's lace tablecloth, a special housewarming present that Grandma Emina had embroidered for us the year before.

"That's pretty. Where did you get it?" Daca fingered the ivory lace. "I need one for my new table."

I looked at Mom, not wanting Daca to have it; Grandma Emina would be upset.

"This is old. There's nicer new ones." Mom rushed to the drawer, frantically pulling out a neatly pressed stack of newer cloths she'd bought. "Which fits your table?"

Daca took three, but thankfully left us Grandma's old one. That night Mom was so grateful, she bent down on her knees, kissing the hem of Emina's gift. I missed the grandmother who baked me cookies, called me "honeybun," and took care of me when Mom was working. I hoped she was okay. We could hear bombs exploding in the south, toward the suburbs, where we'd heard Emina had fled four months ago. With the phone lines cut off, we had no way of knowing whether she was safe. If they bombed the house where she was staying, I was afraid the rubble could collapse on top of her.

The next week Daca took Mom's prized iron from Germany. Losing the iron didn't kill me, but Dad was fuming.

"Those cowardly savages," Dad spat.

"It's not like there's electricity for the iron to work anyway," I said. I didn't understand why Daca and Boban didn't just get a van to cart everything away. Eldin thought they wanted to be less conspicuous; ripping stuff off piecemeal would keep it under the radar of the military brass.

"As long as they don't hurt us," Mom reassured. "Our lives are more important."

Soon Daca's eyes became even larger. "I really like your home," she said one evening, her gun on the coffee table. She didn't need to ask us to get out; she could just shoot us and move in.

"Why don't they?" I asked later. My parents didn't know. Eldin said there was a difference between a crook and a murderer. I wanted to think that Daca and Boban saw we were a nice, decent, harmless family, without a bad bone.

A few days later when Daca returned with Boban, she asked, "When are you leaving?"

"We want to," Mom said. "But nobody will help us get out."

Now I was starting to get the game we were playing. We would trade our stuff and our place if they'd help us escape Bosnia. But then Dad blew it.

"We could cross the front lines to free territory in a prisoner exchange," he added.

Shit. I knew instantly Dad shouldn't have said that. It was obvious that as soon as he crossed over, he'd pick up a gun. He'd basically just admitted he wanted to shoot Boban.

"Aha! So you do want to fight against us!" Boban raised his voice, standing up, towering two heads over Dad, who turned red. When the giant put his hand on his Uzi, I thought he was going to shoot Dad. I gasped. But he just adjusted his strap.

Daca smirked at Dad's screwup.

"Wouldn't you want to be with your mother?" Mom asked. "We miss the rest of our family."

Boban sat back down and lit a cigarette. He took a few drags, then stubbed it out and left. I emptied the ashtray in silence and took a long breath.

"Thank God they didn't hear about Dad's revolver," Eldin told me.

"He still has that revolver?" He'd never mentioned having a weapon directly to me before.

"Any non-Serb with a registered gun is labeled a dangerous resister and shot dead. Dad was on the list," Eldin later filled me in. "But Stevo, this Serb volleyball player Dad trained, came by when you were out getting water. Stevo told Dad, 'Give me your gun now. Quickly. Anybody else but me would kill you. Remember Keka, I was never here.'"

Though the gun was long gone, it made me question why my father had gotten it when he told us we'd be safe here. Was he pretending for us or himself?

A brave Muslim doctor we knew had given us a piece of thread with knots that his mother had sanctified with Islamic prayers to keep evil spirits away. We hung it by our door. This sacred present must have had protective powers. Either that or Dad had nine lives. But I wondered what other secrets he was hiding and lying to me about.

Over the following six months, Daca stopped by every day, bringing me treats and Mom coffee beans, which she ground and added to boiling water. It was a ritual. They'd drink it together, then whatever lights, chairs, cookery, or glasses left in our home that Daca wanted, my mother gave her. At the same time, though, Daca befriended Mom. She showed us pictures of her mother and the son who looked like me. I guessed that even thieves got lonely.

When Boban showed up, he'd try to intimidate us by saying he was becoming the chief of police in Brčko and bragging how many Muslims he'd murdered that week. But I noticed that other military men in the building came back from the trenches muddy, dirty, and exhausted. Boban looked rested; his boots were clean, even in the rain.

"I think he's a pussy," Eldin said. "If we hear mortar shells and explosions all day, then what's he doing sitting here, having coffee with us? I bet he's waiting for the battle to end so he can steal from the pockets of dead soldiers."

We developed a theory that Boban and Daca were grifters from Belgrade aiming to get rich from war profiteering. They may have killed civilians in a botched robbery, but Eldin was skeptical that either had seen combat. I didn't know how to feel about Daca. She talked about her little boy a lot; she clearly loved him. She was gentle with me. I noticed, under her huge fatigues, that she was thin, with narrow shoulders and a flat chest. I didn't think she was a killer. The uniform she wore now seemed a costume for the dangerous role she was playing.

Still, they were armed Serbs, figures to be feared. Downstairs in the stairwell when I went out to get water and bread, I heard my old Serb classmates say how cool and strong Daca and Boban were. "Man, they're dangerous," Velibor said, impressed that they were Arkan's soldiers.

When Daca caressed our white marble table over coffee, we knew that was next to go. It was a present from rich Uncle Ahmet. He'd driven Mom to an antiques store in the suburbs to pick it out. Dad and I loaded up the carriage and took Ahmet's table to Daca's garage. Dad looked bitter. There was no end to this humiliation, as if we had to forfeit every object we'd ever valued one piece at a time until none were left.

But I wanted more of Daca's candy, and her protection. "Is that the same Uzi Sylvester Stallone had in *Cobra*?" I asked her one day.

She nodded and smiled. I showed her my collection of bullets and shrapnel. "I pulled that one hot out of the wall."

"That was brave," she said. "I have more sweets for you. Come for a walk. And bring the painted bowl."

It was a gift Dad had bought Mom on his trip to Romania with his volleyball team. She kept it in a glass cabinet. She liked it even more than the huge wheel of cheese he'd brought back from Hungary. "Be careful of Daddy's present," Mom had said. I was sad to see it go. But I'd never been to Daca's without my father. I looked at Mom.

"Go with her." Mom shooed me toward her. We now felt sure Daca wouldn't cause me harm. I was her favorite. I even thought Mom was using me to soften her up.

As I crossed the courtyard with Daca, my former pals Igor, Velibor, and Dalibor stopped their soccer game to watch us. They didn't say a mean word. They were scared of her. She was my shield. If she liked me, that gave me power. I imagined telling her who had bullied me, so she'd punish my foes and make them stop picking on me. I felt important and cool, the only boy she brought licorice, Bazooka, and Cunga Lunga bubblegum with stickers.

When we got to her place, Boban wasn't there. In the kitchen, I found piles of bonbons, chocolate bars, gum, and Kiki-Riki chewy candy, the kind of stash you'd find under a Christmas tree. But no stores around here had any candy left. I realized right then that she had never gone out to buy me anything; all the treats she'd brought over she'd just grabbed from the stack of stuff she'd stolen from Muslim homes. She had bought my affection with dirty candy I now hated myself for eating. My hunger and greed had caused me to betray my own people.

I helped Daca carry my father's Romanian bowl to her stolen bedroom. It was packed with boxes—yet more loot. To thank me, she kissed me on the cheek with her painted lips. When she went to the bathroom, I looked in the mirrored cabinet and saw the red stain she'd made on my face. I wiped it off. Sitting down on her sofa, I spotted her Uzi on the dresser with an extra clip, the upside showing. I imagined flinging open the bathroom door and shooting Daca right in her face. Then I'd quietly sneak out. Would my family be proud? No. They'd be scared for our lives.

But if no one heard the gun or saw me leave, I bet I could get away with it. When Boban found his wife dead on the bathroom tile, he'd think it was an inside job, that one of their own had offed her. Surely they were competing with other looters. He'd never guess it was the innocent, scared, five foot two, hundred-pound, eleven-and-a-half-year-old little boy she'd given stolen chocolates.

Yet I could see Daca driving our entire family to safety. What if she was the only Serb who would help us get out?

In the living room, she caught me eyeing her slender, pitch-black submachine gun. "Here, you want to hold it, honey?" She handed me her weapon. "It's loaded, be careful."

I held it with both hands, looking up at her. It was heavier than I'd expected. My heart lurched as I pictured blasting her in the chest, her thin body wrecked, walls splattered with blood. Daca stood above me, one arm resting on her waist. She smirked. I stared at her. I didn't smile back. I felt stronger than she was, like Stallone in *Cobra*, the movie Dad took me to twice.

Her smirk vanished. She squinted, as if she could see what I wanted to do to her.

She snatched her weapon back and said, "Time to go."

She slid a midthigh bayonet onto her wide brown military belt. Before tucking the Uzi back inside, she took a nine-millimeter round brass bullet from an extra clip. "Here, you can have it as a souvenir." She handed it to me in her open palm. I was psyched; I didn't have that kind yet.

"Thanks." I slipped it in my pocket.

She handed me a box of waffle hazelnut cookies. It had probably been confiscated from a Bosniak's home too. But I ripped the box open and ate three anyway. They were warm and crunchy and delicious. She watched, looking pleased to be the one giving me treats.

On the way home, I kept thinking that I'd almost become a murderer today. I didn't even feel bad; I would be like a good cop getting a scumbag criminal off the street. I was sure I could have gotten away with killing Daca. I'd just take her weapon with me and walk behind the house to the banks of the River Sava. There I'd wait for nightfall and swim to Croatia. Freedom would be worth the risk of getting shot or stepping on a land mine.

"You okay?" Dad asked when I got home.

"Yup. Just dropped off the bowl. Everything's fine."

I handed him the cookies, not mentioning my dance with Daca's Uzi. It was the first real secret I ever kept from my father.

CHAPTER SIX

Days of Resurrection

The Balkans
July 2011

I needed to see for myself that the bastard was really dead.

Summer vacation for normal thirty-year-old American guys meant partying, romance, hanging out with old friends. I was spending my time visiting graveyards.

I'd already mapped out all the different Bosnian cemeteries. Since second on my list was standing on Pero's grave, I insisted we start there. I walked out of Aunt Bisera's house early Monday morning in a tank top, black jeans, and my black retro Adidas, armed with my camera, pen, and notebook.

"You're going like that?" Eldin asked.

I knew the medieval Bosnian flag tattoo adorning my left arm could cause trouble. But so what if it did?

"I'm wearing what I want."

Eldin clucked his tongue. "You're going to upset Dad."

My father tilted his head, scrunched his eyes, and decreed: "No problems today."

I ran back inside and grabbed a shirt with sleeves that I could use in case I needed to cover up my ink, just to placate my annoying brother. "Well, I'm driving," I insisted. "Don't even try to argue with me about that."

I'd had my license in New York and Connecticut for more than a decade, but I'd never driven in my homeland before. I wanted to prove to Dad and my brother that I still knew my way around, despite everyone saying I'd been too little to remember. I slid into the driver's seat of our rented red Volkswagen Jetta. Dad, wearing jeans and a polo shirt, climbed in back. Eldin, in cargo pants and a T-shirt, sat next to me since he needed more room for his spidery legs. Even in front, his knees hit the dashboard, his size 14 Adidas longer than the brake pedal.

"I should stop to get two bottles of water," I said.

"Why?" Eldin asked. "So you can piss on Pero's plot?"

He knew me too well.

"Don't even think about it," my brother warned.

I navigated the road defensively on the twenty-five-minute ride. Jasenko reminded us that Balkanites in autos were even crazier than on foot—they didn't believe in seat belts, drove drunk, cut you off head-on, swerving out of the way at the last second. The car chaos was an apt metaphor for what this visit was doing to me emotionally. My hands were sweating so much, the steering wheel was damp as we drove up the hill at Groblje, the Serb cemetery. Luka was below, about fifty yards from the entrance. I could feel Eldin's body temperature rise next to me, along with his anxiety. We didn't belong here.

This was underscored when we walked through the entrance and bumped right into a statue of the famous World War II Chetnik guerrilla Draža Mihajlović.

"They have this fanatic gene in their blood," Eldin said.

"It's like entering a German cemetery with a statue honoring Adolf Hitler," I added as my father quietly simulated a spitting noise. But I wasn't letting a bronze Chetnik scare me off. Inside the florist shop by the small chapel, I turned my torso so the flower lady wouldn't see my tattoo. "Excuse me, ma'am. Could you please tell me where Pero Zarić is?" I tried my sweetest choirboy voice. "He used to be my karate coach. He died in 1993."

"He's in the war section. Stay to the right to find him," she said, quickly. I guessed he'd had other recent visitors.

Outside a dozen women in black dresses and skirt outfits stood beside graves. A few maintenance men with shovels were working the grounds.

"I don't want to be in this place," Eldin said, all of a sudden agitated, as if he hadn't known where we'd been heading all along.

"I told you from day one that standing on Pero's grave was on my list," I argued.

"You were that serious?"

"Of course I was. You thought I was playing?" I asked, indignant. "You gave me some items yourself." I realized the ones he'd added were mundane—seeing old friends and relatives and visiting our people's cemeteries to pay respect. My items on the list involved confrontation—just what he wanted to avoid.

"You kept changing your mind and crossing stuff out," Eldin said. "I didn't know I was obligated to do every stupid thing on there."

"If you don't like it, stay in the car," I told him, hurt that he was undermining my game plan. "Or go to the town square and I'll meet you."

"But why are we paying respect to the wrong people?" Eldin asked.

"Yeah, why are we?" Dad agreed with him.

"I'm not being respectful. I need to take a picture of Pero's grave." I wanted to put it in my leather album next to my childhood karate photographs of me and my coach, as a kind of epilogue, to conclude the story.

"Oh, all right." My father was usually persuadable. My brother wasn't as easy.

Eldin and Dad followed me, mirroring my zigzag trail as I checked every marble marker and cross amid the bitter scent of candle wax in the air. Reading each name, aisle by aisle, made me dizzy. I was conscious of sour looks and muttered profanities from people I passed. How dare I walk over their sons' graves with that ink on my skin, I could feel them thinking. In 1992, I would have been shot dead.

"You know, I'm the one who was locked in Luka with Dad. This place creeps me out." Eldin gestured down the hill, toward the concentration camp, now a warehouse again. It was less than a hundred yards away; you could throw a rock and hit it. "I don't want to look at those dark crosses or walk down the aisles between tombstones," he said.

"But think of how symbolic it is," I argued. "I'll walk right over Pero, disturbing his spirit. He'll turn over, cursing, knowing it's me."

"Pero didn't throw *you* into Luka. He killed *my* classmates." Eldin's lips turned downward, a dismal look on his face. "You can't possibly understand."

"Sorry." I relented. My brother had known Pero longer than I did. Since they were closer in age, Eldin had seen him as a comrade and a teammate. He had more reason to fear Pero, who'd killed people he knew; Eldin's life had literally been in his hands. But Pero had been my mentor and father figure, the first man I'd looked up to aside from Eldin and Dad. So I wasn't giving up until I got what I wanted.

"Let's just get this over with already." Eldin slumped over, hands in his pockets.

"You should stand tall. Be proud. I'll take my time and enjoy every second of it," I said. "My friend Fadil came to see the grave of his dad's killer. It can't be harder for us."

Eldin and Dad shuffled behind me, toward the "Veterans Only" section where black marble headstones were embellished with full-body portraits of uniformed Serb soldiers.

"See, you can read who they were." I pointed to the stone slabs engraved with short, telling tributes. I read one aloud: "Survived by two children, his loving wife, and mother. We're all proud of you for defending our home and heritage."

"They're still full of shit when they're dead." Eldin threw up his hands. "Even their headstones lie."

"We're almost there." I led the way, checking every name, section by section. Eldin breathed heavily on my back, impatient and pissed. Dad followed, mumbling, "I knew that son of a bitch. Him too," as we passed old gym clients whose surnames he recognized.

It took fifteen minutes to locate Pero. By the time I found him, I had a headache. His small plot was the size of a single bed. It had a gray marble border, filled with crushed stones. So this was where he'd been all this time. An ash-colored square read: "Zarić Petar 1963 to 1993" in Cyrillic letters, with a cross and what looked like a high school picture of him. Funny, his mother must have chosen the last photograph, taken when he was clean-cut, with short hair. I had never called him by his real name, Peter in English.

I read the words engraved in his stone. There was a short list of survivors: mother, father, brother, sister-in-law. Many tablets here were etched with the phrases "brave fighter," "died for his home-land," or "killed in battle," making it clear that their demise was associated with bravery in the war. It seemed very suspicious to me that Pero's family had chosen the verb *pogino*, indicating that Pero's end may have been accidental; the word, which means "die," made it ambiguous, leaving open the possibility that Pero could have died from friendly fire or even a nonmilitary car accident. He could have fallen off a building. Or been pushed. I was frustrated to not know his exact cause of death.

But I did know for a fact that he had died at thirty, the age I was now. I imagined my life being already over, before my true adulthood started.

Several batches of fat pink and purple roses lined his grave, a half-filled water jug to the side; I bet his mother had recently stopped by to see him. To the right was a wooden bench rotting with mold and pigeon dung that, I decided, mirrored his soul. It looked as though it would crumble if you tried to sit down. I lingered on the sidelines and thought about taking a piss or stomping on top of his head, as I'd threatened. Standing over Pero, I told myself I was six feet high and he was six feet below the ground, so that made me the victor. But then I flashed to my karate triumph at Partizan Sports Hall two decades earlier—the peak moment of my childhood—when Pero placed the brown belt around my neck, lifted me up on his shoulders, and said, "Super job, Keno baby."

With Dad and Eldin right there and other mourners mulling around, I became self-conscious. Suddenly the idea of peeing or jumping on his grave seemed primitive, the foolish and immature fantasy of a twelve-year-old. I didn't want to smash the row of flowers his mother had left. Being here, I didn't feel I'd won anything. I still couldn't reconcile what I'd lost, that my onetime idol had returned to cleanse our building of Bosniaks and take my father and brother away to die.

"He's gone, we're alive," Dad offered.

"And they still have to live next to Muslims." My brother tried to console me. "His time came before ours. He was lucky he got a funeral, unlike many of his victims."

We never did find out exactly what caused his demise. I pictured Pero getting blown up by mortar fire in a trench or being shot in the head by a Bosnian sniper.

"Can we go see my father now?" Dad asked. He was on edge; we all were.

"Don't worry. We'll get to our cemetery to see your father soon. He's not going anywhere," Eldin told him. Then he hit my arm. "Come on. Are you done? I can't do this anymore. We're going to the car."

They left, but I wasn't ready yet. I stayed by myself, rereading Pero's stone, looking around as though I expected him to show up for this showdown. The last time I'd seen him, he'd pointed at me, laughing in my face. I'd muttered, "I hope you die." I knew it wasn't logical, but I was sure my words did him in.

"Look at you now, Pero," I taunted, regressing to twelve, my age at our last encounter. I wanted to hear his voice or get a sign he heard me: the ground rattling below, a sudden wind in my face. There was merely a motionless headstone in stifling summer heat. I'd hoped that seeing where Pero wound up would offer some kind of satisfaction or vindication. But buried in these vast rows of graves that listed ages and causes of death were middle-aged ladies who'd lost their lives in car accidents, kids who'd drowned, army generals felled in battle, next to old men who'd succumbed to cancer. The mix made it seem random and anonymous. I felt nothing.

When my cell phone buzzed I found a text from Eldin. "Hurry up. We need to go. What's taking so long?"

"Okay, I'm ready to see our dead now," I said when I rejoined my father and brother, who were pacing by the car. Back in the driver's seat, I noticed my camera on the dashboard. Damn, I'd forgotten to take a picture of Pero's grave. I felt like turning around to get it, but I didn't want to distress my brother any further. I'd never visited the Muslim burial grounds in Brčko or attended a funeral in Bosnia. The only memorial service I'd ever been to anywhere was for my mother, in Connecticut.

It was a twenty-minute drive on a narrow, two-lane road through town to get to the next cemetery. We passed a flea market and food stands to the left, then a huge mall built after we'd fled.

"What if that broken headstone isn't there and we can't find my father?" Dad said, sitting behind me, leaning forward to stare out the half-open window, agitated. "Sead said they sliced it in half."

"We showed you the picture Sead e-mailed proving it's been fixed. Don't you remember, Dad?" Eldin reassured him.

"Don't worry, somebody patched up his stone," I repeated, rolling my window all the way down. It was a hot, sunny day. I wanted to smell the fresh air outside and hear the Bosnian noises—car engines, people speaking my language on the street, turbo-folk tapes playing in other cars. "How did Grandpa Suljo die again?"

"Heart attack in 1970," my father said. "When he was seventy-one."

Dad was seventy-one now, while I was the age he'd been when he lost his father. The thought of losing him terrified me. My Uncle Sabit had died two months ago at eighty, leaving my father as our oldest living male relative. Since Dad's brain hemorrhage he'd been much quieter. It had taken him nearly a decade to relearn how to speak. I was suddenly worried he could have another stroke here, the last place I'd want him to wind up in the hospital. What if he lost his speech again? There was so much nobody else could teach me about who my father was, where we came from, and the men who made me.

"Grandpa was a good electrician, right?" I wanted him to elaborate, tell me all the details I didn't already know.

"One of the few in town." Dad nodded. "He was a hard worker. He could untangle any kind of wiring. Your grandfather always dressed well. Every day he was proud to go to work in a suit."

Pero worked in that same profession. But in Pero's time there were lots of electrical workers. And unlike my grandfather, my coach wore jeans to work and hated his day job. "You were the closest to your dad?" I asked.

"Yeah, but my parents separated when I was four, in '43." In the mirror I could see Dad sitting back. He closed his eyes, remembering. "I was an only child. I was so lonely. It's not good being the only kid at home."

"Why did your parents split up?" I recalled my mother saying that Grandma Zekija was cold, neglecting my father after she divorced his dad and married someone else.

"Maybe it had to do with my baby brother dying at birth," Dad said.

"What?" I took my foot off the gas and caught my father's face in the rearview mirror. He looked sad. "You had a brother?"

"Yes. But I was only two years old, so I barely remember," he said quietly, looking out the window, into the cloudless sky.

"Dad had a brother?" I turned to Eldin.

"You didn't know?" he asked.

"Hell, no!" I'd always assumed that my grandparents had chosen not to have any more children because they were unhappy. Had losing a baby son taken away their hope? I'd lost a chance to have another uncle and aunt and more cousins in the world. I couldn't believe I'd missed something this essential. I was in college when Dad had the stroke that wiped out parts of his memory. With Mom, Grandma Emina, and Uncle Sabit gone, there were few elders left to fill in my family history. I was furious at myself for not asking Dad more questions about his background sooner. I'd been too preoccupied with my own life to learn more about my father's.

"Oh, strange you never heard," Eldin said. It was old news to him.

As the two-lane road became one, I saw a glass building on the left where an outdoor soccer court used to be. Foreign cars from Switzerland, Germany, and Austria whizzed by. Recent Croatian and Serbian license plates had a flag and the initials of the city where they were issued: BG for Belgrade, ZG was Zagreb. For safety,

Bosnian plates now showed only numbers, with no cities or flags, as if we didn't belong to anyone.

"What else do you remember from growing up here?" I asked Dad.

"During freezing winters when my feet were icy, your Grandpa Suljo came over to bring me gloves and warm boots," Dad said. "I missed him every day after he left. I never got over him leaving."

Now I understood why my father had stayed so close to me and Eldin when we were kids. I didn't know why he was opening up more than usual today, whether it was being back in our homeland together or the barrage of questions I was asking while he sat in the backseat, where we weren't facing each other. But hearing him talk so intimately about his parents' split made me realize that while my clan had nonstop discussions about politics, sports, and food, we rarely shared personal emotions.

When a New York friend wondered if my parents had worried that I was traumatized during the war, I said, "They were too busy telling me to duck." She laughed, but I wasn't joking. After everything we'd been through—watching friends and relatives killed or rounded up into concentration camps, the horrors of ethnic cleansing, our exile, and two debilitating illnesses—we just focused on getting from one day to the next, afraid to burden each other with anything more. Sure, we shared news and nostalgia and recollections of the people we hated. But it was actually astonishing to think how little we'd processed the past together.

"When did they build that?" Dad pointed to a four-story apartment building with copper-colored brick next to a mosque.

"Obviously after the war," I told him.

"Too close to the mosque," he commented. He pulled on his collar, undoing the top buttons of his polo shirt.

"It's so hot out," Eldin said, handing him bottled water.

There wasn't much traffic, but I drove slowly to look for stores and restaurants we used to go to. I recognized a small supermarket that had tripled in size. My favorite bakery had turned into a watch-repair shop, and the hardware store now sold cheap Chinese clothes. Riding in our rental car between Bosnian cemeteries seemed the right time to delve into our history. With Dad in the rare mood to spill secrets of his childhood, I didn't want him to stop.

Veering off from the Sava River to our right, we entered Grandma Emina's neighborhood. Every other house showed signs of destruction from the war, with chipped paint, bullet holes in bricks, windows on top floors boarded up, the renovations still unfinished.

"You used to live on the banks of the Sava River, right?" I asked Dad. I knew he did, but I hoped if I kept probing, he'd reveal important details he'd been hiding.

"Yes. I'll show you where," Dad said. "When Brčko was occupied in World War II, German soldiers moved into the second floor of our house."

"You told me the Germans were nice to you," said Eldin, who sat next to me in the front. He turned halfway toward Dad to hear him better.

"Yes, they brought flour and sugar to my mother. I was five," Dad told us. "If I shined their boots, they'd give me chocolates. They put a helmet on my head and let me ride on their army motorcycle." He smiled at the memory. "One soldier played the harmonica and taught me to sing a German folk song."

When we watched the 1965 film *Battle of the Bulge*, Dad rooted for the Americans. He'd called General Patton "an extraordinary general and a gentleman," lamenting that he'd died in a car accident. Yet I'd noticed that during the Military Channel's footage from the Battle of Stalingrad he'd rooted for Germany. He'd called the Russians *govna*, "human waste," and muttered, "They'd rather build their drunk armies and let their people stand in bread lines." I understood that he'd associated the Russians with their ancestral Serb allies and thought he'd just despised the Soviets. But now it troubled me to hear how close he felt to real German soldiers.

I sipped on water, dehydrated from the heat. "What about the Holocaust?"

"I was a little kid. My mom said the Germans fixed up buildings, churches, and mosques when they were in Brčko," Dad said. "During the war, we had no TV, radio, or newspapers."

"But didn't your parents know what Hitler was doing?"

"When I was older, I learned Bosniaks in town had hidden Jews here," Dad said. "We never held anything against anyone Jewish. I knew Hitler was a psychopath."

"Muslims were getting slaughtered by Serbian guerrillas. They hoped the Germans would save them. They were desperate." Eldin explained Dad's Germanophilia. "You remember what those Chetniks were like?"

I nodded, getting a chill even nineteen years after the black-clad Chetnik in a skull-and-bone hat nearly killed us at the Brčko checkpoint.

"My father had two brothers who died heroically in World War II, fighting for the Partizans," said Dad.

I knew the majority of Bosniak fighters joined the Yugoslavian Communist Party's military arm, led by Tito, an anti-Nazi who was half-Croat, half-Slovene. "But if your family didn't like the Partizans, why did your two uncles fight for them?" I asked my father, confused.

"Because they were idealistic morons who believed in Tito's brotherhood dream with the Serbs. They just used us to drive the Germans out." In the rearview mirror I could see Dad frown.

"Then they created a Serb majority who treated Muslims as second-class citizens, as soon as the war ended," Eldin said.

"Screw those *patlidjani*," Dad swore, confusing Bosnian words.

"You just called them eggplants," I told him.

"Who fucks them anyway." Dad used a Bosnian saying for "Who gives a damn."

"I guess everybody hated everybody," I said.

"Yeah." Dad nodded. "When I was older I found out that Uncle Smajo was killed by the Germans, and my Uncle Halid was killed by Chetnik guerrillas. There was a street named after both my uncles, 'The Trebinčević Brothers.'"

"In fifth grade I used to walk by the sign," Eldin jumped in. "I'd tell my friends, 'My uncles were heroes; this is their street, check out their sign.'"

"Why didn't you tell me?" I felt left out again.

"'Cause you were three," Eldin said.

At the traffic light, I shifted into park and turned to Dad. "I can't believe I'm just learning all of this now." Being back here made me impatient to fill in our family saga—before it was too late. I might never come back here with Dad again. I wanted him to give me a cram course on our ancestors to catch up on who I was.

"Wait, what about Uncle Sabit?" I was mixed up because Grandma Emina's brother fought in World War II *for* the Germans.

"The Germans recruited twenty thousand Bosniaks into the Handschar division," Eldin said. "I saw pictures of Muslim soldiers in Turkish fezzes adorned with swastikas."

"Hitler liked Muslims?" I asked.

"No, but he hated the Jews, Russians, Serbs, Gypsies, and the disabled more," Dad explained. "He didn't see us as Slavs."

"So Uncle Sabit really fought for Hitler?" I hoped he hadn't joined to kill Jews.

"Many Bosnian Muslims refused to defend the Serbs and welcomed the Germans as liberators from government tyranny. They used Germans to get weapons to protect Muslim towns and villages from Chetniks," Eldin recounted. "Out of a hundred and sixty-five Yugoslavian World War II generals, all but four were Serbs."

"Wow. So that explains why Bosniaks wouldn't want to fight under them," I said.

My brother nodded. "World War II was mind-boggling for Muslims in occupied Yugoslavia. They had to decide which side would oppress them least. It was total havoc within a family—brother fighting against cousin."

"You didn't decide by intellect or politics," Dad said. "Your Uncle Sabit joined to fight Chetniks. But his troop was ordered to the eastern front to battle the Soviet Army."

"Imagine how desperate Hitler must have been to recruit swarthy Muslims into his Aryan army," Eldin laughed. "But in 1943, the Handschar was the first SS unit to rebel against the Nazis in France. They executed five German officers. The mutiny is still celebrated by the French."

"Sabit would drink too much on the boat and trash the Russians," Dad recalled. "How he'd shot them in a row like ducks. Sabit's dad was an imam who gave him a lucky Islamic string that was sanctified with prayers. He carried it into battles. He'd have bullet holes in his uniform and dead Germans all around him, but he was untouched. He said the bullets must have been remote-controlled to swirl out of his way."

As we cruised by a dive restaurant where they were roasting a lamb outside, Dad asked, "When are we going to have a lamb roast?"

"Who cooks meat on the sidewalk right next to car fumes?" Eldin asked. "No thank you. You don't want your lamb to taste like diesel fuel."

I wanted to hear more about my uncle, who I used to go fishing with. I was riveted to think he wasn't just a skinny, cranky fisherman buzzed on moonshine. I was disappointed he'd never spoken of his war days with me. When I heard Bosniaks swapping battle stories, I went from feeling lucky I was spared that experience to having soldier envy. "So why did Sabit trash the Russians so much?"

"He hated the soldiers from Russia because they didn't bathe," Dad went on. "He said they had lice and would fight drunk and rape women—they didn't keep a soldier's code of honor like the Germans did."

"Concentration camps aren't honorable," I snapped. "You know that from Luka!"

"I read that Milošević was a fan of Hitler's *Mein Kampf,*" Eldin said. "It inspired him. He'd wanted Muslims to wear green arm bands—like the yellow Star of David badges the Nazis made Jews wear."

"Look, there was a difference between the regular German soldiers we met who were living in our building and the Nazis running Hitler's SS," Dad insisted.

Was there? *A German killed the uncle you loved. Why are you defending them?* I was about to challenge Dad. I didn't know who was worse—the ignorant, deluded people who actually believed in racial cleansing or the pathetic German, and Serb, sheep who'd committed mass murder because they were just following orders. But then I thought of Miloš, the Serb with the AK-47 in our building who'd fought Muslims by day but fed us by night. And Uncle Sabit, siding with Hitler to avenge the Chetniks. I pictured that Chetnik psycho who could have gouged our eyes out with his long sword. I would have instantly aligned with anybody willing to get him away from my family. Maybe you couldn't judge every military man by his uniform. Not every enemy soldier was equally guilty.

"You know the camp they taught us about in school where Serbs, Jews, and Gypsies were killed?" I slowed down before the crosswalk.

"That was run by Ustašas, the Croatian fascist revolutionaries, not the Germans," Eldin said. "The Serbs had two concentration camps for Jewish prisoners: Banjica and Sajmište. The Serbian government sent Hitler a letter bragging they were the first country in the Balkans to get rid of Jews. The Serbs hide their sins like a snake hides its legs," he added.

"After the Germans were defeated, Uncle Sabit was arrested and taken into custody," Dad said.

"Really?" Why hadn't he told me this before?

"Female Partizan soldiers took turns kicking him in the balls," Eldin told me. "They beat the piss out of him."

I'd never heard this odd twist either. My elementary school was named Jelenka Vočkić, after a Serb female Partizan. I wondered if she was one of the women soldiers who'd almost castrated my poor uncle.

Stopping at the light, I saw my old pediatrician, Dr. Ćaušević, crossing the intersection. In his white scrubs and a stethoscope around his neck, he was obviously coming from the hospital, a three-minute walk from here. I beeped and waved. "Doctor!" I shouted. We'd called him from Bisera's to tell him we were in town and make a plan.

"Oh, the Americans are here!" he said, rushing up to our car to greet us. "It's Keka and his boys." He shook Dad's hand through the window, then patted him on the head.

Dr. Ćaušević had been a prisoner at his own job during the war. The Serbs had kept him at the hospital to treat their wounded soldiers. "If he dies, we shoot you on the spot," was how the comrades of a bleeding soldier threatened him. Afterward he'd moved to Florida for a few years. Rumor had it, he came back to Bosnia to be Brčko's chief doctor out of spite, refusing to acknowledge the Serb colleagues who'd turned on him.

"So when can I take you out to dinner?" he asked us.

"Soon," Eldin said. "We'll call you later."

Cars behind us beeped. A guy yelled, "Come on, doc. You're creating a convoy. Get back to work."

"We're holding up traffic," I told him.

"Take your time. Don't worry, they need me to treat them," Dr. Ćaušević said calmly as he waved good-bye.

"His mother was the one who sanctified the thread that protected us during the war," Eldin recalled.

"Picture operating while a soldier held a gun to your head. He has nerves of steel, that guy." Dad sounded awed as we pulled away.

I was still picturing the Muslim men in my own family in the '40s. "So don't you think it's weird that three relatives of ours were overpowered by three separate enemies in World War II?" I asked, having trouble delineating between the German socialists, Chetnik Serbian nationalists, and Partizan Communists.

"Grandma Zekija's second husband, Hilmija, fought with the Croatian Home Guard, siding with fascist Italy and Hitler," Eldin threw in.

"Damn!" I wiped the sweat from my forehead. "How could four pacifist men from our family fight in four different armies?" World War II had torn everybody's families and minds apart long before our war had. I drank more cold water, wondering if that was my problem: I'd spent years trying to understand my homeland when the tribal animosities of this whole place were completely insane.

"I know. Nothing's changed in a thousand years," Eldin nodded.

"You liked Hilmija," I said, turning uphill into the cemetery driveway.

He shrugged. "Yeah, he used to buy me Sandokan superhero shirts in all colors."

It was hard to picture our nice step-grandpa fighting alongside Italian Fascists and the Third Reich. But it remained harder for me to fathom how, in 1992, my family's Serb neighbors had become our Nazis.

"Hey, Eldin, remember the book you gave me that argued Serb politicians manipulated the country into our war by playing up past Serbian victimhood?"

"It was called *The Serbs*." He nodded. "About how Milošević fueled paranoia and demonized us by making up threats of an Islamic revolution in Bosnia in '92. The idiot rallied Serbs to fight Bosniaks—the least radical and most peaceful Muslims on earth."

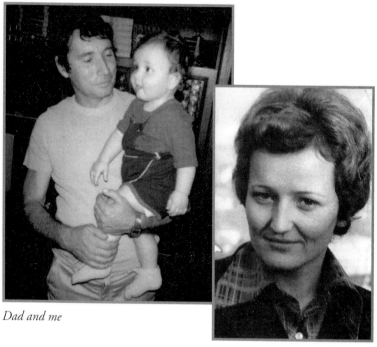

Dad and me

Mom's high school portrait

Dad and Eldin on Eldin's birthday

A portrait of my big brother and me taken by our local photographer on the way to Grandma's.

On vacation in Croatia in 1984

A Republic Day celebration in my teacher Milutin's first-grade class. I am in the top row, fifth from the left, not wearing a traditional red scarf or blue partisan hat. So much for brotherhood.

The day I received my blue belt. Coach Pero is standing behind me.

Thanksgiving Day, 1995, in Connecticut. It was the week the war ended, but we don't look very thankful.

(Right to left) Uncle Sabit, Grandma Emina, Aunt Bisera, Cousin Mirza, and his wife outside Brčko in the late 1990s

Paying respect to the fallen men—many of them Dad's old friends and Eldin's former classmates—in the Bosnian army cemetery in the village of Gornji Rahic, thirty minutes south of Brčko

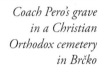

Coach Pero's grave in a Christian Orthodox cemetery in Brčko

Cousin Amela's children, Rusmir, Kemal, and Tidja,
with Dad and Eldin at Amela's home

Dad standing outside the gates at the former concentration camp Luka,
with the bridge connecting Bosnia and Croatia behind him

Watching Coach Boško, a family friend, teach karate inside Partizan Hall

Jasenko and me at Premier, a Bosniak bar and coffee shop in Brčko

Eldin and Dad in front of the hangar at Luka, the former concentration camp

The view from our former kitchen balcony in Brčko

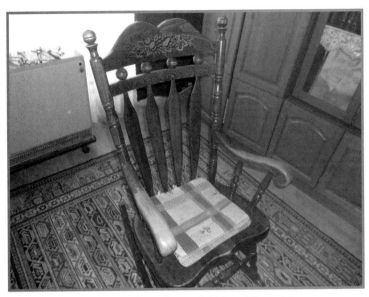

My mother's rocking chair in Miloš and Zorica's home

Cousin Amela with me, Eldin and Dad

Mezarje, the second cemetery we visited, was where Grandpa Suljo was buried. It was only for Bosniaks. As I pulled into the parking lot next to the morgue, I thought: *Even the dead in this land remained divided among ethnic lines.* Walking out of the car, we stepped on rubble from a former shoe factory that had been totally decimated in the war. It was the scene of an infamous seven-day battle. Nobody had cleaned it up yet.

Eldin pointed to the white stones marked with stars and crescents and Islamic names and said, "Now I feel better." We bought five small bouquets at the florist shop.

In front of the entrance was the sign "Europa Hotel." We'd heard it was a Serb joke to place the sign here, a ten-minute car ride from the hotel. Dad shook his head in disgust.

"Well, our people should have taken it down instead of just complaining," I said. I was envisioning sneaking back to this cemetery late that night to spray paint over it when a gravedigger walked by. "Excuse me, sir." I stopped him. "I want to visit my grandfather, Suljo Trebinčević. How would I find him?"

"He's over here," said the short, sweaty guy in orange shorts and a gray tank top. He looked to be in his fifties, with a pointy chin and kind, dark eyes. As he walked us to my grandpa, he told me, "Your tattoo is amazing." He was a Muslim who understood that my ink was a patriotic gesture meant to honor our old Bosnian flag. We belonged here.

Dad laid a bouquet on my grandfather's grave and said a prayer. I took a bunch of pictures. You could see a thin line in the stone where Grandpa Suljo's marker had been cut all the way across. "How did it get sliced in half?" Dad asked.

"From a bomb?" Eldin guessed.

The gravedigger shook his head. "When I was a soldier, I saw

Serbs fighting in this cemetery. When the battles began, the burial ground became the frontline." He stood up straight, turned, and pointed. He spoke authoritatively, like a veteran showing us a map of where the war had been. "This place was pummeled so their army could get an unobstructed view. Horses and tractors ripped up and carried away the headstones. After the war, with donations and my own resources, I replaced the plots and mended each broken marker with cement myself, one by one."

He obviously took immense pride in what he'd done and hadn't been shown sufficient appreciation for all his hard work.

"After the war, it was the first Muslim place we took back and fixed," he added.

Overwhelmed with gratitude, Eldin gave the gravedigger a hundred-dollar bill.

"This is not necessary," he told us, but we insisted.

My father handed him another forty dollars. "For fixing my father's marker."

So Grandpa Suljo's tombstone really had been cut in half and reconstructed. It was carefully cemented back together at its base. Just like we were.

Half an hour later, Dad was still searching for his mother's grave. I was determined to locate my mom's relatives who'd always been so kind to me. We visited Great-aunt Fatima. In 2003, she'd sacrificed herself, to save her granddaughter by jumping in front of a cab that was running a red light. She was supposed to be buried next to her husband, but he'd mysteriously died in the hospital during the war; we never learned what really happened to him. We found Uncle Sabit, Fatima's brother, to pay respects. When the Serbs had stormed his apartment in 1992, Sabit eluded them by hiding behind a bookshelf. The backyard of his house in Brčko wound up being on the front line. Even though he was in his sixties, he'd hopped a high fence and made it to Fatima's place, where he waited out the rest of the war. Hoping he'd take us trout fishing like he used to, I'd been dismayed to hear he'd passed away this summer, just two months before we arrived in Bosnia.

Last, we went to see Grandma Emina and Grandpa Murat. They lay in the same plot with no separation—fitting for a couple who'd been so deeply in love. In Mom's photographs, Emina was a tall woman, stylish and pretty, with black hair and fine jewelry. My grandpa—who'd died before I was born—was a traveling salesman. He sold dress shirts and ties and liked gems too. My mother sneaked his gold Swiss watch out of Bosnia, hiding it inside a ball of socks; I'd inherited it after she died. Murat also had a penchant for exotic birds. Mom said he had a coterie of thirty different parakeets, finches, canaries, and peacocks that he kept in a huge cage and doted on. Aunt Bisera said one night all of his feathered pets began squawking in a frenzy and wouldn't stop. The next day he dropped dead—and all the birds croaked too, in some kind of a synchronized death symphony.

I snapped more rolls of film, thinking what a weird family re-union this was. Then I put lilies on the gravestone of my grandma, finishing number 4 on my list. I kept picturing my mother, the youngest of Emina's three kids, but the only sibling gone. If the war had never happened, Mom would have been here too, resting safe with her folks, instead of displaced, left alone for eternity in a strange plot in Connecticut, where she didn't know anyone. I hoped she wasn't lonely.

Next on my list was to pay homage to soldiers from our side who were killed fighting. After a twenty-five-minute drive, we found the martyrs' cemetery in an all-Muslim village that had been a stronghold during the war. As we passed rows of white footstones etched with Islamic prayers and military pictures of the dead, my father became teary. Eldin's eyes were glassy as he mumbled that he wished he would have fought too. Back home in Queens, I'd found a website online that listed each of this graveyard's 556 soldiers by name. I'd printed it out for my father. For the next half hour I followed Dad around, checking off 99 men he knew. Having an agenda on paper was my way of organizing chaos. I silently thanked God that I didn't have to visit my father and brother here.

Then I pulled out the paper in my pocket and crossed off number 3 from my list.

The fourth graveyard I wanted to see was a burial ground for both Bosnian military and civilians in an old town filled with buildings from the Ottoman Empire.

"Hey, you have to see this guy, he's not one of us," I yelled to Eldin as I read the story of a soldier named Goran. Based on his name, we could tell he was a Serb who had joined the Bosnian army.

My New York friend Shoba spoke of a whole brigade of Serb fighters from mixed marriages that he'd joined. Unwilling to embrace the racist ideals of Greater Serbia, they fought against their own people. Shoba's troop felt it was wrong to kill civilians because of their background. So they chose the side they believed was right. This soldier Goran's family had put him to rest among his Muslim neighbors. I thought Goran deserved the most respect. His moral principles mattered more to him than his ethnicity. If I'd died in my homeland, this would be the place I'd want to be buried. Yet Goran's sacrifice did not change my mood. Any semblance of forgiveness eluded me. It was hard not to feel that all the wrong people were dead.

"You'll never catch me dead flying over Bosnia," Mom often said after we'd escaped. It had been four years since we'd been to see her in Enfield, Connecticut. We promised each other that we'd spread crushed marble stones on her grave so it would resemble Grandma Emina's resting place in Bosnia. My mom's cemetery, just a few hours from where we lived in the United States, was the one I couldn't bear.

"We have to go see Mom," my brother reminded me.

"I know. We'll go for her birthday," I told him.

"That's what you said last year," Eldin said as we got back on the same road that led to the concentration camp, ironically renamed Boulevard of Peace.

It took us just ten minutes to get to Luka, which was now a commercial distribution center that transported sugar, oil, and flour. Truck drivers came here to weigh their merchandise and pay tariffs. The old warehouse buildings were repainted yellow, with new windows and a fence facing the big parking lot. When we arrived, a security guard came out of his cabin. "What do you need?"

I took the lead. "They were both imprisoned here." I gestured to my father and brother. "We've come to see the warehouse."

The guard nodded, lifted the gate. Clearly we weren't the first Bosniaks who'd returned to witness the atrocities that happened here.

We parked, and I put my camera in my pocket to ensure I got a picture of Luka, number 6 on my list. We walked to the open door in the blazing-hot sun. Before we came, Eldin and Dad insisted they were ready and eager to go back there. But once we arrived, they didn't want to go inside. They slouched outside by the two hangar entrances, looking anxious, cowed, somber.

Dad pointed. "Bosniak and Croat men sat on cement and those wooden pallets."

"That's where the camp leaders hung out and where men were taken for interrogations," Eldin said, turning to the right.

"That office is where I went when they called my name." Dad glanced toward an ordinary room now filled with workers, talking on phones and listening to the radio.

It was as if Auschwitz was still in business—as a shipping company.

"That's where Ranko Češić was sitting behind the desk," my father said. "I didn't know what would happen in there. I had a horrible headache. When he asked what was wrong, I told him my head was going to explode and begged for a sip of coffee. Another Serb soldier yelled, 'Fuck off, I'll put you out of your misery.' But after that guard left, Ranko ordered someone to bring me a cup. The woman serving it was my dad's college roommate Valid's wife. She tried not to cry when she saw me. I heard she'd been gang-raped there by Ranko and all the other thugs—who'd made her husband watch."

During the war we'd heard many rumors of Bosnian women being sexually attacked. Yet it wasn't until afterward when I'd been sickened to read that 50,000 mostly Muslim women and girls had been raped, many of them held at Serb-run "rape camps" whose goal was to impregnate Bosniak and Croatian females. It served to humiliate Bosnian men and weaken their family ties. The patrilineal rules of our society meant children inherited their fathers' ancestry. So this was also part of the Serb's ethnic cleansing campaign.*

"Valid's wife survived the war. But after he was shot, his body was never found," my father went on. "That day Ranko told me, 'Just be patient, everything will be fine with you and your son as long as I'm here.' And he kept his promise to protect me."

At the Yugoslavian tribunals, Ranko pleaded guilty to twelve counts of rape, systematic murder, humiliation and other crimes against humanity, and "infringement of physical integrity." He confessed to ordering a Muslim policeman to shake everyone's hand good-bye before beating him to death with a club. He made two

---

* Fifty thousand mostly Muslim women were raped during the war, according to the Bosnian Ministry of the Interior as reported in *Mass Rape: The War Against Women in Bosnia-Herzegovina*, edited by Alexandra Stiglmayer (Lincoln: University of Nebraska Press, 1994).

Bosniak brothers perform fellatio on each other at gunpoint before shooting them.

Now forty-seven, he was serving a mere eighteen-year sentence in Denmark. I wondered how guilty my father must have felt being spared by the brutal exterminator who'd sexually abused and killed his friends and neighbors.

"That's the alley?" I looked out back.

Eldin nodded. He'd played me testimony from other Hague war trials where a comrade from Luka said he was forced to throw wounded men over the wall behind the warehouse, into the banks of the Sava River.

"Savages," Dad muttered, looking spooked.

"We shared a wooden pallet on a forklift the entire time," Eldin explained.

"Did you sleep at all the whole two weeks you were there?" I asked.

Eldin threw me a look that said, "Are you kidding?"

"I kept my eyes open every second," Dad recalled. "I wanted to make sure I was awake so they couldn't take Eldin."

It was the first time I'd heard any of these details. I was moved by my father's sweet fantasy that keeping his eyes open had saved my brother, who believed it too.

"Dad's aura was my shield; even mass murderers wouldn't touch him," Eldin told me.

"There was this man sitting in front of me," Dad said. "A soldier called his name, put his arm around his shoulder, and in a friendly voice said, 'Let's take a little walk.' The door closed, I heard a rifle shot outside the door. The sound echoed off the walls. One bullet. The guy never came back. An hour later, another guy came to sit on his pallet."

I shook my head from side to side. Eldin scanned the outside of the building that he and Dad couldn't enter.

"Every time the guards walked in, I tried not to make any eye contact," my father told me. "I'd look down at their feet. They would walk by us, pick someone to take outside. The guy either came back disfigured or not all."

We passed a gray plaque on the wall etched with a white dove and white Bosnian letters translating to: "At this place from May to July 1992, in the concentration camp Luka, hundreds of innocent civilians were killed, Bosniaks and Croats. May their souls rest in peace."

"Let's take a picture in the warehouse," I said.

Eldin handed me his camera, and I opened the door for him. But then he stopped and shook his head, his eyes alarmed, as if something horrible he'd witnessed inside had suddenly resurfaced, unhinging him. He stopped, unable to walk in.

"Take one outside, with the plaque in the background," he said.

I needed to take a photo of Dad and Eldin here for number 6, but it didn't matter where. "Cool. My camera might catch a ghost in the background," I teased, trying to lighten him up. But locals living in the houses across the fence did believe the place was haunted.

When I snapped a picture of Eldin posed with Dad before the front door, I was sure they were standing taller and prouder than when they came in. It was as if they needed to survive being here again.

I later noticed that Dad's polo shirt was green, an Islamic symbol for life, and I bet that he'd made a point of picking that color and wearing jeans, intentionally *not* dressing up for Luka. Eldin's eyes were shielded by sunglasses, and his Affliction T-shirt was adorned with an angel. I wondered if he'd chosen that on purpose as well. In the frame I took, his arm was firmly around Dad, his hand gripping my father's shoulder as if his life still depended on not letting go. Since they'd returned from Luka, they'd had a special bond, one that I didn't mind not sharing. I was just so grateful they'd both come back unharmed.

A worker on a forklift that held two large white bags stared at me, then went back to his job. As I walked toward the car, I saw my father looking up, with both hands wide in the air, his palms facing him, reciting an Islamic prayer in Arabic. I'd never seen him pray with his arms before. Surviving what he'd witnessed here could make even a secular man reach for God.

"We're meeting Sead at eleven at Boa Café?" my father asked for the third time on Tuesday morning as we had breakfast with Bisera. He was in a suit.

"He's been dressed up and ready since seven o'clock," Bisera said. "I made him coffee and toast when I was feeding my rooster and peacocks."

"Yes," Eldin said. "Sead told the gang you'll be there."

"But what if nobody's around?" Dad fretted.

"Don't worry," I reassured him. "Everybody will be there."

"You look very nice, Keka," Bisera told him.

"Kenan and Eldin got me this." Today he'd dressed up. He proudly showed off his tie, which was navy with yellow fleurs-de-lis, a symbol of old Bosnia. We bought him most of his clothes these days.

"He has to look nice to see all of his old buddies." I patted Dad's shoulder, figuring everybody else would be in casual clothes. Eldin wore jeans and a light blue T-shirt. I was in beige chinos, a zippered sweatshirt, and a black Oakland Raiders cap. I had no connection to that football team other than identifying with a bunch of scrappy outcasts who'd do anything to win.

I insisted on driving us to the town square, only fifteen minutes away. It was a lovely piazza in Brčko that had cobblestone, tree-lined streets with stores, bakeries, and bistros on both sides. Since it was centrally located and no cars were allowed, it had long been a gathering place. Jasenko said Boa Café—which had outdoor and indoor tables—was the new hangout. It was owned by Bosniaks we knew, but just a few doors down, you could end up in a Serb bar.

"I don't know who we're going to bump into," I said. "There are a lot of people I don't want to see."

"Just stay calm," Eldin told me. "Everything will be fine."

We parked and then walked past the regal Hotel Posavina, which had been built in 1891 and was ruined in the war. It had been renovated and now looked fancy, like a European mansion. It was bustling with people coming in and out.

"Hey, did you ever see that photograph taken here in May 1992 of a Serb shooting a civilian in the back of the head?" I asked. "The shooter was a cop who's serving a forty-year sentence as a war criminal."

"They murdered people at this hotel. I'd never stay in such a ghost-infested hellhole," Eldin said, gesturing to the building to our left. "And that Brčko police station became another killing ground."

As I turned back to show Dad, I was shocked to see Slobodan, skinny as ever in a sleeveless shirt and black jeans, a stupid smile plastered on his face. He ran up to my father and patted him on both shoulders.

"Hey Keka! How's Brčko's number-one ladies' man?" Slobodan shouted, smirking. A bunch of people stopped talking and turned around.

My father squinted. Standing in the sun on the sidewalk in his dark suit, he was feeling the heat. He was still drained from seeing Luka and all the cemeteries the day before. And he became overstimulated in crowds. I could tell he was trying to recall that rat's name, definitely not recognizing him. Oh, but I did. Slobodan was my mother's soccer-playing Serb coworker who'd left us at a dangerous checkpoint in the hands of the Chetnik guerrilla we thought would kill us. As if that wasn't despicable enough, we'd learned that Slobodan had later told paramilitaries that Keka's two sons had flown Islamic party flags before the election—a brazen lie that almost got us massacred a second time.

Slobodan wasn't a murderer himself, or even a Serb soldier. He was a coward who let other people do his dirty work. In his expensive jeans and fancy leather shoes, he was known around town as a fake who'd quietly double-cross his prominent non-Serb friends. Meanwhile he pretended to be everybody's pal. "If you look at his face, you'll see his ass," my father once said of him.

"Can't remember me?" Slobodan thrust his big hand out for Dad to shake. "I'm Radovan Karadžić," he quipped, smiling, using the name of a psychotic war criminal nicknamed "The Butcher of Bosnia." It was the equivalent of squawking "Hey, I'm Josef Mengele" to a Holocaust survivor. I wanted to kill the idiot right there, just for the sick joke.

Seeming confused, my father took his hand and shook it. I knew he had no idea who Slobodan was; Dad was just being polite, pretending he did. I had the urge to jump between them, give Slobodan a karate kick with my heel, hard enough to shatter his shin. But I sensed my father's heart was already overstressed from remembering too much at the graveyards and camp. I didn't want to upset him more. I looked at Eldin, who crossed his arms and sneered over his shoulder.

"So where's your wife?" Slobodan asked my father, in a tone that was too familiar.

How dare he ask about my mother! My blood was simmering. I was sure everybody knew of my mother's death from Dad's old gang here. I wanted to spit at Slobodan and yell, "Since when do you care? You left us at the Pirometal factory checkpoint to die, you disgusting, gutless loser." But I was breathing so heavily, I couldn't get a word out. Two cops were standing on the police station's stoop. My dad continued trying to figure out who this creature was. If Eldin turned away for a second, I was going for his throat.

Slobodan reached out to my brother for a handshake. Eldin looked at him, not moving. Slobodan's hand hung in midair. Eldin caught my eye, then Dad's. Seconds passed. Reluctantly Eldin put his hand out partway, lifting a few fingers.

Slobodan took what was offered, shaking quickly, then snatched his hand back. "Why was that so hard?" he asked in a hurt tone, addled, saying something else to Eldin.

But I couldn't hear his words anymore. I went deaf. All I heard was my chest pounding and my ribs twitching. I moved forward. When Slobodan saw me, he leaned in and reached out his hand. Eldin's eyebrows shot up. It felt like the scene was frozen in slow motion on a TV screen. My father looked puzzled, still not getting who this guy was. I glowered. I did not move my hand. If it lifted, it would be to smash his face.

"Okay, fine then," Slobodan snapped.

A buddy he'd come with must have caught the vibe because he said, "Come on, let's take off." He ushered Slobodan to a table in front of the hotel, about fifteen yards from us, where they sat down. Leaning forward on his elbows, Slobodan muttered about me as we glared at each other. I wasn't even sure if he knew what he'd done to my family the last time we'd seen him, nineteen years ago. Maybe his annoying greeting was his usual run-of-the-mill provocation to visiting Muslims. I would have respected him more if he'd ignored us. That would at least show shame. Instead he acted like most everyone else here—pretending that mass murder had never happened in my hometown. If he didn't remember at all, that was worse. I was out-of-my-mind enraged at my country's charade of collective amnesia.

"Keka's younger son is a crazy lunatic," Slobodan said loudly, looking over at us. "You could lose your head in peacetime with someone like him around."

I had had enough of this Serb bozo who betrayed my mom's kindness—twice.

"If I were you, I'd leave right now, Slobodan," I shouted, picking up an empty chair I was ready to hurl at him. I pictured it crashing into his head and then, as he lay on the floor bleeding, I'd kick him in the ribs and remind him exactly what he did to my mother.

Before I could take another step, Eldin grabbed the chair and shoved me back, gripping his huge hand around my neck, squeezing it so hard my joints were locked and I couldn't turn. His left hand jammed under my ribs. He lifted me off the pavement, dragging me across the street. Startled, I was completely overpowered and scared. I didn't even try to fight him; my whole body went limp. He let me down a hundred feet away, in front of Café Boa. I brushed myself off, ruffled and demoralized, my hands trembling.

The last time my brother had overpowered me was when I was eight. Eldin was fourteen and babysitting me one night when our parents were out. I got mad and kicked him in the balls. He fell to his knees and yelled, "I'm going to kill you." He threw me to the ground and kicked me in the back with his enormous boot, making me cry. It was the last time I'd ever picked a fight with him. I had no idea how strong he was now.

Eldin and I stood outside the café, wordless. I sucked in air, my chin quivering.

Dad walked over, scratching his head, finally getting it. "Now I know who that creep is! *Jebiga*, I hate when I don't remember." Dad swore in Bosnian.

Eldin turned to me. "I was wrong to shake his hand. I regret it. I'm pissed at myself. Screw me." His expression was tortured. "But if I didn't, he would have kept goading and you would have insulted and hit him. Then I'd have had to break his face and he'd have to feed himself through a straw for the rest of his life," he rambled. "And the Serb and Bosniak police captains would have rushed out and we'd wind up in jail and what would Dad do without us here? Will you forgive me for shaking his hand?"

I took a few deeper breaths, still embarrassed. I wasn't anywhere near forgiving anyone. Luckily my father's jazz buddy Sead pulled up on his bike, parked, then tapped my dad on his shoulder. They wrapped their arms around each other and didn't let go. It had been nineteen years.

"Look at your two grown sons. Keka; you should be so proud of them." Sead clung to Dad. "You boys have to know how special my Keka is." He kept kissing Dad's cheek. It was hard to stay angry at Eldin as I watched the joy sparkling my father's eyes.

We found an outside table on the patio of the café, underneath the bright green awning. Calming down, I sat on a beige cushioned chair next to Dad, with Sead on his other side. Eldin plunked down next to me and tried to say something, but I turned my shoulder. A few more guys recognized my father and rushed over to say hello. During their greetings, hugs, kisses, and two-decades-long summaries, I kept ignoring Eldin.

My brother tapped me on the back. "It's all good, we're okay, just relax." He looked more freaked out than I was. "Are we cool?"

"If Slobodan only knew today was his lucky day," I hissed, not finished stewing. "You saved his ass. He should thank you."

"Hey, you shamed him in front of everyone, just like he deserved. It's better this way. We don't need the whole police station and the American Embassy out here."

It was before noon, but I needed whiskey to chill out. Slobodan saw me from his table across the street but knew enough to not move any closer. I snarled in his direction, downing two Chivas Regals on the rocks while Eldin had Nescafé, adding milk and sugar to his instant coffee like a grandmother.

"Man, that younger Keka's tough. We heard what happened," said a guy standing by our table. "We need more people like Trebinčević's son in Brčko to show their teeth to the local Serbs."

"What does it say that everybody talks to Slobodan like nothing happened?" I overheard a Bosniak man who told Dad he was visiting from Australia.

"Did you hear he refused that Chetnik's handshake?" asked another guy.

I had never rejected anyone's hand before. Standing up, I was thinking that in minutes I'd gone from feeling like a humiliated child to being almost famous.

I saw a guy in his fifties ride by on a bicycle, catch sight of Dad, and break to a stop. "Keka, is that really you?" He wore overalls and a T-shirt that showed off his beefy arms. I guessed he was a construction worker.

Dad scratched the side of his head, then nodded. "Oh, now I remember you." He broke into a smile and stood up to embrace the man I'd never seen before.

A large table with a group of five Bosnians turned one by one to look at him.

"Kekaaa?" they all shouted, his nickname echoing off the pavement in synchronicity. They rushed over and threw their arms around him. My father hugged everybody, but I knew it would take a while for his brain waves to connect and remember who they all were.

"You're Kenan, his younger son? You're identical," bellowed a volleyball player I recognized.

"Thank you, boys, for taking such good care of your father when he was sick," said an old coaching colleague of Dad's. "It was generous of you two to bring him back to his motherland and pay for it." I'd forgotten how fast word traveled in every corner of this city. People here obviously knew Dad had suffered a stroke in 2001. Now they seemed amazed at how well he'd recovered. "As kids you probably didn't know, he'll always hold a special place around here. Knowing all he went through, we're so happy to see him in such good shape. He's a gem, the same old Keka. I want to buy you all a drink and toast him." The guy was crying so much he got his saliva on my cheek.

"He wasn't only a sports figure," Sead said. "He was a hell of a drummer." He pulled out a picture of their band from a 1958 New Year's Eve jazz concert, showing Dad in his usual three-piece suit.

Sead put his hand around Dad's neck. His nose was runny with tears. I had to look away because my eyes were getting glassy too.

Eldin called out to a tall figure walking by, an athlete in his forties who'd become Brčko's head volleyball coach. I'd heard about this guy— he'd been in the Bosnian army, though now he most likely coached the kids of the fathers he'd once fought.

"I am Zoran, a Serb your father trained in the old days," another man came up to us and said. "I could not pick up a gun and shoot my neighbors, so I left the country." He embraced me.

When Zoran walked away, another Bosniak acquaintance of Dad's pulled up a chair next to me, put his mouth to my ear, and said, "That guy Zoran is a liar. He was my childhood friend, but he sentenced me to death during the war. Luckily someone else saved me."

I was taken aback. "Why would Zoran want to hug me then?"

"He can't live with his guilt," the guy said. "He is dead to me."

It was becoming obvious that everyone we knew in this country was twisted in more knots than I was. I felt fortunate to have a normal American life to go back to.

I saw a guy next to me text on his cell phone: "Get to Boa now! You won't believe who is here." As the news of my father's reappearance in Brčko spread by word, text, and cell phone calls, more people came by. It became so loud everybody in the establishment turned to see what the commotion was about. My brother and I felt like bodyguards, but this time nobody wanted to hurt Dad, just see and hold and celebrate him. I felt special sitting next to my father, proud of our resemblance, basking in his aura. At twelve I'd watched Dad become powerless overnight, thrown out of his home and his office and tossed into Luka. Now his immense popularity and importance seemed to come back, albeit nineteen years late.

My father grinned and nodded and shook hands with everyone who approached him, elated to regain his former glory. I was grateful that Eldin had intercepted the potential disaster and didn't let my reaction to Slobodan ruin this day for Dad. I saw that having a pacifist father and older brother shielding me from harm was saving me from the fate of too many Balkan men here.

"Check that out," I told my brother, surveying the crowd that had gathered. There must have been twenty guys surrounding my father.

"After so many years, look how they still feel about him," Eldin said.

He was so lonely in America, especially after losing Mom. He had only a few old pals left in Astoria. All I could think was: look what they'd taken away.

CHAPTER SEVEN

My Grandpa Murat's Karma

Brčko, Bosnia
September 1992

"Those are not for Muslims," yelled a Serb woman at the makeshift Brčko market, grabbing the red peppers from my hand. But I needed to buy us something to eat. If I returned empty-handed, my father would blame himself for not protecting me. Mom would feel awful she couldn't feed me. We just had soybeans in the cabinet and hardly any more money. Our neighbors hoped we'd die so they could loot what was left of our apartment. Although I was only eleven, letting my family down made me feel like a failure.

Walking home with my head down, hungry and dejected, I looked up to see Pero on the street corner. He wore a blue uniform and held a rifle, and was flirting with a pretty girl who had dark curly hair. I hadn't seen my coach in four months, since his armed police unit invaded our home. I stopped in front of him. I felt no respect or awe anymore; I was hurt and let down. I wanted to ask how he could let his men threaten us by gunpoint. If he was so powerful, why wouldn't he help us escape? He saw me and started laughing. As I walked away, I caught him pointing his finger and cracking up, humiliating me in front of his girl.

"I hope you die," I muttered. It was the last time I'd see him alive.

That night, I was sitting in the rocking chair in our living room, swaying back and forth by candlelight, when the knock on our door made me jerk. I stopped swaying and turned toward the door, scared that Pero had returned to get us. Or it could be Daca, here to steal more.

"Can I come in?" a lady asked. She introduced herself as Zorica and said she was a Bosnian Serb who'd been living in Croatia. Behind her was a shy six-year-old boy, holding her hand. She said they'd moved right below us, into my good pal Huso's two-bedroom apartment. Huso's family had fled the country for safety, in the middle of the night, without saying good-bye. Dad said they had to go fast; they were on a blacklist to be killed. I didn't like that Huso was gone and this woman had taken his home.

I stared at Zorica, who had short, puffy brown hair and wore jeans, a T-shirt, and sandals. No lipstick or makeup. She looked Mom's age. She took her shoes off at the door and instructed her son to take his sneakers off too. Mom let her inside, and she shook hands with my brother and Dad. She wasn't armed or eyeing our belongings. She already had Huso's place. So what did she want from us?

"I'd offer coffee, but we don't have propane left," Mom said, looking ashamed.

"Your father and my uncle were friends from World War II," Zorica told her.

"Kenan, why don't you go show her son your miniature cars?" Mom prompted. I played with the boy nearby so I could eavesdrop.

Zorica told my mother, "During World War II, your father

jumped out of a moving truck to escape the Germans. He ran to the village where my Uncle Novak lived. Your father hid inside my uncle's house for three days."

This stranger knew my grandpa, whom I'd never met? Grandma Emina said he was a handsome gentleman who'd dressed well and was beloved by everyone, especially birds. Aunt Bisera inherited her love of animals from him.

"To thank my uncle, Murat promised to buy his milk from then on," Zorica continued. "So for the next forty years, Novak came on his bike twice a week with fresh farm milk. Your dad could get milk anywhere, but Novak was poor and needed the income, so he helped keep Novak in business. Your father was a good, loyal man."

I had seen that milkman, Novak, at the door once. He was wearing a dark suit and a fedora, like Humphrey Bogart in *Casablanca*, my dad's favorite movie.

"We know you're having a rough time. We want to help." Zorica patted my mother's hand. "Whatever my child eats, yours will eat as well."

Mom started to cry.

Late that evening, Zorica sneaked back with canned meat loaf, chicken pâté, and Milka chocolate. "My father drives to Germany through Serbia, where he fills his car with food," she whispered to Mom, as they sat on the couch by candlelight. Because Zorica's dad was a Serb, he could pass through the checkpoints we couldn't get near without a problem. I was sure that Grandpa Murat's good bird karma from another war was saving us from starvation now.

But I was confused about Zorica. She gave us food, yet she'd stolen Huso's home. When she invited me over to play with her son, Dejan, it felt weird to be in Huso's two-bedroom flat. His family had taken off in such a hurry, hoping to return soon, that they'd just grabbed their clothes and left everything else behind. I resented Dejan for having Huso's toy cards and World Cup soccer trading cards. I was ashamed to be in the bedroom where Huso and I used to play video games. It felt wrong to trespass here without him. One day I would say I was sorry to Huso; I hoped he'd forgive me.

"Take this eggplant for your mom," Zorica said after we finished playing marbles. For all my reservations, she was so nice to me, I began to feel safe at her place.

"Daddy, did you kill any Muslims today?" Dejan asked.

I looked up, startled. It was a late September night. I was playing at Dejan's when his father Miloš walked in the door from a two-week tour, fighting in the outskirts. He was in his dark green uniform. As he took off his muddy boots, he leaned his AK-47 against the wall. My stomach tightened.

Dejan jumped into his dad's arms. "How many Muslims did you get?"

"Dejan! Don't ever say that!" Zorica scolded, her face red.

Sitting on the floor, I finished my Milky Way bar, looking up at Miloš, my neck tingling with sweat. He was over six feet, taller than my father, with huge shoulders. If he was killing Muslims in the field, he could easily shoot me here. Or go upstairs to get my father and brother.

"Can I wear your jacket and gun?" Dejan begged his dad, who handed over his coat. When Dejan put it on, the sleeves reached the floor. Miloš took the clip off his gun and gave it to his son.

"Here, want to touch the rifle?" Dejan pushed it my way.

I took it carefully. The barrel was still warm. That meant Miloš had just been shooting Muslims like me. He might have killed my cousin Mirza who, Dad said, was fighting in the Bosnian army nearby. Outside mortars were firing from across the street. I prayed the bombs weren't landing near my grandma in the suburbs.

"Let's play war," Dejan said.

He gave his father back the clipless AK-47, which Miloš put on top of the dining-room table. Against a constant background of explosions outside, Dejan and I hid at different ends of the apartment and searched for each other. I aimed my plastic Luger-replica water pistol; Dejan put his father's holster around his waist. We weren't allowed to play with his grenade, which he kept on a high shelf that we couldn't reach. I imagined stealing it, squeezing the handle, pulling the pin, and tossing it off the balcony, blowing up my friends who'd abandoned me. We used a pair of rolled-up socks as our grenade instead. I sneaked behind Dejan's back and tossed the sock-grenade in front of him. We counted to three out loud, made a boom noise, then "kssshh." We covered our ears and threw ourselves on the floor so we wouldn't get hit by a second shock.

In the next round, I used thread as barbed wire to trip him. When he fell, I fired my water pistol in his face. Dejan was a nice kid half my age, but I wasn't about to let him win. It was a thrill pretending I was a Bosnian commander conquering Serb bad guys, taking them out one by one, saving my people.

Miloš I wasn't so sure about. Despite what his son thought he did every day, he never knocked bread out of my hand, shot my water canister, or called me *balija*. For the next four months, whenever he visited our place, he took his dirty boots off. He and his wife, Zorica, acted as if they respected my parents. When they brought over their son, my dad taught him chess; Dejan was pretty good for just being six. "Mr. Keka, can we play one more game?" he begged. My dad called Dejan "a good, well-behaved little boy." Still, we were enemies. In my calculation, if Miloš was killed by a Bosniak soldier, Zorica would stop bringing over chicken pâté and chocolate and jam and blame us forever.

One night in October, I was there when Miloš came home, smoking a cigarette, looking shaken. "We lost a lot of men in Vučilovac," he told Zorica, throwing his bag down. "The Bosniak and Croat forces burned the whole damn village. Our T-84 gunner was sliced in half." I ran upstairs, ecstatic. "Their army lost, and this guy on their tank got sliced in half," I told Dad and Eldin, who pumped their fists.

"Is Miloš okay?" Mom asked.

I nodded, incensed. She should worry about the people on our side he'd killed.

The Vučilovac victory gave me hope we'd soon be liberated. Eldin spent hours every day lying on the floor with his ear pressed to the radio so none of our neighbors would hear the Bosnian station he was listening to and think he was a collaborator. One day, he heard news of a prisoner exchange. They were trading Muslim civilians for nonfighting Serbs. Eldin pushed Mom to put our names on the list at the post office so we could join our family in the Serb-free territory and convinced me we had a chance to join Grandma Emina and cousin Amela there. But a compromise couldn't be reached; I was crestfallen when the cease-fire was canceled.

The battles resumed; so did our dismal routine. Daca returned to steal more of our stuff, and to pressure us to give her our apartment. She had the weapons and the power. All we could do was stall and fake-smile and pray.

Daca wasn't our only looter. A soldier named Geca showed up and stole an antique sword my father got in Turkey. At first we were afraid of him, but the next day he walked in wearing a long blond wig he'd stolen from the mall, trying to be funny. We learned Geca was sweet on my mother's friend Ankica, a divorced Serb woman who lived nearby. He was surprised we knew her. Soon—instead of menacing us and taking more of our things—he'd come over with presents of coffee, sugar, and flour that Ankica told him to sneak to us. Another time, when he heard Igor was bullying me, Geca told him to lay off. It worked—Igor stopped kicking me and spitting at me on the stairs.

Still, with no heat or light or water, I was feeling pent-up and restless. Last year I'd had two birthday parties with my pals. Dad got me a Transformer, and Grandma baked me a special dessert. Now, when

I turned twelve on December 9, 1992, I had no friends, no party, no cake. I didn't even know if my beloved grandma or favorite cousin were alive. When Mom wished me happy birthday, I said, "Who cares? The dead Muslims are better off than we are."

I didn't mean to make her cry, but I was desperate for us to leave. Without electricity we'd freeze to death once the temperature dropped. When snow fell, the streets were not plowed. You couldn't tell where the sidewalks were. We had to heat up water in a pot over the propane gas tank. Then I'd sit in the heatless bathroom tub, using the Red Cross soap bar, rough like sandpaper, pouring a cup of water over my head. Zorica tried to help. She had Miloš come upstairs to refill our empty tank. She brought another Milky Way bar for my birthday and gave me one hundred dinars I turned over to my parents for food. Compared to Daca, Zorica was Mother Teresa.

That night, Daca joined Mom and Zorica for coffee, chatting like she was a girlfriend hanging out, not a conniving thug. Daca bragged about all the Serb bigwigs she knew. It gave Mom a new idea: in exchange for documents to get us out, she offered Daca keys and the deed to our apartment, which we owned. Daca agreed to the plan. "I'm going to Belgrade after Christmas. I'll obtain papers to get you through checkpoints at the Bosnian-Serbian border." She promised they'd come through by the end of the year. At this point we understood the new rules: whoever had the biggest gun took what they wanted. The Serbs just typed up their own papers and contracts and stamped them to look official. But we were excited to be going to Vienna in early January, joining Mom's brother there. Daca seemed our last hope.

On Wednesday night, December 30, 1992, my job was to meet Daca at the bus station when she returned at 11:30. That was way past the city's 8:00 p.m. curfew. I felt like a spy on a mission, trudging through a winter storm, the howling wind whipping angry snow through the streets. I waited for Daca in pitch darkness at the station, so cold my toes went numb. I worried the police might round me up. But I felt important to be the one to escort her home with our papers. I wasn't a kid anymore; I was a man my family could rely on for essential tasks. The glass on the streetlamps had long since been shattered. We'd had no light since the war began. Cigarettes sparked in the distance. Men in uniforms were smoking, covered in snow. I spotted the looming headlights of the bus Daca was returning on. As she stepped off, she handed me her heavy bag. I took it, sliding and tripping in knee-deep snow drifts as I followed her.

"I couldn't get the documents for you," she said casually, like it was no big deal.

My face was burning and freezing at the same time. She'd lied; she had no connections to get us out. This would break Mom's heart. Walking behind Daca, I noticed that when she'd slipped me her bag, she'd also put the thin leather strap holding her Uzi over my shoulder. It was my second chance to off her. As we crossed the street, I grabbed the Uzi handle. I only had to lift it and point the muzzle, then pull the trigger. I stopped shivering from the cold and felt sweat coming down the side of my head. Shaking, I placed my index finger on the trigger. *Press it already*, I yelled at myself. "We are not like them," my mother would tell me. I didn't want to hear her voice. I decided I'd call Daca's name first, so she would stop and turn around. I wouldn't shoot her in the back like a coward. I held my breath, gathering strength in my hand.

"I need my cigarettes," Daca said, turning toward me.

Surprised, I dropped the Uzi. It was swinging over my shoulder.

"Wait! You have my gun?" She laughed.

"Oh, it's too dark to see anything." I shrugged, pretending I didn't know I had it.

She pulled the strap over my head, grabbing it back. Again I'd missed my shot. I was relieved, yet still boiling with anger as I imagined my mother weeping when she heard the bad news.

Back in our kitchen that night, Mom looked devastated. "But I thought you said you could help us get to Vienna?" she asked, her voice quivering.

"Well, I'll get you a place in Belgrade," Daca threw out.

"In Serbia?" I could tell my mother was incensed by Daca's stupid idea that we should live amid our enemies where we didn't know anybody.

"You'll stay with my mother there. I need your apartment." Daca was getting pushier. She pulled coffee from her purse and gave me a Mars bar, like a consolation prize. I ate half, saving half for Eldin. I'd disappointed my mother. If I'd killed Daca, Mom wouldn't be crying now. I had no more hope.

"We have to get out of here as soon as possible," Mom said after Daca left. "What other Serbs do we know who'll help us?"

"There's no one," Dad said.

"We need another plan," Eldin agreed.

"Can you go back to Pero?" my father asked.

"Why would you ask him for anything after what he did to us?" I raised my voice.

It was a different Pero, they said, a good guy who used to lift weights at Dad's gym. Good Pero was the policeman who'd helped Mom get Eldin and Dad off the bus, saving them from being taken to another camp. Mom said he might be able to rescue us. But going to the police station was dangerous. We'd heard women were raped inside that building, and that Bad Pero had shot someone to death there.

On the second day of January, Mom took me to the police station to protect her. I was scared as she asked to see this Good Pero, a police captain. A short, pale man came out of his office and shook her hand. He was polite. He was in charge. He spoke quietly, vowing to have our passports drawn up in a hurry. An elderly, white-haired Serb drove Eldin and me to have our pictures taken the next day. We were to pick them up from a Serb woman who worked in the station. The morning of our departure, Good Pero promised to call the border checkpoints to ensure that our names were cleared. It seemed suspiciously easy and straightforward, but we had no idea who might detain us or turn on us.

Before dawn Dad and I sneaked out under heavy darkness, in a blizzard. We hoped we wouldn't run into Serbs who could identify us. If we did, they might keep us from getting on our bus. We walked for ten minutes without seeing anyone at all. Dad opened the front gate of the house we were told to try. He knocked very lightly with his fingertips. The door opened. A Serb woman slipped us an envelope. "Keka, here are the passports and the documents you need. Good luck."

We did not tell Daca we were leaving. "I hope that bitch never gets our apartment," Mom said.

"Snow is good for us," Dad whispered now. "It'll keep everyone inside." We prayed the weather would worsen so soldiers would stay in their cabins at the checkpoints. We told Zorica about our plan to flee at five the next morning. At midnight she came with a few hundred Austrian schillings, plus a bottle of moonshine to bribe the bus driver. We all kissed good-bye.

My parents didn't sleep. I shivered from the cold under a stack of blankets. I could see my breath as we lined up to leave our home before dawn. It was January 3. Our goal was to get on the bus to Vienna, but we had no idea who would try to stop us; we were basically winging it. We each took one suitcase. The snow was waist-high and kept coming down. It was the biggest snowstorm we'd ever seen in Bosnia. I was jealous that my old friends would get to sled down the hill. But then I remembered the slope of the hill led to Luka.

"If we get turned back again, Daca will catch us," Mom warned. If Daca knew we fled behind her back, without leaving her our deed, we feared that she could have Boban kill us.

"Hi, Keka," the bald bus driver greeted my father. He was a chubby Serb who looked to be in his thirties. He wrote down all the passengers' names. At the checkpoint, a soldier would read off the list. If our Bosniak names stood out, our trip would end right there. The driver wrote Dad's initial, followed by our last name, S. Trebinčević," since "Senahid" stood out as more Muslim. He winked at Dad. We smiled. He was on our side—even before Mom handed him Zorica's moonshine.

The blizzard made the drive much slower. There were no checkpoints for three and a half hours, until the bus stopped at the Bosnian-Serbian border. A soldier came out of a cabin. I was petrified as he stepped onto the bus's first step. "Do I have reason to check on everyone?"

"No, we're okay," the bus driver replied. I leaned my head into the aisle a tiny bit, holding my breath, praying he wouldn't stop us. He appeared to only skim the list. *Please God, let us leave.* I hoped the soldier wanted to get back to his cabin to stay warm. The bus was half-filled, twenty other people scattered around empty seats. They looked like Serbs traveling alone. A few couples going on weekend trips. My parents' age or older. Hardly any luggage. I knew that a terrified family of four traveling together, lugging thick duffel bags in the middle of a war, stood out. I was scared that our fellow travelers could tell who we were. We waited for someone to give us up. But the other riders kept quiet. We didn't know why. The snow kept falling. So far the blizzard, a friendly bus driver, and the silence of the other passengers were saving us.

At the second roadblock, we were stopped on the same bridge where we'd been humiliated last summer. We could be forced back at gunpoint, this time in deep snow. A tall soldier in blue camouflage and beret came aboard, bellowing, "Identification," as he marched down the aisle. "Any Muslims?" I stared at my boots. I was sitting beside Dad. Mom sat with Eldin, who was still in more danger. She wanted to protect her son, who was of fighting age, knowing he could be pulled off the bus at any second to be shot or sent to another camp or taken by the Serbian army and forced to dig trenches. I winced as the blue soldier headed straight for us like a magnet drawn to our terror.

"Documents!" he demanded. Mom handed him our passports and the official letter signed by Good Pero. The blue soldier got agitated and yelled "*Senahid* Trebinčević" out loud, emphasizing Dad's first name, which revealed we were Bosniaks. "Get off the bus!" *Please, not again,*

I was praying. Mom pointed to the letter that was supposed to guarantee our passage. He didn't buy it. She said Captain Pero's name.

"Who the fuck is he? You're not going anywhere," he screamed.

"Please, we have the required paperwork," Mom begged. "My young son has the flu."

"So what the fuck do you want from me? Take him to the doctor!" the soldier spit out, ordering us to get off the bus. "You can leave now." He told the driver to take off without us.

"Captain Pero was supposed to call the checkpoint to leave our names with the guards. Will you check, sir?" my mother begged. "Please."

We were hours away from home at the Serbian border, stuck in no-man's-land in a blizzard, past the point where we could return to our apartment. I tried not to cry as we stepped off the bus. We had nowhere left to go. Even if it was possible to catch another bus back to Brčko, Daca would have found us out. We had no friends in Serbia; we'd be killed there. I was shaking and sweating.

"Come with me," the soldier yelled, leading us to a room I feared was a jail cell.

His holster held a handgun and a stick hung off his belt. Inside the small office I spotted pistols and rifles in the open closet. Would he shoot us? If he tried, I'd make a grab for a weapon. Were they loaded? We were safer outside; he might not kill us while traffic passed by. Now the soldier looked around the desk, rummaging through stacks. He grabbed a note on a piece of paper. Wait! Had someone written our names down? Yes, it appeared that Good Pero had indeed called for us. The soldier picked up the phone and dialed. "What's your name?"

"Trebinčević," Dad said.

"Trebinčević," the man repeated into the receiver. "Uh-huh. Yes." I was numb, awaiting the verdict. Would we be allowed to leave or forced to stay? Live or die? Could he kill us right here? "Outside!" he bellowed.

We tumbled back into the snow, shocked to find the bus still outside, waiting. The driver had not followed the soldier's order! He'd pulled off the side of the road, had sat there waiting for ten minutes. He didn't want to leave without us.

"Aren't you letting them go? It's cold out here," the nice driver asked the man in the blue beret who held our lives in his hands.

"Get the fuck back on the bus!" he yelled. We reboarded quickly.

"Thank you, sir," my mother said.

Good Pero's connections worked. His letter and call protected us. So did the bus driver's kindness. But even though we were back on the bus with a protective driver, our ordeal wasn't over. We still had to pass two patrols at the Serbian-Hungarian border. Plus there were still all these Serbs seated near us who could turn us in to any army officer on the road. I worried they were resentful that we'd kept them waiting. No one said a word for four hours. I stared out the window, filled with adrenaline, checking for roadblock ramps or military jeeps that could stop us. In the worst scenario, we'd be thrown out and stuck in Serbia's enemy territory. My stomach cramped. On the Serbian side of the Hungarian border, the guard looked at us for a long moment, then returned our passports.

Our final hurdle was the Hungarian policeman thirty meters farther down. He was in an olive-green uniform with a white belt and visor. He skimmed our identification. "Why isn't your passport stamped?" he asked Dad.

We all stopped breathing. We didn't know if the Serbian border patrolman forgot or if he was trying to cause us trouble. The Hungarian shook his head from side to side. We waited to see what he would do. Finally, he stamped our passports, then got off the bus. The ramp lifted. I looked at my brother, afraid to react. Until the bus was on its way. Then we both raised our arms over our heads, cheering in relief. I pumped my fists in the air. Eldin and I high-fived. We'd made it! My mother smiled and relaxed her shoulders. My father let out a loud sigh of relief. The bus driver let go of the steering wheel, looked at us in the mirror, and clapped his hands. Everyone on the bus applauded, grinned, or nodded their heads. I gathered that the other Serb passengers had been afraid to show they were on our side before armed soldiers, but now we knew they'd been secretly rooting for us all along.

Nobody said anything for the rest of the sixteen-hour ride. I just watched out the window as we passed miles of farmland in Hungary. By the time we finally reached a Viennese town filled with streetlamps and traffic signals, it was nightfall. The string of fluorescent bulbs blurred my vision, so I squinted. It had been ten months since our eyes were exposed to normal light.

CHAPTER EIGHT

Their Side of Town

Grbavica, Bosnia
July 2011

"Don't grill them about the war," Eldin warned me as we headed to our historic lunch date on the other side of Brčko on this warm Wednesday in July. "Don't make Miloš and Zorica uncomfortable."

"They're good-hearted. We'll be guests in their home. Just leave it alone," my father added, as if social etiquette trumped understanding the real reasons our people were almost annihilated.

"Come on. Don't you find it weird that the guy who helped us at night was shooting Muslims by day?" I asked.

"The point is that he did help us," Dad said. "That's all."

While Eldin was in casual beige cargo shorts and a T-shirt and I was in khakis and a hoodie, my father was decked out for a special occasion, in his favorite jazzy fuchsia button-down shirt, black slacks, and a jacket with a matching tie.

I knew Dad felt pure gratitude toward Miloš and Zorica and didn't care to probe the deeper reasons they'd assisted our family.

For me it was much more complicated. I needed to know why these Serbs were the only neighbors who'd come to our aid—though they'd been strangers who mysteriously moved in below us during the war. What had they really been up to? Number 8 on my list was: *Ask Zorica if she felt guilty taking over my friend Huso's apartment.* And Miloš was the only Serb I knew who might admit he regretted fighting against us, so I could fulfill number 10.

"I can't just talk about weather and soccer," I argued, looking for Miloš's taxi.

"Enough with your damn list already." Eldin was walking too close to me. "Can't you just let it go for one meal?"

I wasn't a kid he could control anymore. "Stop being my shadow," I snapped at him as I spotted Miloš leaning on his car's open door.

He was smiling and waving at us with both arms, like a long-lost buddy. Now fifty-five, he'd grown a belly since 1992. I'd never seen him out of the green Serb camouflage uniform I'd despised. Unarmed, in jeans and a short-sleeved shirt, he no longer looked threatening, more like a jovial middle-aged uncle. Yet my twelve-year-old eyes still saw an enemy soldier with an assault rifle over his shoulder.

Miloš had parked in front of the library, a landmark building partly destroyed in the fighting. It had been renovated, repainted to resemble a regal Budapest castle. I took a picture. I'd been capturing images of bombed-out monuments, homes, and office structures riddled with bullet holes and shattered windows that now filled the memory card of my digital camera. I was drawn to the ruins; they mirrored how I felt. I didn't know what troubled me more, sites in my homeland that remained wrecked or ones that were spruced up as if nothing horrible had happened here.

"It's been twenty years, but they say true friends always find each other," Miloš called out when we approached. His six-foot-two frame towered over Dad as they embraced. Then Eldin, who was taller and thinner, hugged him, and they patted each other on the back. "I'd know you anywhere," Miloš said, now reaching for me.

I'd never touched him before—not even a handshake. I flinched, then gave him a quick guy-hug. But he grabbed and squeezed me so hard my feet lifted off the ground. It was odd to think that I was about the age he'd been during the war. At thirty, I still felt like a kid. I wondered why he was so eager to reunite. In two decades, not one of my old Serb classmates had ever made contact. I would have thought Igor, Dalibor, or Velibor would have at least googled us or found me and Eldin on Facebook to see if we'd survived.

"What a nice, clean car," Dad told Miloš, getting into the passenger seat as Eldin and I crawled in back. I was struck that a college graduate had to drive a cab to support his family. Serbs thought they'd be better off without us, yet now they all had less. The taxi Miloš drove, his all-gray hair, and his lined face told me he'd been treading turbulent waters since we left. I wanted to believe that his warmth was meant to make up for his past sins on the battlefield. Eldin put his hand on my knee to stop my legs from fidgeting. I was anxious to get beyond these polite exchanges. I wanted to quiz Miloš to see if he had any regrets.

"There's plenty of food to eat and *rakija* to drink," Miloš told us. "Zorica's preparing everything."

Going to their home felt too intimate. I should have treated us all to a nice meal at a restaurant. But when I'd refused Zorica's offer to stay with them, she'd insisted on cooking for us. I didn't want to insult her. Since so many Muslims from here now came back to spend their summers in Brčko, I hoped they wouldn't ask why we'd waited so long to visit. What would I say—? "We hold a grudge against mass murderers, please pass the potatoes"?

If, like all the other Serbs we'd met here, Miloš complained of the lousy economy, I'd want to yell, "That's what you get for your ethnic-cleansing campaign that destroyed the country." I was hyper to hear answers to questions that had been churning in my gut all these years: How could they just take my pal Huso's furnished apartment, sleep in his parents' bed, use their blankets and sheets, and eat from their plates? I wanted to know why Miloš secretly fed us but then turned around and killed Bosniak boys in the field.

After World War II, Germany apologized to Jewish victims of the Nazis, offering billions in reparations. Yet the German militia who invaded Poland and Russia had no intimate connection to the Jews they persecuted. In the Balkans, it was a classmate or coworker holding a gun to your head, and now they were sitting in your local bar, wanting to share a drink. There had to be one Christian soldier here who would admit that killing their Muslim neighbors was wrong. Miloš and Zorica were the sole Serbs we planned to break bread with; this was my only chance. Yet if I was rude I would shame my father—and the memory of my mother.

Driving into Grbavica, a Serb subdivision, my palms grew damp. It was one in the afternoon, seventy-five degrees outside, and sunny. I hoped we wouldn't sit outdoors and mingle with their neighbors. If Miloš said, "This is Senahid, Eldin, and Kenan," our names would immediately tell their Orthodox Serb crowd our faith. As we drove closer I got paranoid, picturing Serbian flags flying, bells from their churches ringing from all sides. Seeing a poster of Milošević—the Balkan Hitler—hanging in the window of a Serb apartment would make me want to throw a rock through the glass. But I had taken care to wear a short-sleeved striped shirt that covered the old Bosnian flag on my arm. Miloš and Zorica had been respectful of our plight and apartment during the war; I wouldn't disrespect them in their home. But I didn't want to stay long either.

The night before, I'd been frantic that I was just halfway through my list and had only a few days of my trip left. I needed to speed it up to finish what I came for. Number 9 was: *Apologize to Huso for betraying him.* I decided to phone Huso to confess my guilt over our friendship with the Serb family who'd stolen his apartment.

From recent e-mails back and forth, I'd pieced together what happened over the last twenty years to Huso, my old Muslim neighbor and close friend. His mother had worked with my mom. His father, Hasan, was a professor my father highly respected. After Huso's dad had fought with Obren in our building in 1992, their family fled to Croatia and then wound up in London. Hasan—still a bit of a political hothead—had published editorial pieces railing against the British for their pro-Serb stance in the Balkans. Huso's parents had divorced, and he was now living in Sarajevo with his wife and baby daughter. He had a good job working for an American consulting company. I wondered how much he remembered from the war.

Dialing his number, I was nervous; we hadn't spoken to each other since we were kids.

"Oh, shit, you're in Bosnia! What's up, Kendji?" He stunned me by using my old nickname. His voice was deeper and more mature, but he still had his northeast Bosnian accent.

"How did you know I was here?" I asked.

"Caller ID shows a local call," he said. "Are you in Sarajevo?"

"No, Brčko."

"But you swore you'd never return!"

"Only promise I ever broke. But we had to come back for Dad."

"Hope it goes well for him," Huso said stiffly. Then he added, "I don't ever want to see Brčko again."

Clearly I wasn't the only one with lingering resentment toward my hometown. But Huso didn't like his new town any better. Although Sarajevo was once again touted as the cosmopolitan capital of Bosnia, with synagogues, mosques, and Catholic and Orthodox Christian churches side by side, the high unemployment rate was ruining the whole country.

"Last week I was in the grocery store at 5:00 p.m. with my daughter in a stroller when there was an armed burglary, two guys with AK-47s," Huso told me. "There's all these different mafias and ethnic divisions on every level—federal, state, education, the court system. Everyone's corrupt here. Nobody has any money. I want to move to Canada."

As his Bosnian-born contemporary, I sympathized. Yet the purpose of my call wasn't to commiserate about the continued political corruption in the Balkans. I needed to share a shameful secret that had been gnawing at me since I was twelve. I couldn't expect other people to rectify their war sins without atoning for my own. If I didn't share my remorse now, I never would.

Clutching my cell phone, my hand was shaky. "Huso, I have to tell you something that's been bothering me for a long time."

When we were kids, Huso's professor father and neatnik mother had been very strict about which of his friends could come over to their place to play and when. You had to take off your shoes before entering, go straight to Huso's bedroom, and not make a mess anywhere else in the apartment. You couldn't touch any of the crystal or ceramic figurines on their shelves or cabinets or eat anywhere but the kitchen. So I'd felt horrible chasing Dejan through all the rooms after Huso's family fled, as if I was an intruder violating all their house rules. I used to go from their front door straight to Huso's room, so I'd never even seen their whole apartment until Zorica moved in. She'd insisted I play with Dejan on the living- and the dining-room floors, where we'd have snacks and make a mess and leave Huso's toys strewn around.

"After you left Brčko, this Serb family who moved in came up and befriended us. They invited me over to play with their son," I blurted out. "I'm sorry I was hanging out in your apartment without you being there. I shouldn't have invaded your privacy." I pictured how we'd crash Huso's miniature cars—he'd had the same Rolls-Royce, Mercedes, and Volkswagen I did—scuffing up their nice parquet floor. And I'd turn the pages of his 1990 World Cup soccer album, sifting through his beloved trading cards, which I should not have touched. I wasn't brave or strong or old enough to take a stand back then. "I shouldn't have been in your bedroom without you or playing with your toys or . . ."

"Kendji, really?" He cut me off. "Are you kidding me?"

His tone changed; he seemed offended. I was afraid he'd hang up on me. Or that he'd demand all the sordid details and then tell his father, who would lose respect for my dad. But Huso deserved to know what happened where he used to live; it was his story too. Even if I'd sinned, I cared deeply what he and his father thought of us. If I'd left a shadow on our family's name, I didn't want to compound it by continuing the lie.

"That's why you're calling me?" Huso sounded upset.

I felt distressed. "Please don't be angry." I'd hate for him to see me as weak, or a double-crosser who'd betrayed him the minute he left town.

"I am angry," Huso said. "Because you are being ridiculous. We are old friends; you are one of my own. You survived day by day at twelve, when your only job should have been having fun. Instead we were attacked by those cowardly hyenas. It was naked survival."

Twenty years earlier, Bosniaks I knew had called Serbs hyenas, after the animal known for its maniacal laugh—and for ganging up on bigger creatures only in large herds. Sometimes they would steal a lone baby cub, but they never attacked one-to-one when the fight would be fair. Huso wasn't in Brčko for the war; I was glad he understood how bad the occupation was.

"My home was your home. I can't believe you felt bad about it all this time. No need to feel ashamed, Kendji. So we're good?" Huso asked.

"We're good." I let out a long sigh, feeling lighter but a little silly, as if I'd just sped through all the years from twelve to thirty in one phone call.

Huso went on to explain that his dad had filed for property return to reclaim their apartment after the war. While angry they couldn't move right back into their home, Huso's family had made a deal with Miloš: they would wait for him to vacate their apartment so long as Miloš would not rip out electrical wiring, remove sinks, tubs, and outlets, trash the place, or strip it bare, as many Serbs did when they were forced out of the homes they'd usurped. I was pleased to hear him say that Miloš and Zorica had left their apartment spotless.

"Any chance you can come to Brčko?" I asked, sad we'd missed out on so many years of friendship.

"I can't. I'm working and taking care of my little girl. Can you come to Sarajevo?"

"I wish I could." I'd never been there before. But it was five hours away. "I'm stuck here with Dad and Eldin and visiting all our relatives. I'll call you after I see Miloš and Zorica today and tell you how it goes."

"Yeah, good luck with that." Huso's tone was sarcastic, as if I was fraternizing with the enemy.

For a minute I felt like I was entering Huso's place without his parents' permission again. I had committed a sin against my friend, sitting on his bed, eating off his plate, with his fork and spoon. I knew I was just a kid during the war. In fact, Huso would probably be pleased that under his roof, Miloš and Zorica had fed and protected us.

Speaking with him now, I realized that what I'd experienced as unjust nineteen years before was not my imagination. My moral compass was right to point toward shame. What happened in Huso's home was twisted and wrong—it just wasn't *my* transgression. I felt embarrassed, yet grateful to be able to check off number 9. Still I had a nagging sense that I should have been reuniting with Huso today instead of the people who had displaced him.

Pulling into the unpaved driveway of Miloš and Zorica's new two-story house, I noticed that the brick walls had no paint and the front stairs were without railings, as if the work had been halted in mid-construction. I took it as a sign they were broke. Zorica rushed out to greet us. She was heavier, wrinkled, looking older than her fifty-four years. I could tell she'd had it rough since we'd kissed her good-bye that freezing midnight nineteen years ago, when she'd sneaked us moonshine and money to escape.

"You're here." She smiled. "Come in, come in. Keka, I would recognize. Kenan's a younger version of his dad. Eldin I'd never know without his big glasses."

"I got contact lenses in college," my brother said.

I hoped she wouldn't kiss me three times on the cheek, the Serb ritual. I didn't want to impose the Bosniak way of kissing twice, so we only kissed once, American style, an unspoken compromise. Then we embraced. As she ran her hands over my hair, all my old affection for her rushed back. Dad and Eldin gave her one kiss on the cheek too, then deep hugs. We took our shoes off before entering, a Balkan custom we all shared.

As we walked in, we gave them a bottle of our favorite aged scotch whiskey for Miloš and a makeup kit with lotions and perfume I'd picked out for Zorica. She opened hers, put a little cream on her hand. "How nice it smells. You can't get this here. It's the kind my father used to bring me from Germany."

As I looked around, the beige '80s décor of their living room took me back in time. Luckily no photos of Milošević—just a cross hanging in the foyer and a picture of the bearded Orthodox Christian Saint Lazar. Good, I preferred martyrs to war criminals. It was very clean, though it confirmed that they were not well off. Dad went for the couch to my left. I sat on the adjacent sofa, and Eldin took a seat next to me. Although we'd never set foot in this new house, everything seemed familiar. Just visiting a family home in the country of my birth was triggering all sorts of memories.

"I'll open your special scotch," Miloš offered.

"No, that's just for you," I told him.

"To save for another day," my father added.

"Then you must have some of my homemade *rakija*." Miloš poured us shots. We toasted, saying, "*Živili*," meaning "May you live forever."

"Wow, this is smoother than we get in New York," I marveled.

"You don't have Bosnian plums growing in your backyard like I do," he said. "Give it a minute."

Miloš's pride in sharing his best drink with us charmed me as the *rakija* scorched my stomach, the heat expanding upward. "Oh yeah, my eyes are burning."

"It breaks my heart your mother isn't here too," Zorica said, and we all nodded.

Two weeks earlier, I'd found her number in Mom's old phone book. "I was just thinking about Adisa," she'd said when I'd called.

I'd broken the news that my mother had died from ovarian cancer in 2007 over the phone then. Zorica was in remission from breast cancer herself, she told me, after a lumpectomy and radiation. She said she was trying to quit smoking and eat healthier. She asked more about my mother's illness, but I wasn't up for talking about it.

Now I kept glancing around, feeling like I'd been here before though I was positive I'd never visited the neighborhood. "Nice wooden flooring."

"Right after the war, I took these Japanese diplomats around Bosnia. They paid for the parquet floor." Miloš laughed. "I felt bad charging them so much. But they needed to be driven to Sarajevo, four hours away. It cost a mint. Armies were disbanded, but everyone still had weapons. I was scared driving through Bosniak territory, with all those flags waving."

This could be my opening. "Why were you scared?" I asked.

He took out a pack of Morava cigarettes and lit one. Cyrillic writing, a Serb brand.

"I didn't want to be stopped at checkpoints. Or shot!"

I would have loved to witness that role reversal, a Serb military man fearing armed Bosnians. I was about to ask if Miloš still had his gun, but Eldin gave me a look that said: *Don't go there.* I wished he and my father weren't there so I wouldn't be inhibited.

"Rest your feet. Be comfortable." Zorica moved an ottoman in front of Dad. He obliged, lifting his legs up. She put a pillow behind me. "Relax, it's your home too."

Her words took on deeper irony as I spotted my mother's two paintings of red flowers on the wall, still in their copper frames. The matching art-deco acrylics used to hang in our Brčko apartment. I was shocked to see them again. I put my drink down and ran my hand over the four-foot light wood table with a glass top. It had graced our living room when I was growing up. I caught sight of the cabinet against the wall, where I used to store VHS horror tapes that I'd watched with Huso.

Zorica saw how startled I was. "Your mother told us to take whatever we could from your apartment." She stared at the pack of cigarettes on the table but didn't take one. "Kenan, tell me what you recognize."

I looked around more carefully and realized we were surrounded by furniture from my childhood home. I felt misplaced, as if an alien family had abducted my past and was living my former life. How many other Serb houses were the lost treasures of my people scattered through?

"The table, the cabinets, the rose paintings on the wall. And the electric heater," I said. It had wheels on the bottom. I recalled how, when Huso and I would come home from sledding, we'd sit on it to get warm. "And the gold light fixture." I looked up to see its two long, narrow bulbs.

"You should take it all home to New York with you," Zorica offered.

"Don't be crazy," I answered. But if Mom was around, I would have brought her back a token, for nostalgia.

"It rightfully belongs to you," Zorica said.

"No, it's yours, it's yours," Dad insisted. He lifted his eyebrows to say: *If they could afford better, they wouldn't have kept it all for two decades.*

For a moment I considered taking back my mother's roses. But Dad was right, Zorica and Miloš didn't have much. If I left their wall empty, I'd feel like *I* was robbing *them*. The walls of my Queens pad were crowded with Bosnian photographs and posters. Anyway, Zorica was the Serb who most deserved my mother's possessions. I recalled how thrilled Mom was to be reunited with all our old photo albums when Zorica found a way to send them to us a decade ago in Connecticut.

"Think of it as a gift of gratitude from my mother," I said.

"It's nothing, compared to what you did for us," Eldin added.

"This way you'll always be reminded how much you helped us," I told Zorica.

Her eyes became teary. "We have your rocking chair upstairs. You have to see it."

"The one with the painted fruit?" I surprised myself, picturing it so clearly.

She nodded. "You must take it home with you."

My mother brought that chair to our living room when I was nine. I liked it because it reminded me of playing on seesaws and swings on the playground. I'd sit cross-legged on it, watching Bruce Lee movies while pushing back and forth. She'd yell when I tested how hard it could rock before tipping. I wanted to rock in it again, to see if I could still fit.

"You remember more than Dejan," Zorica said. "He'll be home soon. He finished his economics degree, but there aren't any jobs here. He works as a secretary in a socialist party headquarters in town."

I was glad Dejan's party wasn't nationalistic. I hoped he was against Milorad Dodik, the current Bosnian Serb leader, who denied that the genocide ever took place. I was curious whom Miloš was voting for. But that wasn't my battle. My head was still untangling the ethnic upheavals that almost killed us in the '90s, not the ten complicated Bosnian parties wrestling for power in the present day.

I heard gun blasts outside and jumped, turning to the window. "What the hell?" I was about to duck down and crawl on the floor on my stomach.

"Don't worry, it's just a wedding convoy," Zorica said. "They get drunk, drive down the street, and shoot guns to celebrate."

"I'm not worried. It's not 1992." I gripped the couch's armrest and took a breath. Then I got up, moved the curtains, and saw that the convoy was already at the end of the block. When I sat back down, I noticed Miloš staring at me.

"I remember the first time I saw little Kenan from the balcony of our old apartment," Miloš said. "I was in my uniform, smoking." He poured us more moonshine. "I'd just returned from the front. These punks were rubbing a poster of Alija Izetbegović in his face. I yelled at them to stop." Izetbegović was a Bosniak activist the Serbs mistakenly claimed was pushing Islamic fundamentalism, propaganda they'd used to attack us.

"You saw that?" I suspected Miloš was courting my affection by bringing up how he'd protected me from being bullied. First I felt indebted and less alone, then spied on, then embarrassed at how weak I must have looked. "Why didn't you tell me?"

"You were more comfortable around my wife and son," Miloš answered.

Of course I'd been uneasy around him then—he was wearing a Serb uniform and carried the gun he used to shoot my people.

"One of those mean kids was Velibor," Zorica jumped in. "We know his parents."

I still felt hurt thinking of my karate teammates who'd turned on me. "I found Velibor on Facebook. He works for Americans in Afghanistan," I said. All friends on Velibor's wall were Serbs, I could tell from their names. Not that I would ask him to friend me. The Balkanites I'd connected with online were mostly Bosniaks. Even our social networking connections remained segregated. Eldin was virtual friends with a cute Serb girl he knew from elementary school—until he posted news of the war trials on his page, and she defriended him.

"I knew Velibor's father from his birthday parties," I said. "When the war broke out, he stopped saying hello."

"His dad lost a leg in the war and died soon after," Miloš updated me.

That's what he got for being mean to me, I thought, as if I were still in junior high.

"I work out at the fitness center Mondays, Wednesdays, and Thursdays," my father was telling Zorica. "Kenan and Eldin got me the best knee brace in New York." He lifted his pant leg to show her the lightweight gray plastic buckled around his knee.

"Next time don't push a four-hundred-pound cart around," Eldin scolded him.

I looked over at Dad, talking animatedly to Zorica. My legs were jumpy; I needed to go for it. This was my shot to cross-examine Miloš and Zorica, to ask point-blank why they'd taken Huso's home. My childhood was an unfinished puzzle, and they could fill in some of the holes. "Mr. Miloš, why did you and Zorica leave Croatia?" I started amiably, using the polite address. Then I'd build up courage to see if Miloš would admit regretting the war.

He finished his cigarette, poured another *rakija*. I drank more; it was loosening me up.

"We'd lived peacefully in Osijek since college and would have stayed there. But in 1991 my own people attacked our city. We were devastated," Miloš said. "Since I was a Bosnian Serb originally, I was harassed for my background. My neighbors in Croatia decided I was a collaborator and threatened vengeance. A death squad showed up at our door. People who'd eaten at my dinner table the night before suddenly wanted us dead. I sent my family to Bosnia, ahead of me. One night Croatian soldiers came to get me. Luckily I squeezed out the back."

I was beginning to understand why they'd sympathized with our plight and shown us compassion. Their experience mirrored ours: college-educated, open-minded cosmopolitan parents all of a sudden unfairly persecuted by friends and colleagues next door because of their ethnicity. But I didn't like his implication that Serbs were terrorized as much as Muslims during the war.

"How did you get to Brčko?" I asked.

"After we escaped Osijek, we needed a roof." Miloš lit another smoke. Was my interrogation making him nervous? "I told Zorica we had to get a place that was legit, with keys and paperwork. We didn't want to take anyone else's home, but we were forced to leave ours. So we had no choice. Luckily the apartment had been abandoned."

That was what I'd hoped to hear, and the timing checked out—Huso's family had indeed left Brčko by then. Good, Miloš didn't throw them out or greedily grab a second home. Forced to flee himself, he needed shelter for his family, felt entitled to Huso's empty place, and didn't feel guilty. That was my answer. I could check number 8 off my list. But now I was afraid that number 10 would be much harder to nail down. I had to ask Miloš if he regretted fighting against us. I could already tell my obstacle would be Miloš's willful naïveté. He didn't want to understand that an immoral legal system had allowed him to take Huso's home, using made-up paperwork designed to annihilate Muslims and appropriate all our belongings. And Miloš and Zorica had stayed for years after the war ended.

"When did you leave Huso's?" I asked.

"In 2001."

We'd fled Bosnia in January 1993. I tried to calculate when they'd taken our furniture. Had they hoarded extra tables, chairs, and lamps and lived there with both sets for eight years?

"How did you know Huso?" Zorica asked. She appeared taken aback by my link to the rightful owner of her former apartment. It was the first time we'd ever discussed how close we were to the previous occupant.

"My father grew up with his dad," I said. "He was a professor."

"Yeah, he gave Kenan English lessons. He was a tough grader." My father nodded. He seemed to not notice my ulterior motive, as if we were just catching up on old friends we had in common—and not unraveling the fate of a Muslim family just like ours, whose home had been stolen.

"Huso's father was nice to allow us to stay until we built our new house," Miloš said.

I nodded, pleased that this confirmed what Huso had told me on the phone the day before. Still, it seemed surreal that two families we were close to had lived in the same apartment below us for years, sleeping under the same covers and overlapping in our lives, yet had remained strangers—and enemies—to each other. It was like being caught in the middle of a nightmare that nobody could wake or recover from.

"Mrs. Zorica, why did you come up to visit us that day?" I asked.

"Kids were picking on you. We learned you were the only Bosniaks in the building. We knew how it felt, being betrayed by friends. We didn't care about religions; we just saw a family like ours. We heard your name and recalled that my uncle knew your grandfather."

"Crazy coincidence about Grandpa Murat," Eldin said, catching on, looking tense.

Feeling buzzed, I reached my shot glass out for Miloš to refill.

"I'll get lunch," Zorica said. I got up to follow her.

"Where are you going?" Eldin asked, nervously.

What was he, Homeland Security, afraid I'd interrogate her in the kitchen?

"I'm helping her." I brought out bowls of veal soup. Then I carried out trays of her cucumber salad with sour cream and onions, cold baked veal, roasted chicken with peppers and salty sliced potatoes that I ate with abandon. Eldin talked to Miloš about how the Americans were trying to become the next soccer powerhouse. I checked on my dad. He was quiet. As usual, when it came to food, it was just him and the plate. When he was done, Zorica said, "Have more," spooning us both another helping.

For the last five years, I'd missed coming home to the aroma of my mother's cooking, never sure which meals she'd stirred, sautéed, diced, or blended with what delicious ingredients. Even in the cafeteria in my college dorm, my roommates and I could choose from an array of entrees, appetizers, and desserts. It felt so nice to once again be sharing a big spread with a mix of tastes I didn't expect, each dish offering a surprise. I was tired of planning small meals in advance, shopping for myself, preparing everything I ate, mostly alone, at my own table in Queens.

"More veal?" Zorica asked.

I nodded, and she served me another chop. Nothing was made with pork; I was sure it was out of deference to us. Each time I finished eating, she put more food in front of me, patting my head, pleased I was enjoying her meal. Bosnian women were so nurturing.

"Nobody cooks for you in New York. Eat, eat, *sine*," she said, calling me "son." It made me miss my mom.

"I'll never forget how you brought me sweets when I was hungry," I said.

"I wished we could have done more. But when I visited, I was scared for our lives," she told me. "I feared someone might retaliate when Miloš was away fighting. That's why I came up late at night."

"We thought you'd be like Daca, stealing Mom's stuff," Eldin explained.

"Oh, Daca—that bitch. That stupid pig!" Zorica spat out.

Now I was taken aback. Clearly I wasn't the only one with leftover anger. This was getting more interesting.

Eldin woke up from his soccer talk and asked, "Wait, how did you know Daca?"

She looked at Miloš, raising her brows.

"Tell us," I said, intrigued to learn the fate of the sadistic couple who'd menaced us.

"Daca and Boban were how we found your building," Miloš jumped in. "He was hanging around the village where Zorica's parents lived. We were stationed there."

"Boban was in the trenches with you?" Eldin asked.

"No, he never fought," Miloš said. "He roamed around looting, with his uniform and Uzi. I told Boban I wanted to move my family to Brčko. He reached into his pocket for keys and said don't worry, the owner's gone, you can feel at home." Miloš aped Boban's Belgradian accent. The blustery guttural imitation was dead-on, like it was yesterday.

I was excited to have a common enemy. I wanted to connect the dots to this strange story so long after it happened. "How did Boban get keys to Huso's place?"

"Who the hell knows?" Miloš said. "They were Belgrade mafia school."

"So whatever happened to Daca?"

"Oh, you're going to love how her reign ended in Brčko." Zorica smiled. "You guys escaped January 3, 1993."

Every January 3, Eldin and I had a shot of whiskey together, toasting, "This time eighteen years ago, we were on the bus." Zorica knowing the date made me see how intertwined our families were. We would have gone hungry if not for them; their home would be barren if not for us.

"Right after you left, Daca came looking for Miloš to carry something to her place," Zorica said. "He wasn't in, so she grabs my cousin—who comes back three hours later, flustered, his shirt undone."

"She came on to your cousin?" I was fascinated. "Daca had me take stuff into her bedroom!" Had she also tried to seduce me? At twelve? With cookies, candies, and letting me play with her Uzi?

"Honey, she and Boban were filthy criminals," Zorica said. "She managed to find Miloš in the trenches, where she spent nights with the soldiers. She showed him naked pictures of herself, talked him into taking speed, and convinced Miloš I was cheating on him."

"Daca was bad news." Miloš didn't deny she'd come on to him. "Who knows if she and Boban were even married or related?"

Zorica brought us mineral water with a Serb cross and eagle on it. They might be liberal, but they supported their own. I recalled how much my father hated Daca. I looked over to see he was still eating and eating, like he'd just come out of the camp.

"When Boban went back to Belgrade for good and Daca was packing, armed men, some kind of competitive looters, barged into her house. They tied her wrists with wires, beat the hell out of her, and took all her stolen stuff." Zorica smirked. "We heard her face was unrecognizable. Karma got her in the end." She crossed her arms.

Men beating up a woman disturbed me. They should have just taken her stuff and left. "Well, my mom would be happy Daca never got our place," I said.

"Beer?" Zorica asked. I expected the gold Serbian label Jelen, with a deer on it, but was pleased she served Laško from Slovenia, a neutral label, pouring it for us. Even a simple brewski had been politicized in this place. "So right after you left, my mother moved in. She had to leave her home after the Croats took our village. Your mom gave me her keys. A month later armed Serbs barged in and kicked my mom out, saying she had no right to be there. But really they just wanted to keep the place for themselves."

I took a sip of beer. "So Serbs kicked a Serb out of our apartment?"

"Kenan, it came down to greed and power. They were ruthless, using rifles to terrorize an old lady." She sounded like she'd never recovered from the war. None of us had. "Toward the end of 1995, when the Bosnian army got their hands on heavy artillery, it wasn't even safe to go outside. Once, right after Dejan walked in from playing, two mortars fell by the side of the building. All your old friends would have been killed if they hadn't scattered and gone inside minutes before," she said. "We were all packing our bags, afraid we'd be run out of Brčko."

I'd always fantasized about seeing the people who'd taken over my town forced to flee in panic like we did. But if my family hadn't been able to escape, it now occurred to me that we could have been killed by friendly Bosniak fire in our own home.

"I remember the first time I went upstairs to bring you guys canned goulash, Kenan was on the floor playing miniature cars," Miloš said. "As I stood above him, he just sized me up, then looked away. That's when I knew he was a tough guy."

Since he brought up that moment, I wasn't missing my chance. I felt heat in my armpits, sweat dripping down the side of my ribs. "I was only twelve," I said. "What did you expect when men wearing the same uniform as you took Dad and Eldin to the camp?"

Zorica glanced at her husband. Eldin glared at me, crossing his arms over his chest. But I didn't back down.

"It really confused me how you could fill our propane tank and stomachs one day, then shoot Muslims the next," I admitted.

Dad stopped his fork midpotato.

"I was afraid you'd kill us too," I went on.

Eldin rubbed his cheeks, pushing the skin on his face with his fingers. But everyone turned to Miloš, as curious as I was to hear his reply.

"I didn't want to take anyone's life. I tried not to. I hated it." Miloš put out his cigarette, then lit another, squinting, extremely uncomfortable. "I prayed my bullets wouldn't hit anyone. I hoped no soldier would get close so I'd be forced to defend myself."

He looked so intense, as if he'd just come from the trenches and was reliving the worst experience of his life. I heard the sorrow I was hoping for in his voice. I had no doubt he was sincere and rueful. I was amazed. Here was a military man from the enemy side showing remorse. I'd asked him what I came to find out. He had to dig deep and come far emotionally to answer me. I'd waited so many years to have this conversation. But it wasn't enough. Wired, I wanted more. "It was a volunteer army. You know, there were Serbs who fought on the Bosnian side or left the region," I told Miloš.

Eldin sighed loudly to signal me to shut up. Dad put his utensils down.

"Well, every town was different. We heard deserters would be shot," Miloš said, defensively, inhaling smoke. "If I didn't pick up the rifle, I was afraid they'd kill me and my family. Ninety percent of Yugoslavians didn't want this war. Look at us now. Nobody has anything except the politicians. Ten political parties. I told my son if the war ever returned, forget all your stuff. Just grab your passport and leave."

"But who were you fighting for?" I pushed.

My brother cleared his throat, then blew air out of his nose, making noise like a dolphin.

"I was defending Yugoslavia," Miloš said, raising his voice, his arms wide, palms up.

"Defending it from what?" I asked.

"All the secessions from the union that would take our land and rights away," he told me matter-of-factly, flicking his cigarette in the ashtray.

Aha! So that was his delusion: He'd been fighting for Yugoslavian unity. He was brainwashed to think that people from the Croatian and Bosnian republics were some kind of separatists or terrorist rebels who started a war, unarmed and unprepared, just to impinge on his freedom. But Milošević's plans for Greater Serbia were what made the Croatians and Bosnians need to secede in the first place. How could Miloš not know that?

"We used to be one strong, proud nation," he continued. "Then the Croat party demanded independence. And Izetbegović wanted his due. And then Milošević, that loud lunatic . . ."

He got one thing right. But that was all he had against the monster who'd started four wars in eight years. *Loud lunatic* was the best he could do?

"Then the West used our people as puppets to turn us against each other," Miloš added.

First he blamed the victims, now he was pointing his finger at Americans. I couldn't hold it in any longer. "Foreigners didn't detonate our mosques and destroy Catholic churches or murder their own countrymen!" I set him straight. Eldin glowered at me, but there was no way I was quitting now. "They didn't send my brother and father to a concentration camp, or shoot their neighbors in our gymnasium, or drive a tractor to dislodge my grandpa's headstone. Even *dead* Muslims weren't left in peace." My heart was pushing me forward as I asked Miloš the question that had tormented me for nineteen years. "When you came home from fighting one night, I was there when Dejan asked if you'd killed any Muslims. Didn't you tell him that you were going out to kill Muslims?"

"No. I never said that," Miloš answered immediately. "Dejan was only six. What did he know?" He flayed his hand in the air, cigarette between his fingers, ashes flying. "Nothing was ever that black and white. You heard how the neighborhood punks talked. They played patriotic Arkan songs. It sucks you in. Yes, there's a mass Muslim grave outside of town that nobody was held accountable for. But I never killed anyone because of their religion."

Miloš looked horrified that I'd ever thought of him as a murderer. He wasn't angry at all. His eyes caught mine. They seemed to plead for my understanding, my mercy. Could I grant it? He did acknowledge the grave, a small concession. His hurt expression and protests—however naïve—did soften me. I mulled over his case in my mind. He was an educated, moderate Orthodox Christian man. For the first time ever, I tried to see the war from a Serb's viewpoint: Miloš did everything right, the way my parents taught us. He finished college, worked hard, married, and had children like you were supposed to. He had a good life in Croatia. Until he was persecuted for his ethnicity. He was told—albeit falsely—that his government needed him to fight to save his nation. A law-abiding citizen, he believed those in power. So he allowed himself to be taken in by their deception.

No, he was not a brave rebel who stood up to corrupt leaders. He was a family man with a wife and child to protect. But I had to remember that he never became bloodthirsty or power-hungry like

Bad Pero or the murderous Ranko, slitting Muslim throats for sport or stealing for personal gain. He helped us. He was proof that not all Serbs wanted to see us suffer. Some of his people suffered too. Miloš was a decent guy caught in an ugly, unjust battle.

"We would help anyone in need," Zorica piped in, abruptly taking a cigarette from her husband's pack, lighting it, and inhaling quickly.

"Yes, I helped whoever I could." His voice cracked. "When I saved this Muslim guy, Sead Burić, from getting gunned down in his home, I could have been killed by my own men."

"Sead Burić?" Eldin leapt in. "We know him very well."

"We just saw him." I was stunned.

"He's one of the people I came back here to see. My best Bosnian friend growing up!" Dad was buoyed by the coincidence. "He was in my jazz band!"

This miraculous overlap was an undeniable sign. After all, Miloš hadn't saved a former classmate of his or someone he grew up with. Miloš wasn't even from Brčko. He'd stuck his neck out to help a Muslim friend of ours whom my father cherished. I was already leaning Miloš's way, but knowing he'd risked his life for Sead swayed me. Miloš had it rougher than I'd thought. He'd tried to please all sides: protect his family, take up arms with his comrades, while secretly not wanting any Muslims to die. The verdict was not guilty, the defense the insanity of war.

"Is there anything else you want to ask me that will you help you understand?" Miloš's fatherly tone melted me, turning me twelve again.

"No." I nodded at him and stopped asking questions. He gave me what I needed. "Thank you."

Eldin smiled, spent.

"We just saw Sead yesterday! Who knew?" Dad was still marveling at the link.

"So let's have another shot!" Miloš poured us more *rakija* and we all toasted.

I leaned back, relaxed. It was six o'clock, hard to believe we'd been here six hours. Despite myself, I felt safe and comfortable. I had moonshine, beer, and Bosnian food in my belly. I felt heard, respected, cared for in a Serb home. They were treating us like their own.

For dessert, Zorica served crepes with homemade plum jam. "I have Nutella, your favorite, Kenan."

I clapped like a little kid and put a spoonful on my crepe.

I believed the line "All it takes for evil to triumph is for good men to do nothing." But Miloš had done something—he told Serb turncoats not to bully me, he filled our propane tank, gave us food and money to escape. He saved Sead. Yes, I was disappointed with his "everyone was to blame" excuse, rationalizing ethnic cleansing. Perhaps Miloš was too proud to just admit that his side was wrong. Yet this was as close as I'd ever come to an apology from anyone in my country. I could cross number 10 off my list.

"Come on, we're not rationing Nutella." She spooned on a lot more of the hazelnut spread for me. "It's not the war anymore."

When Dejan came home, we shook hands, then hugged. He was slightly taller than me. His eyes and smile were the same; so was his blond hair, except for the short buzz cut. "Should we play war games around the house?" I joked.

"For once I get to win." Dejan smiled. He told Dad, "For years, I beat everyone in chess because of you, Mr. Keka." He told us a little about his life now. He didn't drink, smoke, or go to bars. He was a homebody with a long-term serious girlfriend, though he was six years younger than I was.

"I know some nice Bosniak girls here I can introduce you to," Miloš offered.

"What are you studs waiting for?" Zorica asked.

"They haven't found us yet." Eldin stole my line.

"Yeah, you should find a nice girl here to take back with you," Dejan said.

Now I was the one on the spot, for still being single. If we'd stayed in Bosnia, I'd be married by now. But they didn't understand the limitations I faced. They didn't know that I couldn't support a family in New York; I could barely afford my rent and student loans. With the war and then starting over in a new country where I had to cover my own college and nurse my parents through illnesses, I'd fallen way behind where I thought I should be by thirty, financially and emotionally. I was afraid I could never catch up.

My father and I went out to the backyard to pick a few plums from their prized fruit trees. "They're good people, but we see different worlds through the same binoculars," Dad said, quietly. "If Miloš admitted he was wrong, everything he fought for in the last twenty years would be a lie. It's easier to be disappointed by someone else than to admit you let yourself down."

While Dad's penchant for staying neutral sometimes bothered me, it was probably the reason why we'd all survived.

"I need a picture of all of us," I yelled when we came back inside. "To add to our old photo albums."

"Do you know the story of how they got back to your mom?" Zorica asked.

It turned out the albums' journey to America was as jagged as ours. When we'd escaped in 1993, we each carried one photo book with us, but five albums with our childhood pictures were left behind. Meanwhile Zorica's mother moved into our Brčko apartment. When Serbs threw her out, Zorica quickly rushed our paintings and furniture into their own place, and rescued our albums. Thievery had its upside. Because Zorica and Miloš had taken my old friend Huso's place, I knew their phone number by heart. So when Brčko was reconnected to international long distance phone service in

2003, Mom got back in touch with Zorica. Remembering how Serbs had destroyed and cut Bosniak faces out of their family albums, my mother begged Zorica to get our photographs to Great-aunt Fatima. Before she died in 2002, Fatima handed the albums to Grandma Emina. By 2004 we'd scraped together enough money to fly Grandma to America, where she arrived carrying baby pictures of Eldin and me in her arms.

On our living-room sofa in Connecticut, I sat between Mom and Grandma as they turned through the recovered photographs.

"Look at you, you were one week old here." Mom pointed to my first baby shot.

"Jeez." I knew I'd weighed only about four pounds when I was born, but I didn't recall ever seeing this picture before. I looked like a scrawny mouse.

"Though you were full term, you were just two kilos, much smaller than Eldin," Grandma said, repeating the saga of my birth, which I hadn't heard in years. "The doctor warned us that you were too little and might not survive."

"I yelled, 'You're crazy, I'm taking my baby home to make him bigger and stronger myself,'" my mother told me.

Grandma chimed in, "She told the nurse, 'He'll get fatter and meaner than everyone else, you'll see.' They were so mad when she took you home early."

"And three months later I brought back my eight-pound boy with big fat cheeks," Mom concluded proudly, kissing my face as Grandma rubbed my hair.

Now I filled Zorica in on the sad coda to the story: when Mom died, I took her beloved albums with me to Queens. I put them on a high shelf in my closet. I didn't look at them again until 2011, right before our Bosnia trip. While stressed out and searching for my mother's address book to find Zorica's new phone number, I went to the closet and impatiently pulled down all our recovered Bosnian photography albums. But the bin was too heavy and almost fell on my head. Trying to catch it, I wound up twisting my back into a spasm. "I'm not nervous about visiting our past or anything," I'd joked to Eldin. I showed him what else I'd found among my mother's belongings: she'd kept the silver key to our Brčko apartment, as if, despite her protests, she'd always planned to return home.

I pulled out my camera, posed everyone, and took a bunch of pictures on my digital camera and my cell phone. On my last trip to the Caribbean, I'd snapped ten photos in ten days. In less than a week in Bosnia, I'd already taken five hundred photographs. It was obsessive. But at twelve I hadn't had a camera. I felt a need to document every corner of my country as if to compare the present with the vision stuck in my head.

I impulsively sent one of the pictures of me, Eldin, Miloš, and Zorica to Huso in Sarajevo. I was hoping to sort of introduce them this way. I had a fantasy that I could make peace between our three families, show them we were good people who just got entangled in a bad war none of us wanted. Huso texted me back a second later. "Wow, that cabinet you're standing behind was from my old apartment."

"I'm sorry. I didn't know." I felt queasy and culpable again, as if being friends with Miloš and Zorica implicated me in this ghoulish Serb robbery chain. I was reminded once more that the treasures stolen from Muslim families like mine were scattered among strange homes and could never really be returned or replaced.

"It's okay," Huso texted me back. "Dad said he'd told Miloš, 'Take everything you want, just don't pull out the sinks or the sockets.'"

I looked around their small, modest, unfinished home, filled with other people's ragtag, twenty-year-old furniture. Zorica's Croatian house had been taken from her; her family had also been persecuted for their ethnicity. She'd battled cancer. Miloš didn't want to fight in the war. He was driving a cab to keep this roof over their heads. They were victims too.

Before we left Zorica and Miloš's house, I crept upstairs to visit my mother's chair, which was in the first small guest bedroom. The door was open. Inside, beside a couch, I found the old rocker. I recalled how she used to cradle me, holding me close in her arms. I pictured the last time I saw her sit on the chair in 1991, before the war, when she was reading the book *Život Posle Života*, which meant *Life After Life,* about people who'd died and were medically revived. I'd been interested because we were both superstitious.

My fingers traced the grapes, pears, and peaches painted on the chair's headrest. I sat on the new blue pillow, rubbing the dark wooden arms. They were as smooth as I remembered. I rocked back and forth, hard, crossing my legs like I used to. It was surprisingly sturdy. I was relieved it ended up in a home where it was cherished, and not at some tag sale in Belgrade. For a second I wanted to take it back to Queens with me. I pictured coming home from work to relax and sway back and forth on my little throne, like I used to. Yes, someday when I had a wife and children and enough money, I would reclaim my mother's rocking chair, where I'd rock my own baby in my arms.

CHAPTER NINE

An Argument with My Mother

Stratford, Connecticut
November 1995

"Wait. What is Wolf Blitzer saying?" Mom asked in Bosnian, leaning forward on the couch, straining to listen. "Kenan, what's going on? I don't understand what's happening."

"If you'd be quiet, I could tell you," I said. By fourteen and a half, almost fluent in English, I'd become her interpreter. Sitting on the brown shag carpet with my legs crossed, I inched closer to the television. I put down the Fig Newton I was dipping in milk, desperately trying to grasp the latest developments in the saga unfolding four thousand miles away that could change the rest of my life.

"This peace agreement they're pushing is really a funeral for us," Dad said, also in our native language, standing over the set, clicking his tongue.

"Stop making that noise. I can't hear anything." Eldin raised his voice, getting up to turn the volume higher. He stood next to Dad, listening intently. My brother crossed his arms and shook his head. "I can't believe this! What a mockery of justice."

"*Šta kažu? Šta kažu?*" Mom kept asking me, "What are they saying?" She was impatient for the latest update.

It was the Sunday after Thanksgiving. We'd just finished a dinner of roasted lamb and potatoes; we found turkey—which we'd never had before—too bland and hard to season. We were sitting in the living room of the new, modest two-bedroom house we could barely afford to rent for $900 a month in Stratford, Connecticut. It was the fifth place we'd lived in two years as we scrambled to regain some semblance of security amid many odd jobs and my mother's sickness. While my American classmates had spent the holiday weekend yelling at football players, we'd been huddled around the special CNN evening news, shouting at the anchors reporting the end of the Balkan War.

After another dispatch, Mom turned to me. "*I šta sada?*"

"What now?" she wanted to know. So did I.

For the last three months I'd been elated, getting goose bumps each time I read breaking news or saw video footage on TV of the Croatian/Bosnian forces mobilizing against our common enemy. We were gaining strength, forcing the Serb soldiers to flee my country in trucks and tractor convoys. It finally looked like a Bosnian army victory. I'd been expecting to hear any day that we'd officially won the war. But now I stared at the TV in shock, translating the newscast word for word for Mom, trying to follow the complicated story. Just as the tide was turning and it looked like Bosnian forces could actually win Europe's deadliest conflict since World War II, Serbian president Milošević threatened to step up the vicious attacks on us that he denied making in the first place. Instead of standing up to Milošević's bluff and realizing he was just trying to save face, NATO was pressuring us into an unjust peace.

"*Debil,*" Mom said through clenched teeth as Milošević's photo was shown, calling him a genetically deformed maniac. "*Fuj*," she continued, as if spitting out rotten meat.

"*Magarac*." My father called him a donkey.

Supposedly German chancellor Helmut Kohl and President Clinton were sympathetic to our plight. But special U.S. envoy Richard Holbrooke was threatening our president, Alija Izetbegović, with air strikes until he stopped our troops from advancing. According to Holbrooke, NATO would bomb us if we didn't quickly sign the Dayton Accords. We'd been in Connecticut for two years, but for me, *us* and *we* referred to my old country; I was a Bosniak who didn't consider the United States my home.

"Alija is a dinosaur. He doesn't belong in politics!" Eldin fumed about our leader. "What the hell is he doing? He's a total idiot!"

"Yeah, he doesn't belong in politics!" I echoed, throwing a pillow at the TV.

"That old man should be in a mosque with old ladies," Mom screamed. "I told you he was too incompetent to run our country. Are you taping this?"

I nodded. I had a dozen tapes from recent news programs and documentaries in a boot box in my upstairs closet. I kept up with every radio, TV, and newspaper clip I could find. By ninth grade, I understood a lot more than I had in Bosnia. I wanted to become a history buff, like my brother. I'd traded in my crush on Jennie Garth of *Beverly Hills, 90210* to moon over the smarter, tougher Christiane Amanpour. But she couldn't help us now.

"Alija should have listened to his generals and kept going," Dad raged. "One more week and we would win the war! The Serbs would be swimming across the river to Serbia, where they belong."

This late intervention, by countries who'd done nothing earlier to stop the war, was so unfair. My chest was getting warm. "*Što? Što?*" I screamed. Why?

"NATO's British and French members are kissing Russia's ass," my brother explained. "They have historic ties to Serbia—who can't bear thousands of Bosnian-Serb refugees on their soil. And President Mitterrand won't allow a European country to have a Muslim majority." Eldin shut his eyes, grabbed his head with both hands. "It's over."

I kicked the TV stand with my heel. The set shook, shaking the flower pots behind it.

"Don't do that," my father said.

"If you're going to act like a wild animal, go upstairs," my mother yelled at me.

"Who are you protecting your precious plants for this time?" I asked.

"Stop bickering like lunatics so I can hear." Eldin steadied the TV.

But how could I be rational? Other boys my age memorized baseball stats; my brother and I ran different numbers: a few hundred thousand Bosniaks like us wiped out in the Serb's ethnic cleansing campaign. One million Muslims displaced. Half a million permanently removed from our ancestral land. Four years of my people being attacked, raped, and massacred. Just four months ago in July, at the Srebrenica genocide, 8,373 Bosnian men and boys were slaughtered by the Scorpions, a paramilitary unit from Serbia. (And this was allegedly when they were under the protection of peace-keepers from the United Nations!) Srebrenica was four hours from Brčko; it could have been us.

And now we weren't allowed to finish this bloody fight, even though we could actually triumph at last. We were stunned.

"Bosnia was pummeled with bullets and bombs while Belgrade kids were eating ice cream outdoors," Eldin complained. "Meanwhile the school motto for Greater Serbia is 'Hate thy neighbor.'"

"You're right." I rubbed my hands through my hair, itchy, my forehead sweating.

I'd been so proud of Eldin's outspoken opinions, and of his endless attempts to make Americans understand what was happening in our country. He'd recently gone to a lecture at Stony Brook, the Long Island university he'd started attending at age twenty-one, three years older than most freshmen. Discussing the fall of Yugoslavia, a Serbian-born female professor had denied her side had instigated the war. She'd called our leader a Nazi. Afterwards, Eldin filed a complaint with the head of her department.

Several Bosnian, Croatian, and American student friends were pleased that he stuck up for himself. "Good job. You told the truth," one of the Croatians said.

Then again, we'd also learned that the anger Eldin expressed toward the Serbs, in his essay on why he'd been exiled to America, might have been the reason he was denied a Soros Fellowship for Balkan refugees that would have paid for his tuition. Other Bosnian exiles in Connecticut who'd won the full scholarship told him they'd only referred to "the war," intentionally leaving out any mention of who'd started it and why, knowing there were Serbs on the charity's board.

"Some Thanksgiving this was," I said, punching the floor with my fist.

"What an odd holiday," Eldin muttered. "Americans celebrate the Indians they slaughtered. To apologize they let them run casinos and exempt them from paying taxes."

"And then they name sports teams after them," I added.

Eldin nodded, chugging his Tropicana orange juice. (Mom refused to get us soda, insisting fruit drinks were healthier.)

"Where's Lieberman?" she asked. "I wish he was leading this country now."

We'd loved our Connecticut senator Joseph Lieberman since we'd read that he pushed President Clinton to lift the United Nations arms embargo so Bosniaks in my country could defend themselves against more murders by Serbs. We'd heard Lieberman on television pressing European leaders to fulfill their promise to the world that the Holocaust would never be allowed to happen again.

"The only ones who understand us are the Jews," Mom said.

"You can't believe the hatred and horror until you've gone through it yourself."

She felt that the similarities between what the Serbs did to us and what the Nazis did to Jews in World War II made the Jewish people more empathetic to our suffering. Israel offered Bosnian Muslims refuge in 1993 and took in exiles. A friend of ours saw Israeli planes drop boxes with supplies and military jackets in central Bosnia. Jerusalem's mayor Teddy Kollek proclaimed that in 1492 Bosniaks were the only people in Europe who'd welcomed Jewish refugees fleeing the Spanish Inquisition. Kollek publicized an open letter to President Clinton singling out Serbia's abuse of power, insisting, "If we do not act immediately and decisively, history will record that in the last decade of this century, the democracies failed to heed its most unforgiving lesson: that unopposed aggression will be enlarged and repeated."

This letter was signed by former British prime minister Margaret Thatcher, former U.S. secretary of state George Shultz, writer Susan Sontag, and Nobel laureates Elie Wiesel, Joseph Brodsky, and Czeslaw Milosz. We thought surely the outcry of support would force the U.N. to end the weapons embargo so we could fairly defend ourselves, but it didn't. Every word of news was confirming that our horrific nightmare still wasn't over.

"There they go again." Dad threw his hands up in the air. "The United Nations is our second enemy, right after the Serbs."

"The U.N. and Clinton just want the shooting to stop to get the embarrassing pictures of the war off the six o'clock news," Eldin spat out.

When the phone rang, it was Dad's friend Mujo, Jasenko's father, calling from Germany, where his family had been exiled since 1992. "What the hell are they doing?" Mujo screamed. "The Serbs were on their way out of Brčko! They were packing! Morons! The Bosnian soldiers are crying."

It seemed unfathomable that Serbs would be rewarded for the

atrocities they'd committed against us by being allowed to remain in control of my old town.

"We can never go back there now," Dad said, tears in his eyes.

I realized that ever since we'd escaped Bosnia almost three years before, I'd clung to the hope that our side would be victorious so we could return and resume our old lives. But at that moment, I felt the sudden shock of knowing it was over. I would have no more holidays with Aunt Bisera and our cousins, Amela and Mirza, and their crazy songbirds. No more fishing on the Sava River or karate tournaments at Partizan or soccer with my friend Jasenko. I might never see him again. What girl would I marry? Where were my kids going to be born? What language would they speak? Where would my parents be buried? Would I ever see Grandma Emina again? It felt like my team was losing the most important championship in the world and I wasn't even allowed to play.

"Never," I repeated, my voice cracking.

That week, coming home from an after-school basketball game, I was depressed. Eldin had gone back to his college dorm late Sunday night. I wouldn't see him for a month; I already missed him. Dad returned to his breakneck work schedule, getting home at midnight. He was working by day at the Polystar bottle-cap factory and by night as a bagger at the Stop & Shop. At least he now had a car.

It was worse when we first got here and didn't have any transportation. He'd bike to work and to get us groceries. One night I looked out the window to see him getting out of a pickup truck. In between his jobs, he'd loaded two bags of food onto the handlebars. But on his way home, when it started raining, all his groceries fell to the ground. A kind construction worker stopped to help. He loaded Dad, his bicycle, and the ripped bags and ravaged food into the back of his truck and drove him home. I ran downstairs to help carry in the dented tomatoes and soggy, smashed eggplants. The humiliation never seemed to end. I hated being a broke, foreign high school freshman. I felt guilty each morning, leaving a sick mom home alone, without my father and brother around to take care of her.

Coming home one fall Friday, I took off my new metallic Nike Air sneakers—an early birthday present she bought me—and put them on the mat outside the door. Inside I found my mother sitting at the dining-room table in front of an old Selectric typewriter, a piece of paper in the roller.

"What are you doing?" I asked.

"I'm working on the story of how we came here," she said.

"Why? Nobody gives a damn what happened to us," I told her.

"That's not true! Look at all those important people who signed the letter to President Clinton," my mother argued. "Someday when I'm not around, it'll be documented for you and your kids."

Since she'd been ill, I hated when she said things like that. "Don't worry, I remember every second of the war," I said. We'd been in Connecticut two years, but there wasn't a detail I'd forgotten.

"I know, you have an elephant brain. And you keep grudges forever," she said. "But it's not healthy to hold on to all that anger and stress. Look what happened to me."

It seemed so cruel that she'd survived the war only to discover a lump in her breast on the day we made it to Vienna.

We went to Austria because it was the only destination we could get to by bus from Brčko, and we wound up in Vienna because my Uncle Ahmet's wife had Bosnian relatives there. When our bus pulled into the Viennese station on the evening of January 3, 1993, we took a cab to Ahmet's. We had no idea of the fare, or even how to count Austrian currency, so we showed the taxi driver all of our money—300 schillings. "That's the fee," he said, taking it all. I could tell from his accent he was a Serb. "He ripped you off. The ride should have cost 100 schillings," Ahmet told us when we got inside. A final Serbian double-cross. I swore it would be our last.

Ahmet, his wife, and two daughters were living with a wealthy Protestant family of philanthropists who knew how desperate we were. They let the eight of us bunk in their basement as we waited out the war. Since it had been so long since we had electricity, the lamps hurt our eyes. So we asked Ahmet to dim the lights. There was no bathroom downstairs. It was cramped and windowless, like a bomb shelter. On one part of the floor, Ahmet stayed with his wife and young daughters. He'd shattered his leg fighting in the Bosnian army, so he was on crutches, limping, in constant pain.

We kept to the other side of the room. My brother, the tallest, took the top mattress while Mom and I slept below, on the pull-out trundle bed, feet to head for more room. My father crashed on a flimsy beach chair that kept collapsing in the middle of the night. We'd go upstairs one at a time to use the lavatory and shower, trying to stay out of everyone's way. The toothpaste stung my gums since I hadn't brushed my teeth with anything but baking soda in a year. I assumed we'd be waylaid here for a few months until we won the war and could go home.

In Bosnia, the aroma of dandelions and luscious peach and cherry trees had been replaced by the stench of gunpowder, metal, spoiled food, and dead dogs and cats rotting in alleyways. Garbage had piled up in mounds on the barren street corners. Diesel fuel fumed out of the tanks and other military vehicles that had taken over the roads. Dark smoke swirled from the chimney of Kafilerija, the factory on the outskirts of town, where the corpses from Luka were piled on meat trucks, then cremated. It smelled like death.

Walking around Vienna our first day there, I was stunned by how bright, clean, and gorgeous it was. Surrounded by snowy mountains and hills, everything we saw was pristine and fresh. I breathed in the welcome scents of the crispy clear air, washed by water fountains, and elaborately manicured gardens. The regal, Old World elegance of the cathedrals and museums made the city feel like a magical kingdom. The shapes of windowsills and moldings echoed the Gothic buildings in Brćko's main square. Yet this whole new country seemed made of medieval castles, as if a king and queen might walk out for a coronation any second, like in an old movie. I was lost in a time warp, getting dizzy from looking up at bronzed eagles and white plaster angels.

Honoring their historic ties to my country, the Austrians were very generous to us. They took in 300,000 Bosnian refugees and gave each family 2,000 schillings per month, which we spent on food. I was taken by the rainbow-colored pastries lining the bakery and grocery shelves. My mother allowed me one sweet every day—a sugar donut, a little apple-filled cream cake, or Mozart chocolate bonbons in gold wrapping—that I'd devour with a tall glass of milk.

Eldin and I were given special IDs that allowed us to use all public transportation at no cost. We liked the trolley cars—a fun cross between a bus and the kind of trains we'd taken to Croatia. I'd never been in an underground subway before—I was impressed with how fast and efficient it was and how meticulous they kept everything. Bored, we rode up and down the rails every day, memorizing each stop, picking up bits of German. We visited Prater amusement park, staring at the enormous Ferris wheel that looked like a giant spaceship. Eldin was sad we couldn't afford a ride, but I was relieved since I was scared of heights. We sunbathed at a Danube River beach and took a subway, trolley, and bus and then walked to the edge of town to the Krapfenwalbad pool, where the pine trees and crickets reminded me of my old karate camp. We spent afternoons at fancy toy stores, where they let us play video games for free. We were protected here. But while miraculously far from the war's crossfire, I was a twelve-year-old boy with no school to attend, no sports to play, no teammates to practice with, no friends to talk to. It still felt like I was waiting out a prison sentence.

My brother found a karate club that let him enroll without any payment. He took me along on the forty-five-minute trolley ride to the sports complex outside of Vienna. I watched him join in their freestyle sparring exercises, thinking it was less aggressive and prissier than our teams at Partizan. But maybe that was why the men in this country weren't killing each other. I didn't practice myself, intimidated by the older strangers speaking a different language. It didn't seem worthwhile to start anything new when I didn't know where I'd be the next day.

With my life suspended, on hold indefinitely, I took over Eldin's radio obsession, checking constantly for war developments. My mom, who'd always encouraged artwork over athletics, bought me a notepad and watercolor markers to get my mind off the destruction of our old world. I whiled away hours on the bed, making pictures of boats on the River Sava, sailing under the blazing Balkan sunsets I missed.

One spring night Mom cut out an article in the international Bosnian newspaper we read. It was an advertisement for the contest "Young Artists for Bosnia," which instructed kids to submit illustrations of your current life. I entered one drawing of a white dove embedded in a broken missile, and another showing a boy sitting on a globe, thinking of his homeland, while to the left, bombs were dropping on a cemetery filled with tombstones and crosses. It was titled "Sad Days in Brčko." I won the contest, and my "Sad Days" drawing ran with a paragraph I'd written, listing the names of the Serb boys who'd turned on me and noting that we'd escaped on January 3, 1993. After printing my full name, I'd added our address on Fleishmann Gasse. Both Dad's colleague Truly and Jasenko's mom saw the newspaper in Germany and sent us letters. I smiled as Mom kissed my head and said, "I'm proud of you." She cut the drawing out of the newspaper and kept it in her purse, showing it off wherever we went. I was thrilled my art helped my parents reconnect with our lost friends. It made me feel powerful. It was my first tiny triumph since the war.

Seeing that we were too crowded—eight of us crammed together in their downstairs level—our Viennese benefactors let me, Eldin, Mom, and Dad stay for a few months in a beautiful, sparsely furnished apartment they owned that was between tenants. It was three times the size of our Brčko home, with floor-to-ceiling windows that overlooked a colorful courtyard garden. I loved how clean it was; it smelled like fancy floor polish. Living there made me feel like a normal person again, and not a scared alien. Mom saw a doctor who said she was okay. After eleven months, we unpacked our bags.

I didn't realize what a rough time other Bosnians were having here until one summer morning when Eldin, Dad, and I took the subway to visit family friends. It turned out they were being housed with hundreds of other Balkan refugees in a cold, sterile-looking former hospital, with a broken elevator and just a curtain for privacy. Kids were screaming, their shouts echoing down the hallways. I saw how lucky we were to be living in a nice, private home. But then, early that evening, we returned to find my mother outside the apartment. She was screaming at an officer in an Austrian police uniform. Two Polish workers in overalls were gesturing at each other in confusion. The couch, the bed, and our bags were sitting on the sidewalk. We rushed over to her.

"You can't do this to us!" she yelled in Bosnian they couldn't decipher. "I can't handle this anymore! They threw us out of Brčko. Now they're kicking us out of Vienna."

Oh no, where would we go now? I was afraid we were being ousted again. But when Eldin spoke broken German to our Viennese landlord over the phone, they immediately cleared up the confusion and apologized. It turned out the workmen from Poland had accidentally evicted the wrong tenants. They'd called the policeman, who didn't understand what the problem was.

"Nobody's throwing us out," Eldin told Mom when he came back. "It was just a mistake."

As Dad picked up our belongings and carried them back inside,

Mom sat on the sidewalk, sobbing. "I was alone when the two men stormed in," she said. "Then the cop came with a gun in his holster. I was sure they were coming to arrest us."

My mother had mostly kept her cool during the year we'd tried to flee Bosnia. Now that we were safe in Austria, she was losing it. I sat down next to her on the street. "Mom, it was a dumb slipup. There's no war here." I tried to comfort her. "Nobody will hurt us."

"I'm so tired of being degraded," she said. "We have to have our own place."

Dad, Eldin, and I carried the ejected couch and bed back up three flights of steep stairs. Mom cried for the rest of the night.

I wanted to stay in this spacious, otherwise peaceful residence, but I knew she was right; it was only a temporary fix. We were jobless and country-less exiles who had to apply for new visas every three months. We'd go to the passport office in town and they'd stamp our passports, which still said "Yugoslavia," though that country no longer existed.

The Balkan War was raging, with no solution in sight. Even if it ended, we feared we could quickly be sent back to a hostile land with no apartment to return to. We knew how much competition there would be to legally immigrate to Austria; I bet they wouldn't let 300,000 Bosniaks get permanent residency. We couldn't officially stay there, but we couldn't go home either. After five months in Vienna, we starting looking around for a bigger place, with fewer refugees, to move to. We applied for emigration on several different continents, wondering who would have us.

The family we stayed with, as it turned out, was pretty well connected, and knew the Austrian ambassador. Eldin and Dad did his gardening, to earn extra money. The dignitary liked us and offered to help get us to Canada or Australia, but advised, "If the United States accepts you, go there." Luckily we were soon called to the American Embassy. All four of us went, wearing the casual clothes we'd carried on our backs from Bosnia. We took a subway and a trolley there. Dad and Eldin knew the most English, so it was decided they would speak.

"Make sure you give the man a firm handshake. And call him 'sir' when you talk to him," Dad instructed, buoyed with hope.

In April 1993 we were interviewed by a soft-spoken American man wearing a blue suit. He was tall, with dirty-blond hair and a poker face. He looked about forty-five. We were surprised he knew so much about my father and which prisoners and guards were with him at the concentration camp. From the way he interrogated us about Brčko's war criminals, we guessed he was actually from the CIA. Mom showed him Dad and Eldin's release from Luka, along with another form, signed by Good Pero, saying that we were handing over all our property and everything we owned to the Serb government in exchange for leaving the country and never coming back. She'd kept them in her purse, next to the silver key to our Brčko apartment.

Inspecting the pages, the American raised his eyebrows, nodding. He hinted that he'd like to keep them as evidence. We decided to trust him. Mom handed them over, pleased our documents might help convict Serbian criminals. He betrayed a thin smile and said "Good luck" as we left him with our papers. We gathered that was our ticket.

"Thank you very much, sir." Dad shook his hand. When we made it to the street, my father said, "We're out of here."

Within weeks, we were excited to receive word that America would take us in.

The only money we had stepping off the TWA plane at JFK airport, at 6:30 p.m. on October 20, 1993, was the three hundred dollars Truly had wired from Germany. Along with our tattered luggage, we carried blue-and-white plastic bags with IOM globe emblems that the International Organization of Migration staff gave us before we left Austria. As we walked through the loud, busy terminal in Queens, New York, we were hoarded together with other Bosnian refugees from the same flight by the security team from another group, the International Refugee Committee. We felt like cattle being rounded up. They'd obviously recognized us from the plastic bags we were toting. They made my parents sign paperwork right there, promising we'd pay back the $3,000 cost of the airfare.

At the baggage claim, a man Eldin's height held up a sign: "The Trebinčević family." He had brown hair graying on the sides and wore a sweater with a blue blazer over it. He looked sixty, older than my father. He introduced himself as Donald Hodges, a Methodist minister, but said, "Just call me Don," explaining that he was from Connecticut's Interfaith Council, a mix of churches and synagogues who'd sponsored us. He led us to his van in the parking lot. He had a gentle manner, asking if we were thirsty, handing us paper cups and apple juice. At thirteen, I'd never met a Methodist before.

Reverend Don drove us an hour to his home in Westport. It was a two-story beige colonial with three bedrooms. It seemed nice but a little musty to me, with antique-looking furniture, embroidered pillows, and a piano. We stayed there for four months. Reverend Don and his wife were the only people we knew in the country. Their two kids were grown, so Eldin and I took their places, with our own separate rooms. Compared to our apartment complex in Bosnia and urban Vienna (Austria's biggest city), this new rural, woodsy neighborhood of big houses far apart from each other felt unnaturally quiet and isolated. It smelled like trees. Not wanting to impose on the Hodges, Mom insisted on doing their cooking and cleaning. Eldin and Dad shoveled their driveway. I walked their sweet golden retriever, who started sleeping on the floor by my bed, as if sensing I was lonely.

One morning, Reverend Don drove us an hour on Interstate 95 to Manhattan so we could go sightseeing. We visited the Statue of Liberty, the Empire State Building, and the Intrepid museum on the

Hudson River. At Battery Park, he said, "You can't be in New York if you don't eat a frankfurter," insisting we try Hebrew National beef hot dogs from the cart. To be polite, Dad joined him, trying one covered with sauerkraut and mustard. But the vendors' nails looked dirty to me. Spoiled by my neat-freak mom's home cooking, I was too afraid to eat anything off the street. I did like listening to the crowds chattering in different languages and watching all the taxis, cars, and buses bustling around like in Brčko.

"Hey, why don't we stay here instead of quiet Connecticut?" I whispered to Eldin.

"We have no choice," my brother said, explaining that Manhattan was too expensive and the only people kind enough to officially sponsor us were in the suburbs.

"It's nice in Connecticut. Everything is just starting for you. Your life hasn't even begun yet," my mother kept telling me. Yet on bad days it seemed like it was over.

In Bosnia, I'd taken English lessons with Huso's father and practiced in school. But I knew only the bare minimum when I first walked into my seventh-grade classroom in Westport. It seemed as spacious and clean as the school in my old country, though the rooms were smaller and the ceilings lower. I was surprised the hallways were decorated with Christmas trees, plastic Santas, and stuffed stockings since, in Bosnia, no religious artifacts were allowed. The Westport kids wore baseball caps, which was considered disrespectful back home. Each room here had a flag instead of the picture of Tito. When the teacher entered the room, I stood up like I'd been taught in Brčko. But when I noticed nobody else did, I quickly sat down.

I was paranoid that the big, rich American kids would make fun of my Eastern European accent, grammar mistakes, and small, skinny frame hidden in the worn clothes I'd managed to lug 4,372 miles. (I wasn't comfortable wearing donated shirts and pants in the wrong size.) I was ashamed to tell anyone we were living on the second floor of the Hodges' house because we couldn't afford our own place. I clutched my spiral notebook and a pink pencil in my hands as Dr. Hightower, Bedford's middle school principal, introduced me to the class. When everyone said "Hi, Kenan" out loud, I felt like a stray dog at a humane society, waiting to be adopted.

"I'll show him around," offered a blond thirteen-year-old boy named Miguel. He pulled up a bench and invited me to sit next to him in the front row. He was shorter and skinnier than me. I sat stiffly with my arms crossed, afraid to do anything that would turn the class against me. I couldn't understand half of what these kids were saying in this slower, softer language. I missed my old apartment, my karate team, my Bosnian pals. I wondered if Huso was alive, and what Jasenko was doing in Germany, which felt like a different planet. I hadn't seen or spoken to him in three years; Mom said it was too expensive to call him there.

I had no reason to trust anyone else. Most of my old playmates from Bosnia, along with my former martial-arts coach and favorite teacher, hated me and wanted me to die. I pretended not to care. But I did. I held on to each slight from my past, replaying the demeaning betrayals in my mind. I couldn't let go of the bad memories. Everything was too important to me. At recess that first day of school in America, everyone was pointing to the new foreign kid. Miguel handed me a basketball. I threw the ball at the backboard carefully and made the shot. Miguel gave me a high five.

"What's your favorite soccer team? Mine's Real Madrid," he told me.

"Yugoslavia no more," I said, regretting that my favorite had split up, like my country.

"Are you okay?" he asked. "Are you hungry?"

We sat together at lunch in the cafeteria. I ate the salami sandwich my mother made me. He shared his Tater Tots with ketchup. It was the first American food I liked. Miguel walked me to our other classes that afternoon and put me on the right bus home that night. But it was a freezing, thirty-five-minute walk from my bus stop to Reverend Don's house. I was always the last student dropped off. After a few days, the bus driver asked my name, where I was from, and where I lived. When I told him, he introduced himself as Offir, from Israel, and said that during his stint in the army, they were rooting for Bosnia in the war. From then on, he dropped me off right up to Don's driveway but made me promise not to tell anyone.

Miguel took a different bus home and had a British nanny who sometimes picked him up from school. He invited me to his big, book-filled house, which looked like a villa. We swam in the pool in his gated backyard. They were rich, cultured, successful. Why was he being this nice to me? It turned out he had a Spanish father and a Catholic American mother (why his English was fluent) and he'd recently moved to Westport from Spain after his parents divorced. He understood what it felt like to be alone, sad, and displaced. I glued myself to Miguel. Whatever he did, I did. We biked to the store, where he bought me football cards we'd collect and trade. We played video games that he'd always win. He got me into basketball, football, and water polo. He taught me how to throw and hit a base-ball, a game I'd never tried before. He gave me hockey pads and a mask and kept smashing the puck at me, insisting I learn to be his goalie.

He was the most competitive kid I'd ever known, aside from me. No wonder we got along. It was a toss-up who was more of a sore loser and cheater which, oddly, made me trust him. If I was ahead in our pickup game, he'd say "two out of three," then "three out of five," and keep going until I gave up from exhaustion. If I made a basket, he'd switch three points to two or lie and say I'd stepped on the line. If I was losing, when he'd go for a layup, I'd stick my knee into his thigh to slow down his streak. When I'd intentionally foul or step on his foot, he'd yell, "What the hell, dude?"

I played soccer and basketball with Miguel every free second I had. The athletic field was the only place I was confident, so I relished being a jock. Sometimes I took competitiveness to an unhealthy level. I hated losing more than I loved to win. I believed that second place only meant you were the first loser. I'd cry in the shower from disappointment if my team wasn't victorious. My performance was all I could control. I'd lost too much already.

As if to replenish us on every level, the dignified Reverend Don helped us find an apartment in Norwalk we rented for $750 a month. Members of his Interfaith Council donated beds, couches, and tables. He helped Mom get gigs babysitting local kids and then land a full-time position at the Nivea factory. He introduced himself to the manager at Boston Chicken, who hired Dad and Eldin to roast poultry and make sandwiches there. Reverend Don drove them back and forth to work until a churchgoer gave my father a used Pontiac Sunbird. Unfortunately, it kept breaking down and we didn't have money for new parts. One day, on the way back from an afternoon at the beach, the transmission blew. For some reason the car would only drive in reverse. So Dad drove us home backward—until a cop stopped us. When we explained we were from Bosnia, he had a tow truck take us to an auto shop that fixed it for that week, though it kept falling apart.

Reverend Don also assisted with health-care connections, hooking us up with a generous Jewish orthodontist in town who gave me braces for free and took care of me for two years. "I'm so thankful you won't look like a rabbit," my mother said.

But it killed me that I couldn't do anything to mend her. From the moment we'd landed here, she was out of it. She would sweat all the time, didn't like the humidity or heat, ate cold fruit instead of hot food, and took naps every day. It was totally unlike her. At Norwalk Hospital, she was examined by Dr. Beinfeld, an older surgeon who was Jewish. (We met people of all religions here—except Muslim.) We'd heard Dr. Beinfeld was the best oncologist there. He did tests on the lump on her right breast, broke the news that she'd been misdiagnosed in Vienna, and explained it was cancerous. Dr. Bein-feld, in his seventies, was about to retire. Yet after hearing what we'd been through, he insisted on operating on my mom himself. He made sure she didn't receive one bill for the surgery and chemo-therapy.

She was exhausted by the treatments, but she worked different odd jobs while trying to recover her strength. What little money we had went to her medication, our rent, and the used gray Pontiac my folks needed to get to work. Eldin spent his free time studying for his SATs so he could get into college. I was glad Mom approved when Miguel's mother offered to pick me up on weekends.

"What would you like to eat?" Nancie would ask.

"Whatever Miguel's eating," I'd reply, which made them laugh.

After I told Nancie I couldn't have pork, she was careful never to serve me ham or bacon. She came over to ask my mother if I could join them for Christmas. Mom was glad I'd made a new friend, and Muslims didn't celebrate the holiday anyway. At his house, Miguel and I decorated the tree. There was a stocking stuffed with candy canes and gold chocolate coins for me along the fireplace. Nancie got me a green fleece sweatshirt and fancy rollerblades so Miguel and I could play street hockey. My mom was embarrassed, but said I could keep the gifts. "Did you thank them?" she asked. She had me take them a potted hibiscus with red and pink flowers. Nancie noticed Mom's green thumb and brought over her ailing snake plant, which my mother revived.

Each time my parents switched jobs and we had to move, I was afraid I'd be isolated and abandoned again. I was especially worried I'd lose Miguel, who was my only real friend. But even after I switched schools a second and third time, Miguel stuck by me. Nancie took to picking me up every Friday and dropping me off late Sunday night. At my home, my parents and Eldin were working, stressed out about money, and exhausted all the time. While Mom still cooked us Bosnian food, she was ill and fighting off her disease, along with depression. At Miguel's I could be a kid with no problems for forty-eight hours. We'd play sports, watch dumb American movies, and eat French fries and the cheeseburgers and hot dogs his nanny would grill us. To this day, I remain close to Miguel and his whole family.

At school, my new teachers went out of their way for me. They stopped me at lunch and in the hallways to ask how I was doing. I practiced soccer every day after classes. Slowly I began to feel better. My English improved from daily exposure to my favorite TV shows, *The Fresh Prince of Bel-Air* and *Beverly Hills, 90210*, which my older cousin Amela had turned me on to in Bosnia. I'd been disappointed to see that all American high schools didn't have rich, gorgeous students driving Porches and BMWs to surf at the beach.

In eighth grade I felt honored to be invited to join a local soccer team with three other foreign kids. In Bosnia we'd played soccer since we were big enough to kick a ball, of course, but now the sport was becoming popular in the U.S. Our team went undefeated, finishing first in our league. The town's paper covered our games and mentioned the goals I scored; I cut out the articles and pasted them in a binder. When we won the championship, I jumped on the back of coach Ted Popadoupoulis, a giant Greek guy, who handed me the MVP trophy with my name engraved on it. I hadn't connected with a coach since Pero. It still hurt when I thought of him.

At lunch one Saturday, I told Mom that my assignment for art class was to paint a figure who changed the world in some way. She happened to be playing Madonna's CD *Immaculate Collection*. Since Mom couldn't understand English, she didn't know what the lyrics meant; I didn't offer to translate. The music reminded me of my cousin Amela, whom I missed. I liked Madonna's sexy, rebellious American attitude so I drew a portrait of the singer. My art teacher chose my picture as one of the best of the year.

"With all the time you waste bouncing balls, don't lose your creative talent," Mom said. She patted my back when I won art contests and sports games. But she was more concerned with my report card and always examined it carefully. When I got A's in history and science, she'd give me a kiss and my father would high-five me. My friends' parents rewarded their high GPAs with money, presents, and cars. My folks' response was, "If you don't get all A's, you'll wind up working tough factory jobs with no security, like we have to."

While my brother and I made good grades and friends in school, Mom and Dad had a rougher time. In Bosnia, they were established and prosperous, embedded in a sweet, kooky clan who adored us. Here they were middle-aged misfits with no recommendations, careers, connections, or command of the language. Dad's English improved, but my mom didn't speak a word when we'd landed in Connecticut. The last time I saw her happy was the day she framed my karate diploma in 1991. In some ways, surviving the war trapped in Brčko was easier than establishing new lives in the United States.

My father refused to consider welfare. He took any job he was offered, whether it was painting houses, sanding yachts at the boat marina, or roasting chickens at a fast-food joint. The steadiest was working the assembly line at Polystar, a company owned by a member of Reverend Don's church, where he made minimum wage, grossing $25,000 a year. He supplemented that by working the late shift at Stop & Shop. So he'd leave the house at 6:00 a.m. and return at midnight. I'd watch him fall asleep from exhaustion while eating dinner. While he wasn't studying, Eldin also tried anything that paid. He briefly sold Cutco knives door to door and was a carpentry assistant and a busboy at Pancho Villa's before joining Dad at Boston Chicken and the fruit cup factory. After Mom left the Nivea factory, she became a data processor at a lingerie firm because, like Dad's position, it came with good health insurance. This, unfortunately, turned out to be the smartest decision they'd made.

As far as we knew, we were the only Bosnians in Westport, Stratford, or Norwalk. But at a picnic arranged by the Interfaith Council,

Reverend Don drove us two hours to meet thirty fellow refugees who were also living around the state of Connecticut. Everyone was grateful to be in "the best country in the world," working hard, comparing blueprints for their American futures, filled with ESL language classes, university degrees, better jobs, bigger cars, nicer housing. I harbored a secret plan myself: after Bosnia won the war, we'd all get to go home.

It took us two and a half years, after staying with two different families and then moving to four different Connecticut rental apartments in the area, to finally unpack our bags at our own rented house in Stratford in the fall of 1995. It was comforting to nest, even if our furniture remained a mismatched suite of tables, chairs, secondhand beds, and lamps donated by Reverend Don's Interfaith gang. One neighbor gave me his used bike. I was glad to have it, but it felt weird being a charity case for so long.

"I'm sending the last check to pay back the International Rescue Committee for our airfare here," my mother told me one cold December night.

She felt pride in paying off our debt. Yet I'd been inconsolable because the war had ended in a stalemate. I couldn't understand why the bad guys who'd attacked us were allowed to remain in the land they'd pirated and destroyed, while the innocent people who'd done nothing wrong were further punished with a life sentence of exile and couldn't return. It went against everything my parents had taught me about why you had to be honest and fair and good. Now I was eternally stuck in this tranquil, tree-filled suburb with no sidewalks, where you needed a car to get anywhere, where in winter it got dark too early, everything closed by 9:00 p.m. and everyone went to bed. Eldin and Dad were too tired to play with me. Mom was too sick to drive me around. Nobody came to visit us anymore. I missed my friends Jasenko and Huso. I wanted to see Grandma

Emina, Aunt Bisera, and my cousins, with their turtles and crazy birds. Connecticut was no longer just a way station to tolerate before I could get back to my homeland, where I belonged. I was scared to think: this was all there was.

I tried to remind myself how blessed I was. Too many Bosniaks were dead, maimed, or orphaned. I hadn't lost my father, my mother, or Eldin. I never had nightmares or suffered from posttraumatic stress disorder, like other survivors. Although I'd been close to the fighting, I never saw anyone get killed. Throughout the year we were outcasts in Brčko, at least we had each other to cling to. We never gave up hope. Everyone told me we were fortunate to escape, mostly unscathed, and to have shelter and good food on the table. My brain knew they were right, but inside I felt so angry and lonely and lost.

Indeed, my mother would go to work, then drive to the hospital to get chemo, come home, and cook elaborate meals. Since Dad worked late and Eldin was soon accepted to college, most nights it was just us two. She started out serving me only Balkan food. But once a month when she got tired, I'd talk her into ordering Pizza Hut's mushroom pizza with cheese crust, or going to Stop & Shop for apple pie, which we'd never had in Bosnia, or picking up a mixed assortment of Dunkin' Donuts Munchkins donut holes.

For my fifteenth birthday dinner, I had three helpings of the beef stew and vanilla biscuits she made from scratch. She served it on the new mahogany table she'd bought at a tag sale. I knew she liked it because it reminded her of the nicer one we'd had in Brčko.

"Get your glass on the coaster now! Don't you dare leave stains," she scolded, grabbing a towel to wipe up the tiny dots of water on her secondhand wood.

"Who are you keeping it spotless for this time? Daca?" I blurted out.

"When you can afford to buy your own table, you can be an insensitive slob," she told me. "At least I'm going to enjoy what's left of my life in a nice home."

I put my glass on her coaster.

After the special meal, we sat in the living room. "Let's watch a movie," she said.

I noticed the VHS tape she'd rented for a dollar from the Blockbuster on her way home. "Oh no, not *Schindler's List* again." She'd already seen it five times and had made me watch it with her twice. "How about something lighter? *Back to the Future* is on TV."

"You're one to talk," she said. "You saw all three of those future movies in Brčko with your brother—and you've watched them all here too." She joined me on the beige couch, holding out a bowl of fruit salad she'd sliced fresh for dessert.

"Who wants to see another Holocaust movie? I'd rather watch a comedy," I told her.

"Cars shouldn't fly," she said. "There's nothing you can learn from that."

"Why do you have to be so deep?"

"Why do you have to be so stubborn?"

"The war made me stubborn," I reminded her.

"Eat some fruit." She pushed the bowl and a fork into my hands.

"You eat some." I handed it back to her. But she waited for me to eat first, as she'd done for me and Eldin ever since the war.

"How many times can you cry over the same movie?" I mumbled, chewing on sliced watermelon and bananas. "I don't get it."

"That's why the Jews understand. We share the same story now," she told me. "That's exactly what happened to us."

I rolled my eyes. "It is not. How is a businessman who saved Jewish people from the Nazis in World War II the same as Muslims being killed in Bosnia in the 1990s?" I was annoyed, not sure if the guy was a profiteer whose motive was free labor, or a real hero. "Anyway, there weren't any Serb heroes who saved us. They tried to kill us and we were screwed out of winning the war fair and square."

"I'll never forget those who did us harm. But not all were bad," she insisted. "What about Zorica and Miloš? Obren? We have to acknowledge the good people too."

"Fine, *you* acknowledge the good Serbs," I said.

"We wouldn't be here if it weren't for them," Mom added, always needing to have the last word. "Kendji, promise me you'll never forget the people who saved us."

"Whatever," I mumbled, slipping *Schindler's List* into the VCR, watching as her favorite movie began again, letting her win something this time.

CHAPTER TEN

Finding Amela

Brčko, Bosnia
July 2011

Number 11 on my list was: *Find out why cousin Amela had never kept in touch with me.*

While back in my hometown, I started wondering why we hadn't spoken in decades, troubled by cracks in my memory. I'd been a pint-sized sixth grader obsessed with soccer and karate. She was my cool seventeen-year-old cousin, my favorite babysitter, a surrogate big sister who wore pink lipstick and loved Madonna.

On April 30, 1992, just as the war was starting, Eldin and I were sent to sleep over at my grandmother's house with the other grand-kids since everybody thought we'd be safer in that section of town. We were woken at 5:00 a.m. by ear-shattering explosions; the Serbs were blowing up the Sava Bridge just two hundred yards from Grandma's. In the chaos, when Dad ordered us home immediately, Amela was still in her pajamas and ponytail, waiting for her parents to come get her.

"See you later, Kendji. Be good," she'd said, kissing me good-bye on the cheek. I'd looked forward to hanging out with her that weekend. I didn't see her again for nineteen years.

After lunch with Miloš on Wednesday, he drove us ten minutes to Amela's all-Bosniak subdivision. There she was, in front of her huge, two-story, cream-colored house, which had cinderblock roof tiles and big rectangular windows. She was standing in the garden, watering pots filled with tall red geraniums. She'd gone from an adorable, flirty teenager to a serious, sturdy, middle-aged wife and mother; we'd missed decades of each other.

During the intervening years, we'd exchanged occasional vague greetings through Bisera, but I'd heard Amela's voice only twice since the war. She'd called us the day my mother died in 2007. Then, last week, when I'd phoned her to say we were coming to Brčko, she'd invited us over for dinner. I'd always felt bad that Amela never wrote or contacted me directly. I didn't even know she had a green thumb like my mom. With brown eyes and shoulder-length mahogany hair, she looked so much like her. As Miloš let us off, Amela dropped her hose to run over. "Look how big you men are." We hugged and kissed. She was five foot seven now, two inches taller than my mother.

"We're all so old." I laughed.

"Look how dressed up you are, Keka," she said, while her eyes darted from my father's suit to Miloš's car. "So who drove you here?" She sounded suspicious. She'd obviously seen the sign that said "Hit Taxi," a company only Serbs drove for. Most commerce in Bosnia remained segregated. She clearly would have preferred that we patronize one of our own.

"We're coming from our friends Miloš and Zorica's house in Grbavica," Eldin said.

"How do you know these people?" Amela asked.

"They're the neighbors who helped us during the war," Eldin explained.

"He's a good guy," I blurted out. Was I really saying, "He's one of the rare good Serbs"?

I was anxious to meet Ibrahim, the doctor who'd married and taken such good care of Amela. I was determined to make a good impression, but I feared he wouldn't know what to make of three American male strangers who suddenly appeared at his doorstep, wanting to be part of his family. I worried this new patriarch of our Bosnian clan might find us too foreign, too liberal, too Westernized. Dad had known Ibrahim's father growing up, but we'd never seen him in person. Not even a picture.

The man who greeted us inside their foyer looked like a big friendly bear. He stood six foot three, almost as tall as Eldin, but bulkier, with wide, thick shoulders. He had a nice face with a high forehead, round chin, and soulful, green-gray eyes.

"It's great to finally meet you, Doctor." I gave him a firm handshake. He had huge hands and a strong grip. Then he pulled me closer to embrace me with both arms. He kissed Dad on the cheek, a Bosnian sign of respect. Warm guy, I liked him already.

We high-fived their kids, then handed out the presents Eldin and I had carefully chosen at Macy's: Chanel perfume and Puma sneakers for Amela; a black protective cell phone case for their sixteen-year-old son, Rusmir; Chicago Bulls basketball shorts for Kemal, who was seventeen; a pink Gap hoodie for Tidja, nine; and an XL Kenneth Cole black cardigan sweater for Ibrahim. Bisera had told us that the textile and cotton factories destroyed during the war hadn't been replaced and the only boutiques that sold quality goods were wildly expensive. All the packages we'd sent to Muslim names in Brčko had suspiciously disappeared. So we'd carried the gifts in our own bags all the way from Queens.

We were totally impressed by their four-bedroom house as all five of them gave us a tour. On the outside terrace—filled with spiky flowers and plants—eight people could eat at the wooden table. They had the classiest kitchen I'd seen in Bosnia, with an electric stove, dishwasher, ice maker, bread maker, and marble countertops. It was spotless, the way Mom used to keep ours. If you didn't go outside to see the rest of the country, you'd assume they were lucky millionaires. I kept thinking, *With no war, this was the life I could have had.* If I'd taken over and expanded Dad's fitness business, I might have owned a home as grand as this. But I'd want it closer to my old apartment so I'd have views of the River Sava. I probably would have married a classmate in my early twenties; we'd have children almost Tidja's age by now. They'd have picnics with Amela's kids and spend holidays together as our generation of cousins used to.

"What a palace you have here," my father said as we walked into their spacious living room.

Ibrahim grabbed Dad's shoulders. "Now let me get a good look at you, Keka. How spiffy you look, all dressed up so nice for us."

"Kenan and Eldin got me this." My father proudly showed off the tie we'd bought him, although, I recalled, he'd picked it out himself.

"Sit down, Keka, take off your jacket, rest your legs." Ibrahim hung Dad's jacket over a chair, gently led him toward the maroon leather coach, placed an ottoman at his feet, and handed him a pillow. Eldin sat down next to Dad. I was touched by the fuss Amela's husband was making over my father.

There was a handsome marble bar in the corner, with a row of high stools. I sat on one and leaned my elbows on the corner, trying to be unobtrusive.

"Come sit on the couch, it's more comfortable," Amela said. Her three kids stood silently, gaping at us like we were some kind of visiting royalty.

"Go get your cousins a drink," Amela told Rusmir, the middle child.

"My dad has whiskey, moonshine, and wine," Rusmir said, then ran downstairs to the basement to fetch it. He was a well-behaved boy, like Eldin and I had been.

Kemal, the seventeen-year-old, scrutinized my chinos and my suede shoes, and the Ray-Bans hanging from my button-down shirt. "You dress sly, like a sports agent," he said.

He was my size. I calculated how I could get him a similar shirt and chinos. I'd send it to Bisera's all-Bosniak town so nobody would steal it.

Rusmir returned with Chivas Regal scotch and *rakija*. Ibrahim poured and toasted: "After so much time."

Their adorable little girl kept staring at me, like I was a zoo attraction.

"She had an English lesson today," Amela said. "Tell cousin Kenan what you learned."

"*Ne*," Tidja said. I patted her head, but she jerked away. I was heartbroken. I was winning over Ibrahim, but now their daughter was repelled by me.

"Kenan used to draw too," Amela told Tidja. "He won a big art contest at school. We were sure he was going to be an artist."

"I'd sketch sailboats on the Sava River under the sunset," I told Tidja in our native tongue. "Amela, remember how I used to draw all the time at Grandma's house?" My eyes were begging her confirmation.

"Yes, for hours at a time," Amela testified. "The only way to keep Kenan quiet and out of trouble was to give him paper and watercolors."

Tidja came closer to me and whispered, "Want to see a dragon?" I nodded yes, elated. She led me to her room and gave me a beautiful picture of a red creature with yellow horns that I made her sign for me.

I'd missed her whole life so far; I wished I could catch up nine years in one night. "So who is your best friend?" I asked.

"I play with a lot of classmates from school," she answered. "Mostly boys."

"What's your favorite TV show?"

"*CSI Miami*. We get it by satellite," she said. "I didn't know you could have such big buildings by the sand that don't sink."

I laughed, hoping she didn't think all of America was like that. "I can send you every season on DVD," I offered.

"Probably already saw them all."

I noticed her pink bed, walls, and stuffed animals. "So I know what your favorite color is. I could get you a pink coat." Winters had been freezing in Bosnia lately. Clothes from America would be warmer and last longer. "I'll show you what the stores near me have and you tell me what style you like. Do you have a computer?"

In her brother Rusmir's room, we went online on his Sony laptop. Amela said they'd just had their Internet connection hooked up six months ago. We found Gap Kids, and I scrolled down to girls' coats. "Want to come sit next to me?" I asked, but Tidja, still shy around me, said, "No, I'll stand." She pointed to a short, fluffy, pink down parka. It didn't look warm enough to me.

"How about the next one? It looks warmer." I showed her one that would cover her up below the knees. I'd get her pink boots too, so her feet would never be cold.

"That's pretty," she said. "How many people are in New York?"

"Millions," I told her. She was a happy, confident kid, like I once was.

"I heard the buildings are so high there they go over the clouds," she said.

I found a picture of the skyline for her.

"Whoa, all those houses." She looked awed. "Where do you live?"

I went on Google Maps, plugged in my Queens address, and showed her my street.

"I told my friends at school I had cousins in New York, but they didn't believe me."

I was flattered she'd bragged about me. I hoped to have a smart daughter like her one day. "When you come to New York, I'll take you to the Empire State Building."

"Mom probably won't let me go until I'm eighteen."

I recalled hanging out in Amela's room when I was Tidja's age, watching her blow-dry her long reddish hair and put on makeup and jewelry. She'd had me tape Madonna posters to her walls as she danced around to "Holiday" blasting from her cassette player. I was suddenly overwhelmed with regret that it had taken me so much time to come back and reconnect with her. Tidja and her brothers didn't even know me. I was mad at myself. I should have gotten over my war hang-ups sooner or put them aside long enough to meet my relatives for a beach vacation in Croatia, where I didn't know any Serbs and wouldn't have gotten into trouble.

Rusmir came in and showed me pictures of his volleyball team and medals he'd won for ballroom-dancing competitions. He was apparently quite the tango dancer. On his computer was a picture of him with his arm around a pretty brunette girl in a sexy red leotard.

"That's how I get so many dates," he confided, smiling.

"I hope you're all hungry," Amela yelled, calling us to dinner. "The boys are getting the brick oven on the terrace ready for steak and beef sausages."

On the veranda, Ibrahim took the head of the table. My father sat at the other end. I sat between Dad and Eldin. Islamic prayers blasted from a nearby mosque. As a new guest who wanted to be helpful, I volunteered to carry food back and forth with Amela.

"You had quite a trip. Won't you sit down and relax?" she asked.

"I'm used to it. Nobody serves me at home." I had too much nervous energy. As salads and vegetable dishes were passed around, I couldn't wait any longer. "There are questions I always meant to ask you about when we got separated," I told my cousin. "Do you remember that morning at Grandma's house?"

"I'll never forget." Amela nodded. "After you and Eldin rushed home, all our neighbors were frantically leaving. Some packed cars, others fled on foot. We stayed. It was weirdly quiet. Mom was in the village."

I spooned cucumber and onions mixed with sour cream onto my plate. "Where was your brother?"

"Mirza and my dad came back drunk from a barbecue for the Labor Day holiday."

"Wow, how naïve everyone was." Eldin took the roasted peppers.

"We didn't believe anything bad would happen," Dad said.

"Trucks loaded with soldiers crossed the bridge down the hill from our house," Amela said. "The massacres started downtown on Saturday afternoon, in front of the police station. Muslims were being murdered on the street. Everyone was screaming."

My mouth went dry. I had never heard this story before. "What did you do?" I leaned forward on the cushioned chair. Eldin inched closer to Amela. Dad stopped chewing his okra and rice.

"Ibrahim sent an ambulance to get me to his summer house in Maoča." That was the Bosniak area half an hour south of Brčko that became free territory.

Ibrahim took over the story, speaking slowly, as if he didn't want to remember. "First I got my mother, my sister, and her kids to the house. I figured soldiers wouldn't stop an ambulance." He reached for the scotch bottle, refilling our glasses.

"You weren't driving your car?" I wanted to get the whole picture.

"I figured a thirty-one-year-old Bosniak man in a civilian car could be stopped and killed," he said. "If anything happened to me, Amela would have no way out."

Before the war I'd heard from my mom that Amela was dating an older guy. But I'd never met him and hadn't known he was fourteen years Amela's senior, roughly the age difference between my father and mother. "Did Mirza come too?"

"No, Mirza and Dad went back to the house to get our things first," Amela said.

"How nuts. Did they know they missed the paramilitaries by a hair?" I tapped my heel on the floor and took another sip of whiskey, biting down on the ice.

Amela poured herself club soda. "Years later, an old lady who lived nearby said we left minutes before the street was taken over. Whoever stayed was killed on the spot, or taken to Partizan Sports Hall, Luka, or the police station to be shot there."

Dad gasped, clasping his hands in front of him.

"So you all escaped to the summer house in Maoča?" Eldin asked.

"Ten of us crowded into two bedrooms there." Amela stood up to get us bread and napkins as her boys turned the sausages on the grill.

"Mirza joined the resistance," Ibrahim added. "He was twenty when he picked up a gun. He was in a reconnaissance squad and told us stories of hiding in the bushes. Serbs frantically fired into the woods, yelling for anyone to come out. Mirza said the Bosniaks would wait until Serbs sat at the campfire at night, then ambush them."

"I wish I would have fought," Eldin lamented. He'd been eighteen. He had a worse case of survivor's guilt than I did.

"Once Mirza came over, bloody with rose thorns on his face and neck, shivering from cold and wet snow," Amela said. "He'd walked four hours from a trench to give his wife and newborn baby a piece of bread. He said he had to run through a field. He was the only one who made it to the road."

"Damn," Eldin and I said at the same time. I imagined the different lives we'd have had if we'd gone with Amela that morning. Eldin would have been a soldier. I might have helped Ibrahim in the hospital. If so, I could have been a doctor now too. Dad had wanted me to go to the University of Sarajevo, his alma mater. Medical programs in the Balkans were shorter and cheaper than in the United States. Sometimes at my job, I wished I was an orthopedic surgeon working with athletes. Then, instead of feeling invisible, as I often did in Manhattan, I'd be popular like my father was, as the unofficial mayor of Brčko. Or revered like Ibrahim, who I'd heard was seen as the Bosnian Dr. Oz.

"Ibrahim delivered supplies from Croatia," Amela said as she got up to serve the meat. "The trip was normally five minutes across the Sava Bridge. After it was cut in half, it took three days. He picked the longest possible route so as not to fall into enemy hands."

"What did you guys bring back?" I was excited to hear more of brave Bosnian soldiers in my own family, still wanting to feel part of the resistance.

"I stuffed my medical van inside out with medicine and supplies," Ibrahim said. "I was out of school. Instead of fighting, I treated our soldiers. On the way back, we didn't know who'd be in control of the checkpoints. Luckily they were all on our side."

I imagined Bosniak military men waving us through checkpoints instead of the nasty armed soldiers we'd been threatened by.

"We heard they were torturing and raping Muslim women." Amela lowered her voice. "Ibrahim said he'd never let them take me alive or have us separated. He held my hand, keeping his grenade close to his body in the driver's seat in case." Fear flickered in her eyes as she recalled this suicide pact. "Thank God, we made it back to Maoča. But we were shelled when we got there. When I went outdoors to hang shirts to dry, I heard a roar and saw a low dot in the sky get bigger as it approached. It was a fighter jet. Mortars firing all the way from Brčko bombed the mosque below us."

Tidja dug the middle out of a slice of bread. "I hate crust," she said. She sipped her glass of Coca-Cola, then sang a song. I wondered if she understood this was the worst scene from her parents' past or just thought we were discussing a movie.

"It depresses me for days when I drive by our military cemetery. The parents of my classmates come by to see their dead sons." Ibrahim squinted at the thought.

"A dead body with a bullet seemed human and respectable compared to the ones that were mutilated," Amela said.

"Some were naked, missing a penis, ears, or eyes, or had a slit throat." Ibrahim shook his head. I was stunned he said this in front of his children. I looked at Tidja. It went right past her; she was still singing.

I whispered to Ibrahim so Tidja wouldn't hear, "Dad's friend who fought in Brčko said he'd seen a Bosniak so out of his mind that he tied a dead Serb soldier to the back of his tractor and drove around until only the leg was left."

"If he didn't get me and Grandma out, it would've been over." Amela put her hands on her husband's shoulders, rubbing them gently.

So he was a doctor who saved wounded soldiers, and her personal hero too. I was proud he was in our clan. But what had I done? I'd never seen combat or rescued anyone. I didn't feel I had a right to speak of the war in front of military men or medics who'd been on the front line. All I did now was help people in New York recover from injuries. Still, I'd felt fulfilled watching a sixteen-year-old athlete I treated return to his football team after a bad knee injury and seeing a woman client with a herniated disc heal her dropped foot. When Dad ruptured his Achilles, I put him through a twice-a-day exercise routine that allowed him to walk well again. That felt like an accomplishment. But I always wished I could do more, to make up for what I couldn't do in Bosnia.

Amela added, "I thought we were just going to Maoča for the weekend. We wound up tying the knot there, had kids, and stayed for twelve years."

"When did you get married?"

"December 1993. During the ceremony, bombs whistled over our heads." She laughed. "A notary public came to the house. Ibrahim's aunt and uncle were the only ones there. That night he had to go help the wounded."

"You must have seen insane stuff as a medic," Eldin said, wanting to hear more too, clearly also feeling vicarious pride in Amela's husband's heroism.

"For three years we were never safe. They shelled the villages all the time. There were daily catastrophes," Ibrahim said. "I watched so many of our people die."

"When I walked by my school, near the military base, I saw them fire howitzer cannons in your direction," I told Amela." I prayed the mortar wasn't hitting you."

"We had no idea if you'd survived," she said.

"I was hurt you never kept in touch with me," I surprised myself by confessing. As a twelve-year-old boy, I'd decided she must have forgotten all about me.

"The phone lines were cut; there was no way of communicating. For three years we had no electricity or telephones," she said. "But you never left our minds."

It pleased me to hear they'd been concerned about us back then. But there was something else I needed to know before I could cross the item off my list. During the war, I'd heard of many Bosniaks who'd requested that their relatives join them. "Did you ever try to contact us through the free territory radio? Or enter our names in the prison exchange?"

"Yes, we tried several times to put you on the civilian list," Amela said. "But there were no rules. It was chaotic."

"Oh you did? Really?" I moved my chair closer.

"They told us that since Eldin and your dad were fighting age, they wouldn't release them to come to our side," Ibrahim explained.

"We wanted to help you, Kendji," she said. "Yet it was so crazy. Everyone was scattered. I loved you like a kid brother. But I had my own baby to take care of and worried every day whether we'd survive."

So she had attempted to save us. She didn't forget us. She just had her own troubles. I leaned against the cushioned chair, feeling a cathartic sense of relief and the juvenile comfort of being cared for as a kid, as if I was now both ages at the same time.

"We didn't know you were alive until we got Uncle Ahmet's letter that you were in Austria with him," she said.

"It was the only place where we knew someone who would take us in," I explained.

Amela stood up, holding an empty platter. "What else can I get you?"

"Just some water," I said.

She came out of the kitchen with a few small bottles of spring water and handed me one. "So where did you live in Vienna?" she asked.

"With this really nice wealthy family who helped us out," I said. "Beautiful city, if you had money. The Austrians were great. They gave us monthly schillings. I spent my whole allowance on Viennese pastries."

"Since Austria's on the border, tons of Balkanites drove in to get supplies," Eldin told her. "Kenan and I hung out at this army store where Serbs, Bosnians, and Croats bought uniforms, bandages, boots, and helmets. They'd just glare at each other. Man, we wanted to gear up and join them."

"How did you get to America?" Ibrahim asked.

"The people we stayed with knew the Austrian ambassador," Dad said. "Eldin and I did his gardening. We had a shot to go to Melbourne or Quebec. But then this officer at the American Embassy came through with an offer to get us to Connecticut."

My father's penchant for taking whatever labor was available and my mother's insistence on saving Serb documents wound up giving us choices for our new destiny. To think I could have been speaking French or playing cricket now. How random it seemed.

"Why did you wait so long to move back to Brčko?" I asked.

"Our house was destroyed and we couldn't afford to rebuild it. There were daily incidents between ethnic groups at schools, hospitals, post offices. We didn't even get a long-distance phone connection back until 2004."

"Why didn't you call me then?" I untwisted the top of the bottled water and took a sip, thinking that her brother, Mirza, used to write and phone me from Italy, where he'd settled. But I never once heard from Amela.

"You were safe in America," she said. "We had no money. We became the minority. My kids went to school with Serb kids taunting them. I was petrified they'd be beat up—or worse—every single day."

I'd forgotten how dangerous Brčko was long after the war. American troops fixed the Sava River Bridge and kept the peace between Serbs and Bosniaks until 1999. When they left, animosities boiled over. With bank accounts vanished, life savings were wiped out—no jobs, no money, little help. We weren't the only ones who had a rough time starting over.

By the time Amela phoned us in Connecticut in 2007, the day my mom died, I was out of college. She'd offered me, Eldin, and Dad her condolences. I hadn't heard my favorite cousin's voice in fifteen years. I felt bitter that it took the emergency of my mother's death to prompt an obligatory sympathy call. Amela asked when we were visiting Bosnia. I said, "Never." At the time it was an honest answer.

I was a single American guy in Queens while she'd become a wife and mother in Brčko. We had nothing in common anymore. I was filled with anger and self-pity after losing my mother and grandmother at the same time. When I was with my girlfriend, Nicole—who cooked and cared for me—I'd felt consoled. But after she split, I somehow threw Nicole, my mom, my grandma, and Amela into the pile of women I'd loved but was abandoned by. It felt like my life story. Too much was taken from me again. So in my blustery attitude, I thought: who needed women anyway? I just shut down emotionally.

"You wanting nothing to do with this country meant you didn't want us either. When you said you'd never visit, I felt insulted," Amela said. "We were still here, struggling. It was like you just . . . erased us."

I nodded, taking a long sip of water, astonished by her words, embarrassed that she was right. I'd thought we were the ones who'd suffered more, torn from everything we'd known, sudden strangers in a new town with no friends or family, having to start everything over—penniless, car-less, petrified, stuck in other people's houses with a strange accent and foreign tongue. I'd flown back to my homeland still feeling rejected and bruised and twelve. I'd expected apologies and atonement to heal my old wounds. I had no idea I'd been insensitive myself. I'd been so myopic, I didn't even know that I'd neglected my closest relatives.

"I'm sorry," I told Amela. "We got lost in our own lives. Money problems, school loans, Mom dying, Dad sick. I didn't understand what you were going through."

But now I saw why the gates hadn't swung open until I'd called two weeks ago, to say we were coming to visit. I could finally cross this item off my list. I had learned why Amela and I had lost touch: It was my fault.

Our journey back to each other was a twisted, confusing circle that took nineteen years to complete. In many ways, she'd had it worse than I did. She didn't get to go to college or grad school, while I'd spent six years beer-ponging with my buddies. I'd had a job and a cell phone. I should have been checking to make sure her kids were okay. I vowed to never again ignore my Bosnian blood. Instead of clinging to my hurt and viewing my old country as a horror show of bad memories to avoid, I saw that I could never be finished with my homeland. Bisera, Amela, and her children were here; this place was part of me. Bosnia was not an item on a list that I could check off and forget.

"Let's not waste any more time. I'm going to call you on a weekly basis," I promised Amela. "I'll phone and Skype with the kids and find free phone applications and send you pictures. We need to be in touch all the time."

"I want photos of New York and where you work and live and hang out," she said.

Taking videos and photographs at her house, I couldn't wait to add the new generation of faces to my mother's albums. I'd inherited her role: the archivist of the Trebinčevićs. I had Eldin take one photo of Amela's boys on both sides of Dad with me and Tidja in front. She wrapped her arms around my neck and rested her head on my shoulder as if we belonged together, as if there was nothing lost that couldn't be recovered. Then she grabbed my camera and took a picture of me.

"It makes me so happy that you and Amela have reunited," Ibrahim pulled me aside to say. "She doesn't have many relatives left she feels close to. You have no idea how important this is for her."

Tidja came up behind me, tickling my face with the feather of a peacock she'd played with at Bisera's. "Will you come back tomorrow?" she asked.

Amela and Ibrahim were our most successful kin. Yet even as a well-respected internist, he earned only $2,000 a month, less than a third of what I made. Still, in Bosnia, that had bought him this gorgeous house. I hoped someday I could afford this much room for a wife and kids. Even so, Ibrahim said he was running for political office to represent the Social Democratic Party (SDP) because being a representative paid twice as much as being a doctor.

"That's a multiethnic group, including Serbs who aren't nationalists," Eldin explained as the two of us stood outside on the terrace together.

"I don't think Muslims sharing political power will prevent more mass murders here," I told my brother. "Bosnia should become a member of NATO. That's the only way to stop another genocide."

"I know. That's why Serbs refuse and want to stay separate from us," Eldin said. "So they can keep their dream of Greater Serbia alive."

My brother and I had long been in agreement that an unjust peace accord, the same ethnic hatreds, a lousy economy, and corrupt politicians could only add up to trouble.

"A war could break out here tomorrow," I told him. If that happened, I wondered if Eldin and I would come back to fight.

My brother was obviously thinking the same thing. "But this time we have a stacked army and we won't be surprised again," he said. "We'll finish what they wouldn't let us do last time."

Suddenly I understood the Israelis' military mandate to remain prepared at all times. Being armed and ready to win was the best insurance that we would never be victims again.

After finishing another huge meal, with more of Ibrahim's homemade moonshine and whiskey, I felt like I'd consumed enough Balkan food and liquor in one day to make up for all my past hunger. Both Amela's and Zorica's cooking had the same spices and salty taste, befitting two peoples who had lived side by side for centuries. Both meals had been served by warm, nurturing women who spoke my language, reminding me of my mother. I had to stop being a twelve-year-old, irrationally angry at her for my ruined boyhood and, even worse, for her illness and death, which made me feel she'd abandoned me. In each antiquated image I'd reclaimed, my mom was holding me close, looking at me adoringly. She'd been there when I needed her most. Now it was my turn to take care of the relatives I loved.

"I can get us all donuts from the bakery across the street," I offered.

"How dare you!" Amela yelled. "I'm going to make you some right now."

She marched to the kitchen. Women in my family were dangerous cooks, most famous for whipping up desserts from scratch. Within a half hour, Amela magically created a batch of breaded, plum-stuffed donuts with fruit so hot they burned yet delighted my tongue. I hadn't eaten this delicacy in twenty years, since Bisera had made it for me as a kid. It tasted sweet and crunchy and rough, like my childhood.

Dad downed four donuts in a row; he had a sweet tooth like I did.

"Don't eat so much sugar," I scolded. "I don't want you getting diabetes."

"What about you?" Eldin said. "I never saw you eat so much."

"I feel like a python who ate a deer." I must have gained three pounds in one day.

I bet Zorica, Bisera, and Amela saw me as a motherless boy, and were feeding me to compensate for my loss. It worked, I was full, sated. I kept noticing how much Amela looked like my mother before she got sick. Mom was born in August 1955. Amela was born in August 1974. She was thirty-seven, the same age my mom was during the war. No wonder I couldn't stop looking at her. And staring at Tidja, her spitting image, was like seeing my mom as a child. Tipsy, I had the feeling that I was growing older while watching my mother's faces getting younger all around me. I poured myself another whiskey and put my feet on the ottoman. I felt happy again in my homeland. I'd rejoined my family as a grown-up.

I couldn't believe tomorrow would be our last day in Bosnia. It felt too soon to go. I changed my mind and decided that if I died today, I didn't want to be buried in America. I should be laid to rest here, with my relatives in the Islamic cemetery, near my grandparents. If I could afford it, I would bring my father back here too. It was where we belonged.

"Isn't Bisera meeting us here?" I asked.

"She called to say she's not feeling well," Amela said.

"What's wrong?"

"She had blood in her stool," my cousin told me quietly.

My stomach tightened.

Amela looked worried. "Ibrahim said I should take her to the hospital for tests. Do you think it could be serious?"

My bones told me it was. This was the downside of our shared legacy. When we were alone, I'd have to remind Amela that our mothers, who were sisters, and all the females in our family had a genetic predisposition to ovarian cancer. I was afraid that Bisera had the same disease that slowly took my mother away.

"There's one day from the war that haunts me," Amela said before we left. "I was out with Kemal in the stroller, next to a woman holding her baby son and daughter. One second after I went inside, mortars exploded and both of her children were dead."

I looked over at my young cousins. If Amela had stayed outside a minute longer, I would have lost her then. Her other kids wouldn't have been born.

I thought of all the close calls when we should have perished: The explosion near Grandma's house that killed so many people by the bridge. My teacher Milutin holding his rifle, the one that jammed, to my head. The Chetnik guerrilla we thought would shoot us in the back. Dad and Eldin dragged to Luka where Ranko, the mass murderer, singled them out, not for brutality but for protection. Mom pulling Dad and my brother off a bus just before they were shipped to another death camp. Aunt Bisera bending over when a bullet whizzed by her back, just barely missing her. The Serb soldier who ordered us off the Vienna bus at gunpoint.

"We're the only Muslim family I know who didn't lose anyone in the war," I said. "Someone must have been watching over us." I wasn't sure if it was Allah, or the Bosniak doctor who gave us the good-luck charm he'd prayed on to hang on our door. Or my mother's indomitable will.

I put my arm around Amela. For the first time, instead of being angry and resentful that we'd been displaced, I saw that we might have actually been the luckiest Muslims in Brčko after all.

CHAPTER ELEVEN

My Father's Loss

Norwalk, Connecticut
January 2001

"Ready to get destroyed, Ken-dog?" asked my best friend Eugene, a Jewish genius with a light Slavic accent.

"Yeah, it's Thirsty Thursday. Time to get drizzed, you *malakas*," our other roommate, Kostas, said, calling us jerk-offs in Greek, looking goofy in his Hooters T-shirt and recently dyed blond hair. He put Limp Bizkit on the stereo. "Say good-bye to Bugs," he told Danny, a skinny Portuguese Catholic geek who was getting stoned as Kostas turned Bugs Bunny off our big-screen TV.

Eugene handed out Milwaukee's Bests for our toast. I turned on the black light above the television. Its fluorescent bulb glowed purple, highlighting twenty *Maxim* bikini covers lining the wall and my poster of a scantily dressed Anna Kournikova taped to the ceiling. Man, I loved college. Especially living here with my loyal buddies—except for the piles of laundry the slobs left on the floor. I was the neatest. The other guys' moms brought food when they visited; mine came with cleaning supplies and started scrubbing. Unless she was feeling too sick. But I refused to think about my mom's illness and our money problems right now. I had no Friday classes. This weekend I just wanted to be a normal twenty-year-old junior with a cool girlfriend and great buddies to drink endless beers with.

Of the four University of Hartford suitemates I'd chosen, it was no coincidence that three were foreign-born. In my international posse, I was the Bosnian Muslim athlete, at six feet and 165 pounds, in my best shape ever. I played soccer weekly with Eugene, a bespectacled, brown-haired braino whose dad had been an engineer in Belarus. His family had been thrown out of Russia in 1990 and exiled to a roach-infested shithole in Brooklyn. It took a decade for them to get reestablished here. When he invited me to his new home for Rosh Hashanah, Hanukkah, and Passover, I saw his mother was just like mine: a spotless homemaker and serious cook who fed me latkes with applesauce and matzoh ball soup and kreplach that tasted like my mom's *ćevapi*. Of the fifty-five students in our six-year physical therapy program, Eugene and I were the only ones learning science in a second language.

The most gregarious of our bunch was Kostas, a charming Orthodox Christian ladies' man who studied business. We nicknamed him "Socrates" because he liked to spout his (sometimes nutty) philosophies on everything. When we first discussed how the Greeks and Serbs shared a religion, he'd said, "I hate *your* Serb fuckers. We're not the same." Then he asked what I'd seen in the war.

"Dodging gunfire at twelve, a bullet nicked my forehead," I coughed up. "A Chetnik guerrilla pointed his rifle in my face. Saw dead mangled bodies driven by on meat trucks."

"Mad props for what you survived, man. You're my hero," he'd said. "You know, what they did to you, the Turks did to us."

Kostas's mom had a brain tumor. Though he rarely talked about her, he always asked how my mother was doing. I'd tell him when she finished a round of chemotherapy or was starting a new drug treatment. We were secretly linked by the dual roles nobody else knew we were juggling: jovial American students by day, nervous immigrant sons worried sick over their ill mothers by night. I decided we had the kind of covalent bond I was studying in chemistry class, held together with shared electrons, hard to break.

Danny, our shiest suitemate, was a six-foot-tall computer major with an olive complexion and black hair. His conservative Catholic mom freaked out when she saw our half-naked posters and his ripped jeans.

"Why do you wear clothes with holes in them?" she'd yelled. "We can afford new."

"Mom, they came like this. We're not in a small village in Portugal anymore."

"You spend money for torn pants? That's what I teach you?" She'd started crying.

I'd come out of the shower to catch their fight. I went back and showered again.

I felt comfortable and protected in this melting pot in the middle of Connecticut, though I could afford the tuition only with financial aid, student loans, and a merit grant that meant I had to keep up my grade point average to at least 3.91. Unlike the rich frat boys slated to join their daddies' hedge funds after graduation, my suitemates and I were acutely aware of the sacrifices our families made to get us to this country. Each night we called home. Kostas spoke Greek on the phone to his *mitera*, Danny shared Portuguese with his *mae*, Eugene talked in Russian with his *mama*. I'd catch up with my *mati* in Bosnian. When I couldn't handle hearing how rough her chemo was, I'd try to get her to feel more upbeat, asking about Shadow, our feisty little orange-haired adopted Pomeranian, whom she'd take on long walks to the beach to chase seagulls.

"Don't tell me, you're calling your mommy again?" a New York–bred neighbor across the hall ribbed me. "The whole point of going away to college is to escape your family."

He had no idea the real enemies I'd escaped from. Or how much I worried my mother would die at forty-seven and I'd never get to talk to her again. I thanked God every day my parents hadn't been murdered in Bosnia. I could have been stuck in a Balkan orphanage, growing up with Muslim kids who had no living relatives left and Serb soldiers' rape-babies who'd been abandoned in shame. I couldn't relate to the superficial rebellions of some of my classmates.

"Another international crisis?" asked Matt, our token native-born American. When he heard us all on the phone, he always assumed we were fighting since our original tongues sounded brusque and combative to his ear. He was a chubby, witty Jewish business student with a buzz cut who, I noted, called his folks in Pennsylvania only once a week. Matt would tease me and say, "Hey man, could you please speak English? You need to assimilate already." Since I didn't have a car, he drove me to get groceries, haircuts, dental surgery, and home for the holidays. When I stupidly broke my wrist playing beer pong, he was the one who'd waited with me for four hours in the emergency room.

These guys had my back.

"Hey, Ken-dog, Molly and Rachel want to meet us at my frat house later," Eugene suggested. "You up for it?"

I nodded. Eugene and I liked to double-date since Rachel and Molly were both in our program. I said sure, though I wasn't an official fraternity member like most of the 5,000 students on campus. The richest frat was filled with Jewish and Catholic suburban kids. Another was upper-middle-class New England natives. A third house seemed a poorer and scrappier mix of Irish guys and Jews, with a few blacks thrown in. The divisions reminded me of Yugoslavia. While the Balkans split along lines of religion and ethnicity, here the fraternities seemed to be divided by money and class. Instead of crosses, mezuzahs, or the Islamic symbol of a star and crescent moon (as I sometimes wore around my neck), your car showed your identity. The used navy Volvo I'd left in my parents' driveway wouldn't have fit with all the Mercedeses and BMWs in the school's parking lot. I longed for nice wheels too, vowing to buy myself a good car someday.

As the guys drank and played video games, I e-mailed Rachel: "Up for a party later?" adding, "Stay at your place tonight?"

In high school I'd wound up in bed with a cute cheerleader a few times. But Rachel was my first real girlfriend. She was a brainy New Jersey brunette who wore pink lip gloss and lilac nail polish. Her mom was a Polish Jew whose relatives survived the Holocaust. People banished from their countries intrigued me; our shared histories made me feel less alone. Rachel always brought me Gatorade punch on the football field—that was how I knew she was into me. After I got my U.S. citizenship in 2001, she and the guys threw me a red, white, and blue party with balloons, flags, and a "Welcome to the American Dream" poster.

Before I changed clothes to meet up with Rachel, I planned to call my parents. But at 9:30, my landline rang. It was my father's factory boss. Something was wrong. Had Mom been rushed to the emergency room again?

"Kenan," Dad's boss said in a solemn tone. "Your father had a stroke. You need to get to the hospital now."

I squeezed the receiver, in shock. I'd expected another setback in my mother's battle with cancer. But my sixty-two-year-old dad—who never even got colds—was strong as a bull. My face must have gone pale because my roommates were all staring at me.

"Yo, what's up?" Danny paused his video game. Kostas turned the music off.

"I need a favor," I told Matt, my voice cracking. "I have to get to Norwalk Hospital."

I left Rachel a message: "Have to cancel. My dad's sick. Going home. Sorry."

Matt grabbed his keys and led me to the parking lot without a word. On the two-hour drive through the darkness, I felt torn, not wanting to leave the dumb bliss of a perfect college weekend to deal with another family catastrophe. Then I hated myself for not feeling compassion for my father. He'd dodged armed enemies and betrayers to get us out of Bosnia safe, without ever picking up a gun. For the last eight years he'd humbled himself every day to pay for our food and shelter in a new country. Why couldn't I focus on that? Because I was sick of being mature and fed up with all the bad news.

A year before, Mom had been rushed to this same ER with abdominal pain. She'd recovered from breast cancer, but a CAT scan found a tumor on her ovary. After a hysterectomy, she needed a brutal course of chemo. She had to drive herself to and from the treatments, since nobody else was available. My parents insisted that my brother and I stay at school and not move back home. Eldin was still living on the Long Island campus of Stony Brook, finishing his graduate studies. Dad only made $25,000 at the fruit-cup factory, but he had health insurance. On early mornings and weekends, he painted houses for a few hundred bucks a pop. Now, on the way to the hospital where Mom was still getting her weekly chemo, I felt guilty and helpless. Working so many hours at menial labor was killing both of my parents, grinding them down in a series of rotating medical disasters I couldn't save them from.

"You okay, Ken-dog?" Matt asked as he parked in the hospital lot.

"Not really."

I ran to the intensive care unit, irrationally rushing to speak with my father. I found him lying in a coma with tubes stuck in his mouth and flabby arms. He was so pale and skinny, he looked already dead. I joined Eldin, Mom, and the doctor in the hallway. Matt leaned against a wall in the corner, not wanting to intrude. I waved him over. After all, my college buddies were my family too. I had nobody else in this country.

"If I were you, I'd pull the plug," the neurosurgeon said.

His advice stunned me. I thought America was supposed to have great health care and not let people die. Even emergency room care here was a million times better than in Bosnia during and after the war. Mom looked over Dr. Williams's shoulder toward the ICU as if she didn't trust the doctor and needed Dad's advice on what to do.

"He's breathing on his own," the doctor told me. "Surgery could drain the intracranial pressure, but it's too risky. He probably wouldn't make it. Even if he survived, the whole right side of his body would be paralyzed."

I refused to listen. The fact that Dad could breathe with no tube gave me hope. If he wasn't brain-dead, he could wake up. Eldin tried to console my mother in Bosnian. But his eyes were clouded in despair, probably thinking what I was: how many calamities could we take? I leaned on the counter at the nurses' station and closed my eyes. Mom asked for water. Her treatments often made her nauseous. How old and tired she looked, her face bloated from steroids. The chemo had stripped away her long blond hair. Short strands had grown back a dry reddish brown. She'd aged decades in the eight years since we'd left Bosnia. Who would take care of her now that Dad was too sick? I was afraid that I would have to leave school, and that seeing my father this sick would drain my mother of the little strength she had left. But she turned to the doctor and said, in perfect English, "Don't be ridiculous. We will never pull the plug on Keka!"

The doctor rolled his eyes. I felt like he was thinking, *You're not only an ignorant foreigner, but you're out of your mind.* I thought of the other people here who'd underestimated us: the Connecticut church lady who asked my mom if she knew what a washing machine was, the high school guidance counselor who advised me to be a mechanic because science would be too hard for me to learn in a new language.

"Remind your mom how long he was passed out before she found him," Dr. Williams told me. "Six hours. The longer someone's untreated, the more irreparable the damage." The doctor crossed his arms, seemingly annoyed that we weren't heeding his warning: if Dad came out of his coma, he'd be a vegetable forever.

"He will be fine!" Mom insisted, crossing *her* arms. "Keka is a very strong man."

She later told us, in Bosnian, how Dad had returned home from his house-painting job at eleven that morning, had his lunch, then changed for the factory. She'd left for her doctor's appointment. When she got home at half past five, she was confused to see his car still in the driveway. Upstairs in the bedroom, she found him on the bed, face up, his feet resting on the floor. His arms were spread out, his eyes rolled back into his head, his mouth open, vomit everywhere. She couldn't wake him. She'd followed Dad's ambulance in her red Dodge.

"But Dad never had high blood pressure," I told the doctor in the hall. "He wasn't a smoker or drinker. He was in good shape, aside from falling asleep in between his two jobs. He'd come home exhausted, worried about finances. Do you think stress caused this?" I asked, as if logic could fix his brain damage.

"He had a weak artery in the brain that burst," Dr. Williams said.

"His mother had a stroke," I recalled.

"Who knows? Could be genetic. These things happen."

I was reluctant to accept the doctor's assessment—until Eldin sneaked a look at Dad's chart on the counter of the nurses' station and read it to me. "Middle cerebral artery, cerebral edema, intracranial pressure, hemiparesis, hemiplegia, facial droop, Broca's and Wernicke's aphasia."

"Shit." From my class on neurological pathologies, I knew how dire it was. He'd never come out of this as himself. Nobody could.

"What are you guys, doctors?" the neurosurgeon asked in a condescending tone.

"We're both in school for physical therapy. I just came from a neuroscience exam." I read my father's thick chart, filled with test results from his CT scan, PET scan, EKG. When other physicians confirmed Dr. Williams's pessimistic prediction, it hit me that we might be losing my dad. I felt winded and had to sit down.

"Will you break the news to Mom?" I asked Eldin.

"That his brain is fried and won't ever get unfried?" His tone was bitter.

"His right side could be paralyzed," he told Mom, in Bosnian, as she joined us outside Dad's room. "Even if he comes out of the coma, he won't be able to chew food or speak normally. His language is damaged."

"So he won't read or understand or talk well?" she asked. I nodded. She bawled, then wiped her eyes with Kleenex and said, "I don't care. I'll take care of him. Nobody pulls any plug on Keka."

A month later, he woke up. He didn't recognize anyone or know where he was. He was thrashing around. Mom phoned me at school, hysterical: the nurses had tied him down.

"It's for his own good, so he doesn't fall on his face," I told her.

"He's no prisoner," she insisted. Since she was on medical leave from work, she came to the hospital every day at 7:00 a.m. He was moved from the ICU to the rehab wing, where she'd clean him up, shave and bathe him with moist pads. When he'd speak gibberish, she'd answer as if they were having a nice talk. She taped pictures of us around his room so he'd remember us. He learned to recognize her but couldn't say her name.

The first few times I visited, he didn't know who I was. He looked at me like I was a hospital employee. It shattered my heart that Dad didn't remember me anymore, that we'd never again have a conversation. We hadn't talked in two months, the longest we'd ever not spoken. I couldn't call him from school. He didn't even know what a phone was.

"Patients neglect their weaker side," I told Mom as she fed him, sharing what I'd learned in class. "So force him to pick up things with his other hand."

She put a spoon between his right fingers. He tried but spilled his applesauce on his blue hospital gown. He burst out crying, then hit himself on the forehead from frustration. I'd never seen my father cry before. I hated it. I sensed he understood what was happening to him and was embarrassed. Of all we'd survived, I feared this was the blow we couldn't recover from.

Mom told him to slow down. "Keka, *polako*." She rubbed his hair to calm him. He tried again, holding the utensil steady for a little longer.

Six weeks later, when I was on spring break in March, Dad seemed to be improving. He still didn't know who I was, yet he stared at me intently, as if he recognized me but wasn't yet sure from where. He'd started working out. He hadn't been able to take the time to exercise since we'd left Bosnia. Now, Mom told me, he'd sit on the edge of his bed and pump his arms. Still weak, he'd walk up and down the hallway, smiling and greeting the nurses in a made-up language of garbled Bosnian, along with a friendly "hi" in English.

In the rehab room, I watched him spinning an arm machine. He couldn't raise his right arm or leg, he had a facial droop, and his motions were uncoordinated. Yet he was so focused you'd think he was competing in an Olympic race. He counted in Bosnian out of order: "*jedan, dva, tri, ćetir, pet, dva, osam, jedan.*" I winced; he seemed like a disabled child.

As he spun away on his arm-bike, Dad glanced up and saw me. I waved, bracing myself for him not to know me again. But he stood up abruptly, with a surprised and thrilled expression on his face, as if he were being reunited with someone important to him that he hadn't seen in ages. His eyes widened and his mouth opened. "*Sine!*" He yelled the word for "son" in Bosnian.

"Yes. It's me! Your son!" I pointed to my chest. "I'm here, Dad! It's Kenan!"

"Ke-Ke," he tried. We slapped our palms together, like we'd just won a big sports championship. Then we hit each other on the shoulder and hugged. I held on longer than usual, overcome with joy that I had my dad back.

He broke away and pointed to his temple, gesturing with a clenched fist, squeezing his palms open and shut, muttering incoherent sounds, making a "boom" noise by clapping his hands. He was trying to tell me that his head had exploded, sharing the story in his new made-up tongue.

It was a rough spring break. When I returned to school, I got hit by a second blow. Rachel came to my dorm room but didn't kiss me hello. She took a seat on the couch across from me.

"My mom doesn't want me to date a Muslim guy," she said with no preface.

"Why?" I felt my stomach tighten. I'd been kicked out of the Balkans because of my religion. Now I was being thrown out of Rachel's bed for the same reason?

"She doesn't want me with a non-Jew. She was crying about it."

Rachel and I had been good friends for a year before we went out. I'd met her Polish mother and thought we'd bonded over our Eastern European backgrounds. But I was only good enough to be Rachel's friend, not her lover, even though I was a gentleman who held doors and treated on dates, like Dad taught me. When Rachel was sick, I'd instant-messaged to see if she needed medicine. The thought that her mother cried because we were dating made me wish we'd never met. After all this time I couldn't believe she didn't see why I'd find her words devastating.

"Did you tell her that's unfair?" I yelled. "Did you defend me?"

She didn't answer. All of a sudden I was far away from Rachel and my Connecticut dorm and my new country. I was back in Brčko with Igor, Velibor, and Dalibor. I was adding her to the list of betrayers who'd rejected me as a kid.

"You should go." I couldn't look in her eyes.

After she left, I went to Eugene's room. "Since I'm not a Jew, I'm not good enough for Rachel."

"It's not you, man." He looked up from his computer and took his glasses off. "My mother hates that Molly's Catholic. She always tells me to break up with her. That's just how Jewish mothers are. They're crazy. Don't take it personally."

Kostas burst in and screamed, "Fuck that bitch! I never thought she was good enough for you!"

Danny walked in, hollering, "Her Polish Jewish relatives were thrown out of Europe during the Holocaust! And she shoves you aside for your religion?"

I knew that romantic choices had nothing to do with genocide. But I couldn't be rational. My hurt felt epic. I had close comrades from all races, religions, and ethnicities, but I haven't kissed a Jewish girl since.

Still, I had no doubt true love existed. My parents had never used sweet endearments or exchanged romantic presents. But for six months we watched in awe as my mother healed my father, pouring all of her adoration and energy into getting him back to health. Then, in December, right before I turned twenty-one, we learned that her cancer had spread. Over the next five years as Dad got better, relearning to talk, walk, and cook, she became weaker and weaker. She seemed to be shrinking. Just as we were getting Dad back to his old self, we were losing Mom. He seemed determined to return to strength so he could care for her now.

The last picture of my entire family together was taken by Eugene at our graduation. Sitting in the outdoor auditorium, Eugene asked my father how he was doing. It was a bad day. Dad pointed to himself and said, "Headache." When Eldin said, "You want water?" Dad answered "What's water?"

Mom, pale and nauseated, stood in the shade. "Now that my boys have graduated, I can die in peace," she said.

"Stop saying that," I told her.

She was proud when I landed a fantastic physical therapy job in Manhattan. I'd be working 12:00 to 8:00 p.m., with full benefits and three weeks of vacation. I found a small one-bedroom apartment in Queens near Eldin's. But right before I signed the lease, Mom's cancer metastasized. Her doctor prescribed Valium and a hospice. She refused, wanting to die drug-free at home. I stayed in Westport. For six months, I took the Metro-North from Connecticut to Grand Central to work in the city. On the way back I'd pick up food and bandages, arriving home at ten at night to take over Mom's care from Dad. Then I'd walk Shadow, who took to grabbing the leash in his mouth whenever he saw me arrive. Mornings it was agonizing to hear my mother moan from the burning pain caused by open wounds all over her body. What upset her most was when Shadow, her devoted companion, stopped sleeping next to her, as if he was afraid to be so close to death.

In February, as my mother's breathing became more labored, a hospice nurse began staying overnight. One evening she whispered, "She'll probably fade away by morning." Dad, Eldin, and I stood by as the nurse closed Mom's eyes the last time. The funeral home people took my mother away in a black body bag. Watching her deteriorate and die, we all agreed, was worse than the war.

But for me, the two calamities were intertwined. Studies have shown that the leading cause of death for Bosnian women who survived the war was breast cancer, with malignancy and mortality rates four times as high as their American counterparts. So I blamed the stress of the 1992 conflict for the disease that ravaged her. Was it the smoke and poisonous chemicals used in weapons we breathed when our homeland became a battleground? Or the lack of doctors and screening available in the aftermath, or some deadly combination of factors? Researchers haven't definitively established a correlation. But I saw it as another endless aftershock of the ugly battle in the Balkans that none of us could fully recover from or escape.

At my mother's funeral on February 6, 2007, Dad, Eldin, and I were the only three mourners. The closest Bosnian Muslim cemetery was hours away, so we'd picked a small Arab-run place nearby. The grounds were not well kept. There were none of the flowers she'd loved. My college buddies had wanted to come. But since Muslims bury their dead within twenty-four hours and my friends were dispersed around the country, nobody could make it on time. The three female mourners I really wanted to see were on the other side of the world: Aunt Bisera; her daughter, Amela; and my Grandma Emina, who'd been kept in the dark about her daughter's cancer all these years. My mother had decided not to tell her. "How could an old Bosnian lady help her sick daughter, five thousand miles away?" Mom had asked in her typically self-effacing style.

When I told Bisera, she said, "We'll plan a service here," sobbing into the phone so hard I could barely make out her words. I was too numb to cry. It wasn't fair that my life and Eldin's had improved in this country while my parents' had deteriorated.

"Don't have a big service," I warned Bisera. "Grandma will be in shock. She has horrible arthritis and high blood pressure. She won't be able to handle it."

When our ringing phone later showed Bisera's area code in Bosnia, we learned my premonition had come true. Upon hearing that her fifty-two-year-old youngest girl had died, Grandma Emina dropped dead of a heart attack, right after the service in Brčko. My vision became blurry, but I still couldn't weep.

My college pals arrived from all directions the next day. Eugene's car had New Jersey plates. Kostas was living in Framingham, Massachusetts. Danny had driven from Boston and Matt from Hartford.

That they'd come so far just to spend a few hours cheering me up made me feel loved.

"Yo, I got you," Kostas said, giving me a guy-hug.

"Anything you need, man." Danny put his arm around my shoulder.

"And don't be afraid to talk about it," Matt added.

"We're here for you," Eugene reassured me as they took me out for pizza.

"Your mom let you dress like that?" Kostas asked Danny, pointing to his torn jeans.

"Hey, remember when Danny's mom freaked over his ripped jeans and Ken-dog ran back to take another shower to avoid her?" Eugene said.

"Hey! Why is everyone picking on me?" Danny wanted to know.

"Because you got stoned and watched cartoons for four years," Kostas answered.

We shared more silly memories, but real-world troubles had deepened our bond. We'd all stood together at Kostas's mom's wake the year before. Hers was my first wake; the Greek Orthodox traditional open casket spooked me. I was relieved that our Islamic service didn't display my mother's body.

A week later, our little dog Shadow died. Now tears poured from my eyes, a torrent of shock and built-up grief. I flashed to the Road Runner cartoons I'd liked as a kid in the Balkans, when I'd perversely rooted for the coyote. I felt like him now, the pathetic character who kept losing, no matter what. He got shot, blown up, burned, squashed like a tomato by an anvil landing on his head. The hits kept coming.

Yet there was also relief that Mom's thirteen years of pain in Connecticut were over. She looked so sick in the headshot on her 2007 driver's license, which I still have in my wallet, next to my own. I preferred to picture her back in our apartment in Brčko, young and beautiful as she framed my karate diploma on the day of my big Bosnian tournament in 1991, the last time we were all happy.

Amazingly my father, the extraordinarily resilient Keka, learned to speak again—in almost fluent Bosnian. Both his motor and language skills miraculously improved when we moved him to Queens, where he could hang out with his old countrymen. Word-wise he completely recovered—everything but his English—which vanished somewhere between his left frontal lobe and his lips. All those years of practice and usage in America just disappeared, as if his stubborn heart took control of his brain, refusing to remember we'd ever been forced to leave our homeland.

CHAPTER TWELVE

Crossing Enemy Lines

Brčko, Bosnia
July 2011

"I have to see Petra again. One last time," I told Eldin. It was Thursday afternoon and we were walking through the entrance of my old Brčko apartment complex, trailing behind Dad. We were on our way to have a last lunch with Truly in our former home.

"That's a really bad idea. You already saw her. You said, 'No one has forgotten.'" Eldin quoted me. "Point made."

I'd listed—and already accomplished and checked off—confronting Petra. Yet now I saw there was so much more to ask and say. Talking about the war with Miloš had lit my brain on fire. If a Serb soldier who'd seen his friends die in battle had no hate and could admit he felt sorry, wouldn't she feel rueful too? I desperately wanted to find out. Both Miloš and Obren—Petra's late husband—had protected my family, whereas Petra stole from us. So she had more reasons for guilt and lament. Did she miss her Muslim neighbors? Yet it was more personal than that. I was suddenly dying to know how she felt seeing me again. Like a lover spurned long ago, I wanted to know if her life was worse without me. Would she confess to feeling guilty about her cruel actions and attempt to apologize for her past sins? Did she have regrets?

"You're going to cause an ethnic commotion in the building and the police will be called," Eldin argued, his teeth clenched. "If it's a Serb cop, you'll be all over him. Then I'll have to get involved and call the American Embassy and you'll upset Dad."

"How are you going to upset me?" my father turned around to ask. He'd been oblivious to our argument, looking around, lost in his thoughts. Or was he was just pretending he didn't hear?

"Don't worry." Eldin herded him toward the stairs. "Let's go find Truly."

As we trudged up the first flight, my father stopped to say hello to a former neighbor on the second-floor landing. I looked at my watch. It was four o'clock. I had only one day left here. Since Truly lived right next door to Petra, I knew, despite Eldin's warnings, that I couldn't resist. "This is my last chance."

"What do you need to speak with Petra about anyway?" Eldin's face was red and ruffled.

"I'll ask if she enjoyed the stuff she stole from Mom. I wonder if she still has anything."

"What if she does? Are you going to steal it back and wind up in jail?"

"I want to see her reaction when I knock on her door," I told him.

"After what you already said to her, she'll refuse to open it."

"I'll wait on the stairs. She has to come out eventually," I said. "I just want her to know we're doing well. That we're better off than everyone else in this building now."

"Why do you fucking care what she thinks?" Eldin was sweating. He pulled his T-shirt away from his chest and blew inside it to cool himself off.

"I need to hear her side of the story," I said as a pretty, dark-haired woman in jeans and a tank top who appeared to be about Eldin's age passed us on the stairs, followed by a little boy with a blond buzz cut. The woman looked vaguely familiar.

"*Dobar dan*," she said, offering a "good day" as she walked by.

"That was Petra's daughter!" Eldin whispered. "She looks just like her father."

I watched her climb to the third floor and go into Petra's place. "Petra's probably home too! I'm going to talk to her," I said.

Eldin shook his head, fuming. "But you already checked her off your damn list."

Inside our old apartment I paced around, practicing what I'd say to Petra. "Did you enjoy trading in your Muslim neighbors for new ones?" I'd ask. "See, you couldn't get rid of us," I'd say. Or I'd spot one of our paintings on her wall and scream, "This looked better over my mother's sofa, you thief!" as I took it back.

I was wired and out of breath. While Eldin and Dad watched soccer with Truly, I worked up my courage. Finally, I slipped out of our apartment and knocked on Petra's door softly so my brother wouldn't hear, remembering how hard the Serb soldiers used to bang on ours.

Petra's daughter opened her door a crack, with the chain still on. Her son came up behind her, wrapping his arms around her leg. Seeing the kid looking scared threw me off. But I wasn't backing down now. My heart was thumping. "Is your mother here?"

"She's not home yet. What do you need?"

"I'm Kenan, your old neighbor. Keka's son. I'm visiting from New York."

"I thought it was you when I walked by!" She opened the door. "Remember me? I'm Jelena."

"Yes, you're tall like your dad," I said. She had his high cheekbones and brown eyes too.

"Not quite as tall, thankfully. He was six foot four." She laughed. "Come in. Look at you. You're a grown man."

"I grew up twenty years ago," I blurted, and she chuckled, catching the war reference.

Her boy continued to cling to her jeans leg, staring up at me. I stood in the tiny hallway that separated the dark, cluttered living room from the kitchen. I flashed to being inside here with my mother in 1992, when Petra invited her over for coffee. It seemed much smaller and more crowded now, half the size of my Queens one-bedroom. I smiled at the boy, who sat down with us at the table, drawing a picture with crayons the way I used to. I scanned the floor for my mother's rug and artwork, but I saw nothing familiar. Just Orthodox Christian paintings and crosses.

"Excuse the walls," Jelena said. "My son leaves fingerprints everywhere." She reached for her boy, smothering him in kisses, the way my mother used to kiss me. I didn't want to like her.

"Who is this sir?" the boy asked his mother politely.

"This is Kenan. He was our neighbor." She patted his head, smiling, then looked at me. "I remember when you were his age. You'd zoom by everyone, skipping stairs, out of breath. You always ran. Mom said you couldn't fall asleep without my dad bringing you jam."

"Your father said I couldn't fall asleep without jam?" I was mesmerized to think of Obren talking about me. I guessed Petra bragged to her daughter that they'd helped Muslims during the war. Obren really had; without him my father—and Jasenko's father—might have gone to Partizan and never returned. I replayed what happened. My father protected Obren at the political meeting in our building right before the war broke out. To thank him, Obren shielded us with his warning. He was a fair man whose actions saved our lives. So did that mean his whole family deserved a pass now?

"Yes, Dad said you needed something sweet to eat before you could fall asleep."

"Ha! I believe that." Though with all the fighting going on, I doubt that anybody slept.

"My parents sent me to stay with my cousins in Germany," Jelena told me. "For safety."

I guessed she was divorced, living with her mom. "Where is Mr. Obren?" I pretended not to know, feeling like a double agent in a James Bond movie.

"He died in 2006 from lung cancer," she said, lighting a cigarette.

"I'm sorry. I remember your dad let me play with his AK-47. He showed me how to load it."

"Really?" She didn't seem the least bit threatened by me, which was disarming. But I was hot and itchy. If I wasn't here for some kind of war restitution, what was this, a social visit?

"Obren saved my dad from being killed at Partizan Sports Hall," I admitted. But she looked blank. I considered telling her that her people had turned our gym into a slaughterhouse to kill my people, but I didn't want to upset her son.

In the kitchen Jelena poured me blueberry juice and put out cookies filled with orange jam. I ate one. I could tell she was a little confused by my presence. I was too. I thought of asking if Jelena knew her mom used to rob Bosniak apartments. But Petra's daughter had done nothing bad to me. I wasn't about to make her ashamed of her mother in front of her little boy. The reason I still hated Petra nineteen years later was because she'd embarrassed my mom in front of me.

When the door opened, I jumped up to greet Petra. But it was my brother, who didn't bother knocking. He rushed in and sat down next to me. Damn it, I didn't need a babysitter. I was stunned that he'd stormed in to abort my mission. She must have wondered who the hell he was.

"I'm Eldin." He reached out his hand to her.

"I remember you," she said as they shook. "You were two years younger than me in school."

I was pissed off. This was my show, not his. Was he worried I was going to toss Petra off her balcony? Was he here to save her, or me? I wanted to storm out and come back alone another time. But I didn't have another time. "So where's your mom?" I asked Jelena, crossing my legs and bouncing my foot up and down. Eldin stared at me, raising his eyebrows.

"She should be coming home from school across the street. Let me call her to tell her she has visitors." Jelena pulled out her cell phone. Two days before, I'd acted threatening to Petra, and she seemed afraid of what I might do. When Jelena told her mom we were here, I feared Petra might say, "Get them out of there now" or "Call the police."

"Mom, you'll never guess who came by to visit. Your old next-door neighbors. Keka's two sons," Jelena said into the receiver. "She'll be right back," Jelena told us. "She's at her hair appointment, but she's going to rush home so she can see you."

I couldn't exhale, as if my trachea was collapsing. I imagined Petra worried for her daughter and grandson, rushing home to protect them. Jelena poured Eldin juice, offering him the cookie plate.

"Oh, tell her not to rush." Eldin gobbled up four cookies quickly. "We should go now."

What? I'd waited two decades for this! He was not going to screw it up because Petra wasn't finished getting a blow-dry. I shot him a look to shut him up. Without words I tried to send him a message: *Get out of here! Leave!* As we all kept chatting, I stared at the front door, tapping my fingers on the table, eating another cookie, nervous to see how Petra would react when she caught me here.

"My favorite place in Brčko to have *ćevapi* is Haso's," Jelena said, letting us know she ventured to the Bosniak side of town to get barbeque by a Muslim chef, as if all Muslims here knew each other. She mentioned Dr. Ćaušević, her son's pediatrician, saying, "I trust him implicitly."

"We know Dr. Ćaušević!" Eldin said. "We just saw him."

"He took care of me from birth," I added, weirdly proud to hear that Petra's daughter and I shared the same hero pediatrician, a man from our faith. It was true that all the Muslims here actually did know each other.

I felt like I had bricks in my stomach. My watch said 4:15. I heard footsteps coming up the stairs. I leaned forward. Finally the door swung open. It was her. Boy, was she done up for a sixty-five-year-old grandmother, with a knee-length beige skirt, purple silk blouse, strappy sandals, and lots of makeup and poufy hair. Such a difference from the first time I'd caught her, two days before, on a chore-filled Sunday. Now here she was after work, dolled up from the beauty shop. I expected her to say, "What the hell are you doing here?"

Instead she said, "Let me look at you handsome men. How long has it been? Twenty years?" She smiled, appearing delighted to see us, and extended her hand.

Was she really glad we'd come? I assumed it was phony social bullshit. Not wanting to play her game, I considered ignoring her attempt at a handshake, as I'd done with Slobodan. But he was a male coming up to me on the street, pretending he hadn't left us to die at a checkpoint. Here I was the one approaching Petra, wanting something from her. I was taught to always be polite to women. Plus Obren's protective aura was hovering. I decided not to disrespect her in her home, in front of her daughter and grandson. Instead I stood up and gave her a formal shake. Eldin followed. Then Petra sat down and lit a long white cigarette, the Bosnian equivalent of Virginia Slims, the brand Jelena was also smoking.

"Who did you come with?" Petra asked in a warm tone.

"Dad's next door. Our family friends are living in our old apartment over the summer," I explained.

"Keka is here? Oh, I've always admired your father. Where is Adisa?" she asked.

"She died of cancer in 2007," I said.

"She suffered for a long time," Eldin added.

"Oh, my dear Adisa. After all you went through, she had to deal with cancer." Petra put her hand on her chest, leaning back into the chair, as if the news of my mother's death caused her pain. She seemed so honestly moved, I almost bought into her mind game. Until I distinctly recalled her taking my mother's skirt and saying with a grin, "You might as well give this to me, you won't be needing it soon. You Muslims will be defeated by next week." What a convincing act Petra was putting on now. She belonged on Broadway.

"I remember when those animals came to kick you out. It was devastating," Petra said.

I was startled she'd called her own people "animals." Was she pretending to be on our side?

"I managed to get your bedsheets and a few paintings. I put them on my wall. Your mother gave them to me," she said. "To hold until you guys came back."

I didn't see any of our artwork here. And I was stunned by her blatant lies. But instead of calling her out, I nodded, fascinated to see where this would go. She was coming across as genuine, as though she believed what she was saying.

"As soon as you left, soldiers knocked on my door, asking whether I took anything." She put out one cigarette, then lit another. I couldn't tell if she was anxious or a chain-smoker, like everyone else we met in the Balkans. "I'd never take things from Adisa that she didn't give me. I swear on my mother's grave. That would be a sin. I told them she'd given me a few things to hold on to for safekeeping. A bunch of police officers and soldiers moved into your apartment. How dare they take your home, those lowlifes."

Did she think Eldin and I were in diapers and didn't remember her stealing from Mom? I wondered if she'd rehearsed this speech for us on the way home from the hair salon or spent twenty years rewriting history. I gathered this was the story she'd reinvented to live with herself.

"So what's it like here now?" I hoped to hear how horrible it was for Serbs living in a garbage-strewn postwar hell of their own making.

"I'm so glad you don't have to deal with the crooked politicians. All the good neighbors left. It's a living disaster," she said. "The new people came from the villages and woods. They get drunk and sing in the bar downstairs every night till four a.m. They howl like wolves." She sounded disgusted. I recalled that Petra had come from a radical Serb village in eastern Bosnia like the ones she was now disassociating herself from.

After World War I, Serbian folk mythology touted as heroes the innocent "mountain men," supernationalists hiding in villages who popped out to rescue poor Serbians from infidels; these myths perpetuated an underdog image that the West by and large bought. The reality was less heroic. During the war, a friend of ours had seen a Brčko house taken over by Serb settlers from the countryside who'd turned the garage into a barn with pigs and cows. When the wife first saw the washing machine, she asked, "What's this metal box?" So did Petra's complaints mean that urban Serbs were now realizing they preferred civilized Muslims like us over their uncouth country cousins? It was a little late. I wondered if the fact that Bosniaks were well educated and cultured had played into the Bosnian war. Before World War II, the German people had resented the prosperity and intellectual achievements of the Jews, which made them an easy scapegoat.

"What are you boys doing now?" Petra asked. "Tell me."

"We went to college and graduate school to be physical therapists in New York," I reported.

"Oh, good work. That's excellent." Her eyes glowed with misplaced pride. "You know those hoodlum friends you used to hang out with? They don't do anything with their lives. They're thirty and waiting to spend their parents' pensions. But you boys made something of yourselves. *Mashallah, mashallah.*" She repeated the Islamic word that meant "God willed it," to praise us. Muslims used the expression the way my roommate Eugene would say "*Mazel tov*" upon hearing good news. I glanced at Eldin. His eyes bugged out, sharing my disbelief. She was saying everything I wanted to hear, validating my life. But even if it was true, I tried to figure out if she was being manipulative, charming me into not being angry—or hurting her. Not that she seemed the least bit worried.

"Looking at Kenan, I see a younger Keka," Petra said. "Where is Obren to feed you your jam? In kindergarten he was like a fly you couldn't catch. He never rested." Jelena laughed as Petra flailed her arms in a flourish, then took a drag of her cigarette.

"You knew me from kindergarten?" I asked.

"Knew you? I was one of your teachers," she said, shocking me again.

"I didn't see you in my school pictures."

"There were different classes," she told me. "I remember how well you used to draw boats on the river at sunset. Waiting for your mom to pick you up after school, you'd play on the seesaw. And Adisa dressed you up so nice when Santa Claus came over the holidays."

Talk about being disarmed. I drank more blueberry juice, completely floored. I had zero recollection of Petra ever being at my school. Yet the details checked out. She knew much more about me than I'd ever known about her. It was bizarre, but Petra was managing to make me feel special, as if out of all the boys, I'd stood out in her memory. If this was a Bond movie, I was being seduced by Pussy Galore.

"You wouldn't believe how different it is here now," she went on. "Dr. Šabanović is the only old neighbor who came back. It's nice to run into him. A great man, from a classy family like yours. Nothing is the same. It'll never be as nice as it was before. But I'm glad you're not stuck here. You're lucky. You look good. You're successful. I'm proud of you."

I took in her monologue, trying to decode each line for the subtext, not sure there was one. She didn't apologize or accept personal blame. Yet in a remorseful tone, she'd acknowledged we were hurt during the war but had succeeded in the end. I had wanted to hate her and stare her down and make her cry out of guilt and shame. But I found her venom toward our replacements and her praise of our classiness oddly gratifying, considering the source.

"So how does your father like New York?" She lit another smoke.

"He loves it," Eldin said. "He's got his crew."

"When are you all coming back here?" she wanted to know.

"Not for a while," Eldin answered.

"Well, I need to see my old neighbor then." She jumped up and strode out the door. Eldin followed. Looking at her little grandson, I took ten marks out of my pocket, the equivalent of about six dollars, and handed it to him. "For ice cream," I said. He smiled and stashed it in his pocket.

"You don't have to," Jelena said.

"My mom said never visit someone empty-handed," I told her.

"Thanks." We shared a friendly good-bye handshake. She had no idea that she'd interrupted my intentions and ruined my plan. Or had she? Watching how sweet Jelena was with her son made her mother more human. It reminded me of my mom in the old days, before the war.

I walked out in time to catch Petra strolling right into our apartment. She still hadn't learned to knock. I followed her inside. She went straight to my father in the living room.

"Oh, look at that well-dressed, handsome man. Keka, it's so good to see you. I'm sorry about Adisa." She hugged and kissed him on the cheek. My father seemed startled. I wondered what he would do. Eldin turned to me, awaiting the verdict.

"Thank you, Petra," said Dad, smiling. He'd immediately recognized her. He didn't return her kiss, but he did hug her back. When in doubt, Dad erred on the side of kindness to everyone, regardless. "Yes, we finally came for a visit."

Before she left, she turned to me. "Come to Mrs. Petra." She gave me a strong embrace. I stiffened. Then she grabbed my face and planted a flurry of kisses on my cheeks, like I was a little boy.

It was easy to lie with words, but her body language seemed open, needy, filled with longing. I stopped pushing away and hugged her back, as if she was one of my relatives here who'd treated me sweetly in peacetime. Or an educator exalting her star pupil. My teacher Milutin had threatened me with his gun; my coach Pero had betrayed my whole family. Petra had stolen from us. Yet I was suddenly proud to accept her praise and affection, turning back into an innocent, well-behaved student, before I'd learned to steal, lie, hate, and hunger for revenge. "You did good for yourself," she said, but the subtext I picked up was: "You did better than the boys who betrayed you. They're a disappointment. They have no future. You had it rougher. You were homeless and had to start over. I'm sorry this happened to you. But you surpassed all your neighbors. You're the clear victor now."

On an unspoken level I felt sure she knew she'd wronged us, felt guilty, and was grateful I'd come over. She couldn't confess her sins to me, apologize, or share the kind of deeper, darker tête-à-tête I'd had with Miloš. Yet I accepted her kisses and kind words as her way of atoning. I bet she'd taken my reciprocal politeness to mean that I was granting her forgiveness. Or she could have seen it as a kind gesture, with no idea of my original—more sinister—intent. But she hadn't sent us to the camps with blood on her conscience. She was a petty thief turned into a lonely widow, stuck in a city her people had destroyed. She was probably soothed to see familiar male faces from better days that she associated with her husband, who had saved us. She'd loved him. She was basking in his quiet heroism. I let her, allowing a better, more complex conclusion to our saga. I hadn't ever pictured any kind of reconciliation scene with Petra. The possibility had never existed in my mind before today. But it felt right and redemptive, as if I needed to salvage a nice sliver from the wreckage of my childhood and my country.

"Good-bye, Petra," I told her. "Until next time."

She shook Eldin's hand, and with a wave, she was gone. I stared at the door.

"Ah, so that's why you were pacing," Truly said.

"I can't believe she just did that," Eldin said.

"I know. You didn't get a kiss," I joked.

I was disoriented by the way my big confrontation turned out. So many Serbs we saw in Bosnia acted the same way as Petra, casually asking, "How are you? Where've you been?" as if mass murder was something anyone could ever forget. It seemed surrealistic, a *Twilight Zone* episode. I was visiting an alternate universe of a species in collective denial. Everyone blamed everything evil that happened on "the politicians," implying "Look what they did to us," as if the leaders held a remote control that powered all the different sects of Yugoslavia to slaughter each other at the press of a button. Everyone in my country had whitewashed the war. No wonder nothing had grown or prospered or been repaired and no redemption could happen here. If the wound didn't exist, it couldn't be healed.

"Well, it's good you got it all off your chest," Truly added.

I hadn't finished. In fact, I'd barely started. But by admitting my hurt and facing down the people who'd scarred me here, I did feel unburdened. The ugliest chapter of my life was becoming less painful in the retelling, as if taking the reins of the story now could quell my emotional turbulence.

"Come have some *rakija* and grilled chicken," Truly offered.

"I'm so glad you weren't rude and didn't let her know you were onto her lies," Eldin said. "If you were hostile and disrespected her, she'd only think, *I'm so glad we threw these* balijas *out.* But you listened and let her talk. You were a gentleman, like Dad."

"Mom would have called her out," I said.

"Definitely. But I'm proud of you." He patted me on the shoulder. "You have no idea what you did by acting so civilized. You hurt her worse. You took away her reason to justify what they did to us.

You turned it around and did the opposite. No wonder the country is still in disarray. You just reminded her how they lost their best people."

Hungry, thirsty, and spent, I wanted to eat, then take a long nap. But my past wasn't through with me. To cross number 7 off my list, I had to return to Partizan Sports Hall, the second home I'd lost in Brčko. As a kid, I'd planned to be a coach here myself. I wanted to put on a karate robe again and attend practice one last time. I bet I'd be the only member of the old squad to come back.

I kept thinking of Pero. How could I get closure from a phantom who'd already been punished by death? Seeing his grave among hundreds of others wasn't personal enough; everybody expected gloom at a cemetery. It just left me feeling more empty. But converting my childhood sports arena into a horror chamber was a specific crime that my mind couldn't reconcile. Pero used to be the first one at Partizan, unlocking the doors to let me in. I wanted to reclaim his former territory by marching in there without him. If Partizan was the house of Pero's betrayal, I could at least confront the damn building.

"Come on, let's see a kick," my dad said when we got out of the car, holding his hand wide open. I tried, hiking my hip up. In a slow motion I extended my foot, barely making contact with his palm.

"Told you, ya still got it," he said, but I felt stiff and slow.

The "Partizan" sign was pinned against the building's gray stone wall outside. In elementary school I'd learned the name came from the band of resistance fighters Tito had led against the Nazis in World War II. The Partizans had tried to preserve the rights of each ethnic group as they fought the Germans. How ironic that Nazi concentration camps inspired the atrocities that wound up ruining our namesake gym.

It was the first time I'd ever been here in street clothes. Wandering around, I was let down by how much smaller and dingier it was than the grand emporium of my memory. Dad had a separate gym nearby where he'd trained athletes. This place used to be my domain, where I'd run around, make noise, and cause a ruckus, kick the ball against the wall and be cool—while being singled out as an example for the other students. It was a symbol of my success and physical prowess.

Now the same thick glass windows were intact, the sun streaming into my eyes. I squinted, my throat parched, trying to get the image of this space as a slaughterhouse out of my mind. The same two basketball hoops stood hinged on the walls, now painted pink and blue. The same ropes we'd climbed still hung from the ceilings. The hall extended through a small door into an auxiliary gym where I'd practiced karate kicks. It was empty, the lacquered floors removed. Two decades later, it was still undergoing a never-ending reconstruction, like I was.

Eldin and Dad stood against the wall. I sat on the wooden bench by the basketball court, watching the karate students in white kimonos with different-colored belts lined up for their 5:30 practice, horsing around, like we used to. I recalled my last competition here, twenty years ago, when Pero stood over me with my brown belt. The image of Pero standing over dead Muslim bodies intruded.

"This place gives me shivers." Eldin tucked his head into his shoulders like a turtle.

"They say that the souls of people murdered roam around and don't find peace until their remains are found," I said.

A man rushed over to greet us. "Aw, Keka, it's really you." He flung his arms around my father, kissing his cheeks, patting his back, all lit up.

"Boško, my buddy." Dad was teary.

I remembered Boško, the new karate coach, from the old days. He was a colleague of Dad's, a black belt who'd been a fellow chaperone of our karate camp on the Croatian coast. It was on top of a hill, with wooden bungalows.

The coach clapped his hands together at the sight of Eldin. "Look at this huge hawk."

"After practice we're taking you out to dinner," Eldin said, hugging him.

"Are you kidding? Don't worry, I already had fresh trout caught just for you. This is the little ninja?" He grabbed me. I squeezed him and lifted him up, almost throwing out my back. What was I thinking—the guy was fifty-five now, six four and 230 pounds, all muscle.

"So how's Mr. Submarine?" he asked, using the nickname he'd given me at camp, when Dad taught me to swim in the Adriatic Sea. "Your legs are quick, like a propeller," Boško had said, sneaking underneath and pulling my ankles, pretending to be a shark.

Coach Boško was from a mixed family. Since he had a Serb name and father, he'd been a soldier on the Serb side during the war. And yet he'd come—without weapons—to see us. When we were hungry, he'd twice discreetly brought us a loaf of bread and checked to make sure we were okay. Boško was a hard worker who by day was the superintendent of local schools. We heard he'd mobilized the authorities postwar to reestablish the karate team. But a Bosniak coach stole our old team name, Lokomotiva. He gave it to a Muslim team he started on the other side of town. The Partizan team was stuck with its nickname, "Lokosi," instead.

Dad handed Boško the bottle of whiskey we'd brought.

"Thanks, you shouldn't have gone to the trouble of carrying it all the way for me." He read the label. "Ah, the real American whiskey."

"It's actually Irish," I told him and he laughed.

"So how's the team doing?" Dad asked.

"It's split in two. No surprise," he said. "I'm no good in this town. To Serbs, I have a Muslim mother. To Bosniaks, I carry my father's Serb name." I felt for him; he embodied within his own skin the ethnic conflict that almost killed us all.

I ventured into the locker room. To my right, two teenagers were changing into kimonos. I had envisioned putting on a robe again to join in the practice and considered asking coach Boško for a spare one. But who was I fooling? Eldin had done karate in Vienna and joined a karate club in college, while I'd completely left the sport behind in Bosnia twenty years ago. Being back here with the new young team, I felt awkward and old and washed up. I no longer knew the kicks and katas that won me a brown belt twenty years ago. The new generation was half my age, with probably twice my speed and dexterity. I'd discredit the martial art I loved if I put on a brown belt now. I'd have to start over with a beginner's white sash. I couldn't do it. I would never be that agile, carefree kid again. I would rather keep my memory of being a winner than try to pick up my karate practice now. It was over, something else the war had taken away.

Inside the locker rooms, it was obvious the showers hadn't been used in decades. There were no faucets or showerheads or doors, though I heard an eerie drip coming from an invisible source. The cement floor around the drain had dark stains. I imagined it was dried-up blood from the bodies that had been butchered and stacked here. It made me nauseous, but I pulled out my camera and snapped a photograph to capture it.

"You're taking a picture of the town's shame. Look how dirty it is. We can't even use the showers," a guy's voice said. I turned to see a young, clean-cut Serb college student. "I should take a picture myself and send it to a TV station."

I didn't know if the "shame" he mentioned referred to the inadequate plumbing or to the town's tainted war history. Imagining the latter gave me hope that the younger generation could admit to the sins their parents denied.

I noticed his kimono was tied with a black belt—the level I'd never achieved. His black sash looked thicker and wider than our belts had been, made from a higher-quality fabric. When we'd fled, I'd left my old brown belt with my white robe in a sports bag under my bed. "You won't be needing it anymore," my mother said.

I'd learned there was only one male here who'd earned a black belt (and two girls). I'd heard about him. He was the captain now, coach Boško's star player. That was supposed to be me. No matter how old I was, I would never stop feeling ripped off.

Back in the auditorium, I recognized a man around my age sitting on a bench, talking to Eldin, who stood nearby with his arms crossed like he was uncomfortable and on guard. When I sat down by him, the guy turned and stared at me. "You're Kenan."

I nodded. He was shorter than I was, five foot eight, with blond hair that was half gray. In sweats and a T-shirt, he looked exhausted, and very familiar. I could see his boyish face hiding behind the circles under his brown eyes. "You're Milorad," I exclaimed.

A Serb, he'd been a teammate, a blue belt in my day. At karate, he was shy and respectful. He never used to smile and he wasn't smiling now. I shook his hand lightly. I hoped he didn't expect a friendly chat, as if this was still a fun place to hang out and not a haunted death trap.

"Your bro's arms look like he works out. That's your old man? He looks great. He always stayed in shape." His eyes scrutinized my plaid dress shirt, Levi's jeans, and sneakers. "You look good too," he said. He seemed intrigued that we'd come back here to visit. "I don't practice karate anymore. Those are my daughters." He pointed to three young girls running laps.

"How old are you now?" I asked.

"Thirty-six."

That meant Milorad had been sixteen during the war—too young, like me—to have been a soldier. I wondered if his father fought.

"Remember karate camp?" he asked. "Good times."

"I know, I still have pictures." Those summers I spent in Croatia with Dad and Eldin were the best times of my life.

"My girls don't get to go. They closed it," Milorad told me.

"I heard they turned that shoreline into a strip of hotels and condos," I added.

"Eldin said you're physical therapists in New York. What's it like there?"

"They only care if you do a good job. Nobody persecutes you for your religion." I gave him a jab. "What do you do?"

"Transportation." He paused. "When the Americans were here, I was a truck driver."

The Americans hadn't been in Bosnia for years. I immediately thought: he's probably not working, but I am, so I'm doing much better than my old teammate. Then I recognized the way my defenses kept working. Being back at Partizan made me see that I was stuck in a sports competition that had been going on since I was eleven. I couldn't win the war or recapture what we'd lost. I couldn't even practice karate anymore. But I could be more successful professionally than the classmates who betrayed me. That was all I felt I had over them. Surpassing old enemies in terms of job security and income seemed my only way to triumph. And yet having a nice life in America—with two college degrees and steady work at age thirty—didn't make up for the pain I'd felt as a kid. It never went away. It still hurt.

"You came all the way here to see the disaster we live in?" Milorad asked with a self-deprecating lilt.

In Bosnia it seemed people were still judged by their name, religion, and political party. To get more power or money, you had to bribe the right corrupted official—a disastrous recipe. In my new country, your drive, talent, and personal values mattered most. That was how you made a name for yourself.

"Yeah, something like that," I told Milorad. As we shook hands good-bye, I felt nothing against him. I had no reason to blame him for anything. He was just a player. He wasn't a coach. He hadn't been a soldier. He'd never murdered anyone.

Standing next to Eldin as the karate drills started, I asked, "How many people do you think Pero killed?"

"More than you want to know," Eldin said.

I'd never actually seen my exalted sensei personally hurt anyone. I recalled the time Pero walked home with us after practice and Mom invited him in for dinner. Out of all the kids on our team, he was eating moussaka and homemade rice pudding with me at my house. I felt chosen. I'd loved being his star protégé. I couldn't accept that our closeness was a lie. It still didn't make sense to me. Could you fake six years of caring?

"Did you ever wonder why Pero didn't shoot us?" I asked. "I mean, he could have, easily. He was in charge. But you said he didn't look you or Dad in the face at Luka when he walked down the line of prisoners. He looked away and chose not to make eye contact. He didn't hurt either of you. The last time I saw him, he mocked me—but he never lifted his gun. When Mom asked for help, he didn't touch her. He just told her to get back to the apartment."

"What are you saying?" My brother leaned against the wall.

"Even with all Pero's savagery, maybe he couldn't kill us because we treated him with respect and kindness. He felt just enough guilt to keep us alive."

Eldin exaggeratedly rolled his eyeballs. "Then what about all the others who were nice to him that he shot and mutilated?"

"So why didn't he pull the trigger on us?"

"Only he knew that," Eldin said. "Kenan, you weren't old enough to know who Pero really was. I was eighteen, I hung around with him in town and at bars while you were playing hide-and-seek." He paused. "He didn't change overnight. He was always pissed off and arrogant and second-rate."

"Wasn't he the best martial artist in town?" I asked.

"Not even close. He was average. You know, Dad put in a good word with the judges for him. That's why he got his black belt."

Eldin crossed his arms. "In two years you would have surpassed him athletically."

"Seriously? But I thought his talent was why he was so popular."

"He was thirty years old, living at home. He never went to college. He wasn't going anywhere. So he envied everyone who was better, smarter, and bigger than he was." Eldin sounded adamant. "Pepa, the Croat kickboxer, was the true talent and hero, and Pero knew it. So at the start of the war, Ranko and Pero smashed Pepa's hands with a hammer, then shot him in the head. Right in front of the police station."

"*Jebote-život!*" I said, the Bosnian equivalent of "fucking life!"

"You know, during the war, Pero even stole money and jewelry from his closest Serb comrades, the ones he was supposed to share the loot with," Eldin went on.

I pictured Pero wearing his nice leather jacket and fancy black belt, surrounded by pretty girls. My twelve-year-old mind denied what my brother was saying, but at thirty I recognized the truth of Eldin's portrayal of Pero. "Why didn't you tell me all this before?"

"I tried, but you didn't want to understand. You have no idea who this creep really was," Eldin said. "The more I talk to people who knew him here, the worse he seems. He was always a bad guy, even before the war."

I did recall that Eldin used to say Pero was a bad guy. But I'd thought he meant *after* Pero had taken up arms as a Serb soldier, not beforehand, when he was my coach.

In an odd way, I was mollified to learn that my grand master had been depressed and bitter all along, that he hadn't changed overnight because of the political unrest or something I'd said or done. From ages six to eleven, I'd only seen Pero at Partizan and at karate competitions, where he was in charge, representing our team, with all the kids looking up to him. We never talked about anything but sports. I realized there were no words I might have spoken or action

I could have taken to stop Pero. Knowing that his choices during the war had nothing to do with me took the sting out. I was just a kid, not stupid or weak. He did care about me at one point. I hadn't been taken for a ride. The age difference between us was to blame for my gullible outlook. I needed to be back at Partizan with my brother to see the whole picture of who my onetime hero really was.

Coach Boško drove us all to dinner in his new blue Volkswagen Jetta. From the backseat I asked, "Do you know how Pero died?"

Boško nodded. "At the height of his reign in '93, he got into a fight with another Serb soldier over a girl. Pero went to look for him. When he got to the apartment and called out his name, the guy was drunk and fired his automatic rifle through the closed wooden door. A bullet hit Pero in the chest. He died instantly, in the hallway." Boško pulled into the parking lot and slowed the car to show us where. "Right in that building."

So this solved the mystery of why his gravestone implied it was an accident. But how did Pero get buried in the veterans' section if he didn't die on the battlefield? I rolled down my window to get a better look, but I still didn't feel anything.

"He had a brother, right?" I asked.

"Pero's mom buried her other son just last week," Boško said. "He lived in Holland. He was burned alive in a car accident. I saw her bring flowers to his grave."

"The good brother suffered, but Pero's end was too easy," Eldin said. "He didn't even see that a gun was pointing at him through the door. The bastard."

"Rotten soul," Dad mumbled, scrunching his face.

Seeing where Pero had been shot and hearing how stupid his murder was didn't change anything. I was still processing the conflicting facts and memories. So he wasn't the top karate guy in town. Yet with Dad's help, he had reached the level of black belt—higher than I'd attained—and he was a good teacher for a time. I supposed that level of achievement wasn't enough for him. As an ambitious athlete and his devoted disciple, I was also obsessed with winning, willing to do anything to reach a higher level. Pero probably wanted to be stronger, more skillful, better respected. But he wasn't capable, no matter how hard he tried. Martial artist stars in the Balkans were treated like Hollywood celebrities; he must have longed for that kind of fame. Yet the best athletes around here—like the late, great Pepa—were more talented and more humble.

Desperate for acclaim he could never reach, Pero had become drunk, first on alcohol and women, then on stolen loot, then on the power the war granted him. I guessed that he kept reaching for more prestige and money to overcompensate for the failures and limitations he couldn't face. But it probably never filled in what was missing inside him. I bet he wasn't acting out of true political or religious conviction, but from a psychological need to become more than what he felt himself to be. Trying so hard to be a big man had made him smaller. He'd lost his life arguing over a girl, playing the role of tough guy. He didn't die *for* his people; he died because he couldn't even get along with his own people.

I recalled how my relationship with Pero went sour after he'd argued with my father over not getting a raise. I imagined he felt frustrated. At thirty, he couldn't marry and start a family if he couldn't afford his own place. In our Balkan town, not being married by your third decade meant something was wrong with you. I knew what it was like to feel small and inadequate. I guessed that Pero resented us—and others who were more prosperous—and the war became his excuse to settle personal vendettas. Could resentment turn you into a monster? All you needed was a charismatic leader who blamed your misfortunes on a common enemy—and not your own failure. If you took a man already miserable and handed him a government mandate and a weapon, would he become evil? Would I?

Late that night I used my international phone card to call Brian, my college friend's father. He was a forensic psychotherapist in New Jersey who'd worked with the CIA, profiling serial killers. I spilled the whole Pero story to Brian, telling him how many Muslims had been murdered by Pero and his buddy Ranko. I admitted I was stuck, unable to figure out why our lives had been spared.

"For six years, you showed Pero reverence and admiration. So Pero, a sociopath, didn't want to extinguish the rare flame of respect that illuminated his worthless ego," Brian explained. "Killing you would have made him feel less powerful, not more."

I'd never seen it that way before. I liked knowing Pero fit this sociopathic personality type across the board—and wasn't a rare case who'd singled me out. It seemed the only way I could feel calmer was by retracing the chaos of war.

I did not regret visiting Bosnia. I'd needed to reclaim the part of myself that was ripped away nineteen years ago. I'd confronted my country—with all its ugliness, ridiculousness, and complexity. While I would return to visit Bisera, Amela, Tidja, and others I loved here, I never wanted to see the Partizan Sports Hall, or Luka, or all the different graveyards again. I was finished rattling the dead. Finally.

Or so I thought.

One week after I returned from the Balkans, a dream threw me right back to Partizan. Eldin was there too, with my former teammates. It was a big reunion, our first practice in nineteen years.

"I see you remember how to tie your brown belt after all this time," a familiar voice joked, in Bosnian. I turned to find Pero, with a thin beard, his hair a mess of dark blond curls, in his white karate pants and red warm-up jacket, his black belt worn and faded. He waved, thrilled to see me, then yelled for everyone to line up.

I was angry that he was in charge again. He no longer deserved to lead us. For the first time, I refused to obey. I stepped out of the formation to protest.

"Kenan, get back in the row. You're holding us up, kid." He winked at me.

"Pero, don't you have something to say?" I asked in English, a visitor here now.

He shrugged. I shook my head in disbelief at what he was trying to pull off.

"Tell the new guys who don't know what you did," I ordered him. My old teammates floated out of their columns, protesting too.

"Pero, what happened to you?" I kept demanding. "Were you out of your mind?"

His smirk vanished. His face turned a brighter red than his jacket. He took a step toward me, put his feet together, and clasped his hands. "Don't bring that up now." His voice was nervous, pleading. "Let's just start the new fall season."

I shook my head, refusing.

"But aren't you excited we get to do it all over again?" he asked. "See, the place is fixed up. Look how shiny the wooden floor is."

"It's over, Pero. There's no way to fix this. You can't be our coach anymore," I decreed.

His eyes lowered. He shuffled away to the locker room. The rest of the team faced me as I stood where Pero had been. Suddenly I was in charge. Pero's lower body slowly fading into darkness; only his torso still visible. I wondered if he knew he was dead.

Opening my eyes, it took me a while to gather it was the summer of 2011 and I was safe in my apartment in New York. Pero was buried in the Bosnian cemetery by the time he was thirty. I was thirty now. Even after seeing where he'd been killed and visiting his grave, I was still trying to fathom how my childhood idol had become so monstrous. Ultimately I pitied Pero. He lost his way, his humanity, his life. I accepted that the hurt I felt at twelve would never fully heal. It would stay with me, a scar less visible but more permanent than the old Bosnian flag on my arm that I'd chosen to always keep me company.

Sitting on the edge of my mattress, I felt satisfied. In reality, there was no happy ending. There was not even a clear military defeat that we could mourn and start to recover from. The war was an open-ended, ongoing disaster, with no point, no positive outcome, no conclusive wisdom, no closure. But I couldn't settle for that unsatisfying stalemate. So apparently my subconscious had called out Pero, demanding that he show remorse, forcing the reconciliation that was impossible for us to have while he was alive. I'd crossed him off my list, crumpled up the page, and left it in an ashtray the last day of my trip, right before I'd left my old country. And yet I couldn't help but feel that Pero was sorry, so he'd returned to my dream, offering me a better finale to our shared tragedy.

In Dreams Begins Forgiveness

Queens, New York
January 2012

Six months later, I had another dream, this one about my mother. In the five years she'd been dead, I'd only dreamt of her sick, in pain, emaciated, and hairless, as she'd been during her final decade in America. But last night, my mind had restored her to health. She'd regained all the weight she'd lost. She was young again, completely strong and healthy, with long golden-blond hair the color of lilies from our flag's fleurs-de-lis.

I was leading her through our old Brčko neighborhood, giving her a tour.

"Is everybody coming?" She sounded excited.

"Yes. See all the freshly painted white houses?" I asked her, in Bosnian. "Remember when we walked through these ghost streets during the war?"

The last time we were in this neighborhood, where she'd grown up, we were returning from the dentist after the area had been bombed, hot blue flashes exploding in the sky, leaving the houses roofless. The residents were dead or gone. The remaining walls were pockmarked by bullet holes like standing slices of Swiss cheese; you could see inside. But now everything was new, beautifully rebuilt.

As Mom and I went down the hill and crossed the bridge together, I yelled, "The whole family will be here. Grandma Emina too!" My voice echoed. I spun her to our old apartment, a twenty-minute walk, in seconds.

"It's so great you're back," said a Bosniak neighbor who used to live across the street from Grandma. "You should've come last year."

"I couldn't, I was dead," my mother said.

Their conversation felt rushed, as if we didn't have enough time. Then, all of sudden, we were swept up to the balcony of our Brčko home. We were on the top floor, the tallest building within miles.

"See, they're all running away." I looked down at our old enemies, happy to watch them leaving with tattered, pathetic suitcases in their hands. They stared up at us with fear.

"The tables have finally turned, and I lived to see it happen," Mom said.

"The town is a hundred percent in our hands, not divided anymore," I replied.

Mom smiled. But then she pulled me toward an abandoned cobblestone building, the warehouse in Luka, where Eldin and Dad were taken. The structure was getting smaller as we approached. It was the size of a kiosk by the time we stood in front.

"Why did they build new homes around here, yet leave this monstrosity? It's so dark and creepy," Mom said.

"As a reminder," I told her, gently.

"Everything is close and small because you're all grown up now," were the last words she said.

I woke up and blinked, confused. Above my desk in Queens I saw a picture of me, Dad, and Eldin crossing the Sava Bridge into Bosnia last July. Next to it was a black and white photograph of Mom when she was my age, looking through binoculars. I'd found typed recipes of Bosnian desserts she'd left. Yet I was never able to find the pages about our escape that my mother planned to write. She must have been too tired or too sick by then. Or perhaps it was too hard for her to remember.

It was time for me to finish her story and tell my own. She'd once yelled, "Enough with the sports already! Can't you stay inside and read a book?" She would be shocked—and thrilled—that I was writing one. On the day I finished the first draft of *The Bosnia List*, a white mailer showed up at my Astoria mailbox addressed to Adisa Trebinčević, though she'd never lived in Queens and had died five years before. Inside was a book about Muslims who'd had supernatural powers. Normally I'd assume it was a promotion sent to everyone with an Islamic-sounding name and toss it in the garbage. But I took it as a sign—for a few seconds anyway—that she was sending me her approval.

I thought of all the sacrifices my parents made for me. Had I ended my journey by avenging the people who'd betrayed us in our motherland, I would have failed her. I pictured being thrown into a Balkan jail, causing an international upheaval, leaving Eldin and Dad to fly back to Queens without me. That might have given my father another stroke; it could have killed him. Instead, by tempering my anger the way he taught me, my worldview was altered.

After visiting my hometown, I saw that the neighbors and classmates who'd turned on us were stuck too. But they were mired in the aftermath of their weakness and bad decisions, grappling with a lousy economy, political chaos, personal confusion, irrevocable regrets. They hated their lives. They were worse off in peace than I was during wartime.

For two decades I'd been clinging to my rage over what the Serbs did to us. The resentment might never totally disappear. After all, I had just dreamt of sharing the battle victory we were never allowed. I couldn't change my subconscious. Yet during my trip to Bosnia, giving up on getting real revenge, something internal was repaired: I came back more trusting and hopeful.

Returning to New York, I realized that if we'd never been exiled, Eldin, and I would be running Dad's sports business in the Balkans, coasting by on his good name. We'd be married to local girls in the town where we grew up, knowing only one language and culture. While I didn't choose this rougher, more complicated route, I relished my double identity, being bilingual, traveling the world. Proud to be a Bosnian Muslim, I was also privileged to be American. Here I was able to turn my childhood passion for sports into a solid career in a healing profession, where helping others made me stronger. Close friends and colleagues of all backgrounds were sensitive to my past and respected me. I was beginning to feel more lucky than bitter.

In retrospect, there are many ways I did win the war. My war.

Eldin said that everything Mom told us while we were trying to escape Brčko turned out to be true. Now, five years after we lost her, I recalled her insistence that in all religions and races, you could find those who were both good and evil. I heard my mother's voice echo: "Don't ever forget the people who saved us."

There weren't many, was my first thought. But I could suddenly see there were exactly enough to keep us alive. I went to my desk, pulled out a piece of paper, and started another list. This one was filled with names of the Serbs who saw only a family in need and came to our rescue.

I retraced the trail of guardian angels who'd watched over us during that harrowing year, leading us to safety. Two decades later, the faces of the Serbs who'd helped us survive resurfaced in a flourish. It felt like an affirmation of my mother's faith that even during the most tragic times, there were flickers of goodness that must be remembered. It was her final, unexpected gift to me.

The New Bosnia List

1. Thank God for Obren, who warned Dad and Mujo away from Partizan Sports Hall
2. Toast Stevo, the volleyball player who discreetly confiscated Dad's revolver so he wouldn't be taken away for good
3. Visit Zorica and Miloš, who brought us sardines when we were starving, filled our propane tank, and gave us schillings for Vienna
4. Find Ranko, the convicted war criminal, at the Denmark jail to ask why he protected Eldin and Dad at Luka
5. Search online for Ankica, mom's friend who sneaked bags of coffee, sugar, and flour for us
6. Wish good health to Geca, the soldier who delivered Ankica's care packages and made Igor stop bullying me
7. Send gratitude to Jovo, the coworker who held his bus till Mom returned with papers to pull out Dad and Eldin
8. Honor the officers who drove Mom to the bus that Eldin and Dad were being taken away on
9. Buy older Irish whiskey for Coach Boško, who checked on us and brought us bread
10. Never forget the white-haired man who drove us to a photo shop to get our passport pictures taken
11. Thank Good Pero, who made calls for us and typed the paperwork we needed to get us out of the country
12. Say a prayer for the last bus driver who waited for us in a blizzard to drive us to Vienna and our freedom

ACKNOWLEDGMENTS

Immense and eternal gratitude to:

Intrepid WME agent Kirby Kim, who sold this book during the hurricane.

Brilliant Viking/Penguin editor Wendy Wolf, whose gravestone will be inscribed "She died defending truth, justice, and the serial comma."

Esteemed newspaper and magazine editors and producers who first said yes: Hugo Lindgren, Sheila Glaser, William Vollmann, Honor Jones, Nicole Angeloro, Sarah Hepola, Mark Lasswell, Robert Pollack, John Reed, Erol Avdović, David Mairowitz, Dick Gordon, and Rachel McCarthy.

History aces, fact checkers, fellow travelers, protectors, and close companions I will always look up to: Eldin Trebinčević and Senahid Trebinčević.

My loyal, beloved Bosnian crew: Bisera Kazazović, Amela and Ibrahim Kamenjašević, Mirza Širbegović, Ahmet Ćaušević, Truly Busch, Said Muminović, Gigi Džidžović, Sead Burić, Djila and Jasenko Alimanović, Huso and Nadina Rončević, and Miloš and Zorica.

The best, coolest, and most generous boss in the universe, Patrick Walsh.

Generous, helpful, kind Penguin staffers: Maggie Riggs, Lindsay Prevette, Maureen Donnelly, John Fagan, Barbara Campo, Alan Walker, Megan Halpern, Tiffany Tomlin, and Kent Anderson.

Website artist Todd Jackson and computer geniuses Dorri Olds and Eric (EB) Shapiro.

My treasured mentors, teachers, and sponsors in this country: Dr. Glenn Hightower, Mr. Bauer, Dr. John Gagnon, Lazlo Papay, Catherine Certo, and Reverend Don Hodges and his family.

Lyrical early readers and perceptive critics: Kimberlee Auerbach, Merideth Finn, Stan Mieses, Royal Young, Jerry Portwood, Kate Walter, Paul Brownfield, Judy Batalion, Keysha Whitaker, Amy Wolfe, Sara Karl, Jill Krasny, Rich Prior, Alice Feiring, Amy Klein, Tony Powell, Lisa Lewis, Aspen Matis, Justin Matis, Gabrielle Selz, Sarah Gonzalez, Pari Chang, David Sobel, Jason Schneider, Sarah Herrington, Noah Wunsh, Liza Monroy, Abby Sher, Seth Kugel, Louise Sloan, Emily Rueb, Stephen Gaydos, and the rest of the Sunday workshop.

Astute editors, consultants, and advisers: Julie Just, Tom Reiss, Larry Bergreen, Sandy Frazier, Gerry Jonas, Tom Zoellner, David Margolick, Molly Lyons, Nicole Bokat, Ryan Harbage, Danielle Perez, Betsy Maury, Julia Leiblich, Esad Boškailo, Bob Cook, and David Brand; storehouses of war knowledge Jack Shapiro and Michael Shapiro; and the amazing Charlie Rubin, who—luckily—loves ćevapi.

Important comrades, colleagues, and ardent supporters: Lauren Testa, Gaelyn Rogers and Emmi Freimark, Jimmy Silber, Ed Maloof, Mark Sackett, Edward Rose, Matt Forman, Rich Mocarski, Douglas Wells, Christopher Morgan, Ryan Cohen, Eugene Katsnelson, Kostas Klokelis, Andy Menneto, Katie Caporta, Nancy and Allyn Arden, and my fellow never-ending bad sport Miguel Peman, my first American friend who taught me how to trust again.

GLOSSARY OF NAMES, PLACES, AND TERMS

NAMES

Adisa Trebinčević (Ada): Kenan's mother

Admir: Friend of Kenan's brother

Ahmet: Kenan's mother's older brother

Aleks: Serb classmate of Kenan's

Alen: Bisera's neighbor

Alexander Karadjoredević: Serb army commander who became king in 1929 and changed the country's name to the Kingdom of Yugoslavia

Amela: Kenan's cousin; she and her brother, Mirza, are Bisera's children.

Arkan: International war criminal; he ran paramilitary unit, Arkan's Tigers.

Dr. Beinfeld: Jewish surgeon at Norwalk Hospital

Bisera: Adisa's sister

Boban: Serb husband of Daca; they stole from Kenan's family.

Boško: Karate coach after Bad Pero

Brian: Kenan's friend's father, a forensic psychotherapist

Dr. Ćaušević: Kenan's old pediatrician

Ceca: Serb pop singer

Daca: Serb wife of Boban; they stole from Kenan's family.

Dalibor: Serb childhood neighbor, friend, and karate teammate of Kenan's

Danny: Kenan's Portuguese college roommate

Dejan: Son in Serb family who befriended Kenan's family

Donald Hodges: Methodist minister who helped Kenan's family settle in Connecticut

Eldin Trebinčević: Kenan's older brother

Emina: Kenan's mother's mother

Esad: Kenan's father's friend in Astoria, also originally from Brčko

Eugene: Kenan's Russian college roommate and close friend

Fatima: Emina's sister

Gigi (Ruždija Džidžović): Bosnian entrepreneur in Astoria

Halil: Bisera's second husband

Hasan: Bosniak neighbor on the second floor

Hilmija: Zekija's second husband

Huso: Bosniak childhood friend, the son of Hasan

Ibrahim Kamenjašević: Amela's husband

Igor: Kenan's childhood friend, a Serb

Jasenko: Kenan's childhood best friend, a Bosniak

Jelena: Daughter of Petra and Obren

Jovo: Serb coworker of Kenan's mother

Kemal: Son of Ibrahim and Amela

Kemo: Bisera's third husband

Kenan Trebinčević: Author

Kostas: Kenan's Greek college roommate

Kristina: Works in hair salon in Astoria

Magbula: Truly's wife

Maršal (Marshal) Tito (Josip Broz): Moderate Communist dictator who, following World War II, ruled Yugoslavia until his death in 1980

Matt: Kenan's token native-born college roommate

Miguel: Kenan's middle-school classmate and first American friend

Miki: DJ at Marshall's bar in Astoria

Milan: Serb soldier

Milisav: Serb friend of Kenan's father

Milorad: Former karate teammate of Kenan's; a Serb

Milorad Dodik: Serb leader

Miloš: Father in Serb family who befriended Kenan's family

Milutin: First- to fifth-grade Serb teacher

Mirza: Kenan's cousin; he and his sister, Amela, are Bisera's children.

Molly: Eugene's girlfriend

Monika: Croatian hairdresser in Astoria

Mujo: Jasenko's father

Murat: Kenan's mother's father

Nancie: Miguel's mother

Nedjo: Bisera's first husband

Nicole: Kenan's ex

Obren: Serb next-door neighbor; husband of Petra

Pepa: Croat kickboxer

Pero (Bad Pero): Serb karate coach

Pero (Good Pero): Serb policeman who helped Kenan's father and brother

Petra: Serb next-door neighbor; wife of Obren

Rachel: Kenan's college girlfriend

Ranko Češić: Serb war criminal; currently serving an eighteen-year jail sentence

Rusmir: Son of Ibrahim and Amela

Sabit: Emina's brother

Sead Burić: Kenan's father's childhood friend

Senahid (Keka) Trebinčević: Kenan's father

Slobodan Milošević: Serb leader indicted by the UN's International Criminal Tribunal for the Former Yugoslavia for crimes against humanity

Slobodan Tešić: Serb coworker of Kenan's mother who refused to help the family

Smajl: Fatima's husband

Snježana: Serb bartender in New York

Srdjan: Chetnik guerrilla

Suljo: Kenan's father's father

Tidja: Daughter of Ibrahim and Amela

Truly: Friend of Kenan's father

Velibor: Serb childhood neighbor, friend, and karate teammate of Kenan's

Vojislav Šešelj: Ultranationalist Serb

Zekija: Kenan's father's mother

Zoka: Sidekick of Bad Pero

Zorica: Mother in Serb family that befriended Kenan's family in 1992

PLACES

Balkan Peninsula (aka the Balkans): Geopolitical and cultural region of southeastern Europe

Bijeljina: Bosnian city

Bosnia: Country in southeastern Europe on the Balkan Peninsula; sometimes called Bosnia-Herzegovina

Brčko: Town in northeastern Bosnia on the country's border, along the Sava River, across from Croatia

Luka: A river port and warehouse facility in Brčko whose buildings were used by Bosnian Serbs as a concentration camp from May through early July 1992

Maoča: Bosniak area south of Brčko that became free territory

Mostar: Bosnian town ravaged in the war

Partizan Sports Hall: The local gymnasium, where Kenan and his friends practiced karate; the name is taken from the military arm of Tito's Communist Party.

Sava River: River in southeastern Europe; considered the northern border of the Balkan Peninsula. Its central part forms the border between Bosnia and Croatia. About 615 miles (990 km) long, it rises in Slovenia and joins the Danube River at Belgrade, Serbia.

Vukovar: Croatian city two hours north of Brčko

Yugoslavia: Country in the western Balkans during most of the twentieth century; consisted of six socialist republics—Slovenia, Croatia, Bosnia, Serbia, Montenegro, and Macedonia—that, along with Kosovo, became independent nations in the 1990s during the Balkan War.

TERMS

Balija (plural: balije): Derogative ethnic slur for a Bosnian Muslim

Bosniak: Regional term for a Bosnian Muslim

Bre? Eh? (Serbian)

Burek: Baked or fried filled pastries made of thin, flaky dough (phyllo) filled with beef

Česma: Fountain

Ćetir: Four

Ćevapi: Beef sausages

Djesi: What's up?

Dobar dan: Good day

Dva: Two

Evo ti plavi pojas: Here is the blue belt you earned.

Fuj: Phew

Govna: Human waste

Hvala: Thanks

I šta sada? What now?

Imam: Religious leader who leads prayers in a mosque; the Muslim equivalent of a rabbi or priest

Iz Brčkog: From Brčko

Jebiga: Fuck

Jebote-život! Fucking life!

Jedan: One

Magarac: Donkey

Mashallah: God willed it.

Mazel tov: Congratulations

Osam: Eight

Pasoš: Passport

Patlidjani: Eggplants

Pet: Five

Pogino: Died

Polako: Slow

Pršuta: Long strips of lamb

Rakija: Homemade moonshine usually made of plums

Sine: Son

Šta kažu? What are they saying?

Što? Why?

Stojadin: A man's name and the nickname for a poorly performing Yugoslavian car model, the Zastava 101; the nickname is both a pun on *sto jedan* ("101") and the folk phrase *sto jada* ("a hundred woes").

Štrudla sa jabukama: Apple strudel

Tri: Three

Zadavi ću te: My hands will be around your throat.

Zeljanica: Spinach-filled pie

Živili: May you live forever.

RECOMMENDED BOOKS

All the Missing Souls: A Personal History of the War Crimes Tribunals, by David Scheffer, Princeton, N.J.: Princeton University Press, 2012.

Balkan Ghosts: A Journey Through History, by Robert D. Kaplan, New York: Picador, 2005.

The Balkans: Nationalism, War, and the Great Powers, 1804–1999, by Misha Glenny, New York: Penguin, 1999, and *The Fall of Yugoslavia: The Third Balkan War*, third revised edition, by Misha Glenny, New York: Penguin, 1996.

Himmler's Bosnian Division: The Waffen-SS Handschar Division 1943–1945, by George Lepre, Atglen, Pa.: Schiffler Military History, 1997.

The Serbs: The History, Myth, and the Destruction of Yugoslavia, by Tim Judah, New Haven: Yale University Press, 1997.

Wounded I Am More Awake: Finding Meaning After Terror, by Julia Lieblich and Esad Boškailo, Nashville, Tenn.: Vanderbilt University Press, 2012.

Yugoslavia: Death of a Nation, revised edition, by Laura Silber and Allan Little, New York: Penguin, 1997.

INDEX